With Casement's Irish Brigade

Written by Michael Keogh (RIP)
Compiled by Kevin Keogh
Editor: Brian Maye

ACKNOWLEDGEMENTS

It was Michael Keogh's youngest son, Kevin, who commissioned this book. He wishes to thank especially his own son, also called Kevin, who was responsible for discovering the whereabouts of Michael Keogh's long lost papers. The story of how those papers went missing is an interesting and curious one and is narrated in the introduction to this book.

Both Kevin senior and his wife Mary wish to make special mention of their granddaughter, Janice Doyle, who has shown a particular interest in her great-grandfather's life and his writings about his time with Casement's Irish Brigade in Germany from 1914 to 1916. Janice has written a useful and insightful school project on the topic.

I would like to express my gratitude to Kevin and Mary Keogh for the opportunity to edit this fascinating first-hand account of what it was like to be with Casement in Germany, an account by a man who took so close, intrinsic and leading a part in trying to realise Casement's ambition to form a brigade from Irishmen in the British army who found themselves prisoners of war in German prison camps in the early stages of the Great War. Michael Keogh's story is by far the most comprehensive inside account we have of what it was like to be part of that enterprise. What makes it of special value is that the first draft of it was written so close to the time of the events with which it was concerned.

It has been one of Kevin Keogh's longest-held and dearest wishes that his father's story would be published in book form. My hope is that Kevin is satisfied with the way I have edited and presented his father's story.

Robert McKenna, head librarian in Griffith College Dublin, was most helpful and generous in his suggestions about how to locate particular sources of relevant information and he also very kindly took the trouble to supply many of those sources via his contact with other libraries. His assistant, Dimphne Ní Bhraonáin, also gave generously of her time.

The editor also gratefully acknowledges the patient and unfailing courtesy of the staffs of the University College Dublin Archives, the National Library of Ireland, the library of Trinity College Dublin and a number of Dublin City Council libraries, especially the Pembroke branch.

Gratitude also goes to Seamus Ó Síocháin for his advice about other sources to consult for Casement's time in Germany. His recent monumental and superb biography of Roger Casement will not be easy to surpass.

Finally, a special word of thanks to Ann, my wife, and Elizabeth and Andrew, our children, for their continuing love and support and, above all, patience. To them will always be dedicated, with love, the fruits of my labours.

Brian Maye
Dublin, March 2009

PREFACE

In the Vanguard for Irish Independence: the Irish Insurrection of 1916 in the Making

Roger Casement's Irish-Ireland military and diplomatic mission in Germany from 1914 to 1916 remains an event of which very little is known. For all that, it was an event of no small significance historically – whether we consider the history of the World War 1914-18 or the history of Ireland. In the case of every incident of war, some time must elapse before its completely detailed and satisfactory history can be written; this is so even in the most favourable of circumstances. But in the matter of the Casement military mission, circumstances were such as to make a full and accurate presentation of the details a very difficult proposition indeed.

Up to the present time,[3] the following data for the history of Casement's mission have appeared in print:

1. Newspaper narratives of his well-planned voyage from Ireland to the USA in July 1914 and thence to Germany, which he reached in October 1914. And of his last expedition in a German submarine, which so faithfully escorted the Aud's cargo of 20,000 stands of arms and 10,000,000 rounds of ammunition, to wait in Tralee Bay on the south-west coast of Ireland for 22 long hours for the Irish Volunteers who never came on Good Friday morning, 21st April 1916.

---

[1] Michael Keogh originally wrote his account in the 1927-32 period. Elements were added and removed thereafter up until around 1962, a few years before his death.

[2] Sir Edward Poynings was Lord Deputy of Ireland for Henry VII (king from 1485 to 1509) and is mainly remembered for his law which subjected the Irish parliament to the control of the English king and council. In fact, the statute under which Casement was tried was a treason law passed in 1351.

[3] The details concerning Casement listed here may be surveyed in a number of his biographies, especially the most recent, *Roger Casement: Imperialist, Rebel, Revolutionary*, by Seamus Ó Síocháin (Dublin, 2008). In 1795, Wolfe Tone and other leaders of the United Irishmen spent a few days in McArt's Fort on Cave Hill outside Belfast planning the independence of Ireland.

2. The famous trial for his life, in London in June 1916, as a so-called "traitor" to the Anglo-Saxon Crown, under the 1492 Poynings' Act of the English King Henry VII.[2]

3. The criminal revenge of Ireland's 750-year-old common enemy in publicly hanging Roger Casement, "the Irishman", at Pentonville Jail, London, on 3rd August 1916. He died so manfully, unrepentant and uncompromising, on the cruel cross of an infamous British Empire. He was a true friend of the Boers in the South African War during their fight for freedom; the justifiable enemy of King Leopold's "red rubber" slavery in the Congo of Africa; the ever-trusty pathfinder in showing up Fleet Street and Threadneedle Street London financial interests in drawing the redder human blood from the "bottom dog" native in the Putumayo region of South America; the much-needed provider of succour to our own Irish fever-stricken, poorly clad and starving peasantry in west Connacht and the more northerly seaboard of Co. Donegal; and lastly, and above all, the 20th-century torch-bearer of the liberty first implanted by that other Irish chieftain in the Red Hand province at Cave Hill, Belfast, in 1795 in the personage of Wolfe Tone.[3]

4. References in official naval histories of the World War 1914-18 – about a page or so in the English, twice as much in the German, because Casement was a real friend of the entire German people.

5. The English parliament White Paper documents relative to the Sinn Féin movement 1921.[4]

6. Roger Casement's diaries (for the most part never intended for publication by the Irish patriot but such parts as might serve for the guidance of future Irish-Ireland negotiations with continental powers in Ireland's struggle against Seán Buidhe [John Bull]), as edited by Dr Charles Curry of Munich University, Bavaria.[5] This edition was afterwards recopied in serial form by Dr J. Maloney of New York for *The Globe* newspaper of Boston, Massachusetts, in a vain attempt to concoct anti-German propaganda, and obviously to strike "a home run" for Mother England and Lloyd George's "duress" Anglo-Irish Treaty with its supercilious veiled threat of immediate and terrible warfare

---

[4] *Documents Relative to the Sinn Féin Movement* (His Majesty's Stationery Office, London, 1921).
[5] C.E. Curry, ed., *Sir Roger Casement's Diaries: His Mission to Germany and the Findlay Affair* (Munich, 1922).

against the liberty-loving Irish people.[6] A partitioned Ireland was quite sufficient in fomenting civil and fratricidal strife in 1922 in the former united camp of worthy sons of Irish freedom.[7] English and West-British dastardly intrigue succeeded where the Dublin Castle pets and imported jailbird Black and Tans had failed in thwarting the Trojans in the IRA and Ireland's integrity as a "small nation" – though not deemed worthy of freedom according to the frame-up Treaty of Versailles in 1919.[8] It remained in the end for Churchill's salvoes of field artillery to deliver the imperial coup de grace which counteracted the honourable process to amalgamate Irish-Ireland militancy by means of the historical Collins-de Valera general-election pact, which would have seen each side proportionally represented in a new Dáil Cabinet formed to guide the destiny of a sorely tried Irish people.[9]

7. Captain Karl Spindler's soul-stirring narrative of bravery on the high seas, despite Britain's cajolery in 1916 that her bombastic navies ruled the waves. The book tells the story of the good ship Aud and her gallant crew of Viking-German sailors and their "gun-running for the Irish patriot, Roger Casement".[10] We can still further note the recorded bravery of the Aud's expedition in scouring the furthest artic, ice-bound waters during April 1916, in the attempt to augment Casement's Howth guns of 26th July 1914, by hoping to place a further 20,000 much-wanted rifles in the hands of the home Irish Volunteer army.

---

[6] The reference is to the concluding stage of the negotiations between the Sinn Féin delegation and the British government in December 1921 leading to the Anglo-Irish Treaty, where Lloyd George, the British Prime Minister, threatened unleashing widespread war on Ireland unless the Irish delegates agreed to sign an agreement.

[7] This conveys the mistaken view that it was partition that provoked the Irish Civil War, whereas what in fact caused that conflict was the oath of fidelity to the Crown contained in the Treaty.

[8] Ireland failed to gain recognition as a separate nation at the Paris Peace Conference that followed the First World War, although Britain had claimed to be fighting for the freedom of small nations such as Belgium during the war.

[9] Before the June 1922 general election, Collins and de Valera signed a pact which provided for the pro- and anti-Treaty sides to be represented in the government that would be formed after the election in proportion to the electoral support they received.

[10] Karl Spindler wrote his own account of the voyage of the Libau, as the Aud was called beforehand by the Germans, which was published in 1920. The English edition was published in 1921 under the title, *Gun Running for Roger Casement*. The second edition, published in 1931, had the title, *The Mystery of the Casement Ship*.

Captain Chatterton of his Brittanic Majesty's Navy, in his book which refers to the 12-day trip of the Aud from Wilhelmshaven on the Kiel Canal to Tralee Bay in Co. Kerry, gives the title of seaworthiness to Capt. Karl Spindler and his crew. "Sailors all. A near thing for England's sea-conquering prestige," Captain Chatterton wrote.[11] The world conflict saw these Anglo-Saxon and German cousins at war to the dagger's end (they are now at peace with the remnants of Germany's Ironclads rust eaten in the watery grave at Scapa Flow). Spindler tells a tale in some few hundred pages of Teutonic chivalry in true keeping with Casement's master mind as revealed in his pre-war essays on "The Freedom of the Seas" and the prophetic paraphrasing of the writing on the wall, with the wily Briton's back right up against it.[12]

To know the intellectual forecasts and inspiration for the bare truth of Ireland in the sea-pirate's deadly tentacles, it would be well for every Irishman and German, alive or worthy of the name, to read Rory of the Gael's[13] treatise published in the USA immediately before the World War under the title *Ireland, Germany and the Freedom of the Seas: a Possible Outcome of the War of 1914*. In the near future, who cannot vouch but that Ireland will produce yet another John Holland, the Irish Fenian and first successful inventor of the submarine?[14]

It is the naval supremacy of England that holds a boundary-divided Éire in bonded slavery despite the flippancy of some of the nation's spokesmen who taunt a people's courage into believing an English statesman's word of honour as coequal with England's bond in empire partnership. We must awake once more to adhering to the more fearless teachings of Casement when he wrote: "The

---

[11] Edward Keble Chatterton (1878-1944) was one of the most prolific writers on maritime themes. The editor hasn't been able to establish which of Chatterton's books this quote is taken from, but it may be from *The Big Blockade*, which is about the British naval blockade of Germany during the First World War.

[12] Casement's pamphlet, *Ireland, Germany and the Freedom of the Seas: a Possible Outcome of the War of 1914*, was published in New York in 1914.

[13] Michael Keogh frequently uses this pseudonym for Casement; the latter used it as a pseudonym (in its Irish form, "Ruairí na nGael) for himself in some of his journalism.

[14] John Philip Holland (1841-1916), who was from Liscannor, Co. Clare and who emigrated to America where he joined the Fenians, is generally regarded as "the father of the submarine".

Downing Street London types of honourable statesmen are akin to an equal amount of sea pirates in evening-dress."

8. The veteran Irish Fenian John Devoy's editorial articles and memoirs in the New York *Gaelic American*. These narratives concerning the Easter Week 1916 Irish Insurrection and Casement's mission with his Irish Brigade in Germany tell how some over-enthusiastic Irish leaders in the US went all out in negotiating behind the Irish-German lines of communication at Berlin during 1915-16. But, no amount of doubling-up tactics and secret wire-pulling could have procured better conditions for militant or naval action by the Germans in going to the assistance of Irishmen willing to take up arms in Ireland. The Casement-Zimmermann Ten Article Agreement[15] had been accepted by the Irish revolutionary tribunals in both the USA and Ireland as far back as January 1915; yet, it can be related from facts only too true that Casement, Plunkett, Monteith and co. were frustrated in clinching a "whole measure" plan in accordance with the Irish-German War Treaty (i.e., the Ten Article Agreement) negotiated in November 1914.[16]

The "save our face" explanation on the part of certain Irish extremists in the US, who in March 1916 struck discord in the heretofore straight-issue plan of campaign, can serve now only as tantamount to a death-bed confession of failure. They dared to exploit the acceptance of a half-measure scheme, contrary to the original plan, and that plan was the only hope of gaining an equal chance against a modern, fully equipped army of occupation which sustained the English and West British alliance in Ireland.

Let it be clearly understood by all Irishmen and Germans today that Casement and his compatriots in Germany, as well as the Irish Volunteers at home, were greatly hampered by the intriguing methods of other Irish so-called "insurrectionists". Some in the USA, and undoubtedly their counterparts in Erin, played important roles in paving the way so that some apparent whole hoggers might gain foot-stool political prominence through compromisory tactics. It's an old story: in warfare of the Gael against the Gall, Irishmen of the passive-resistance

---

[15] Arthur Zimmermann (1864-1940) was German Under Secretary of State for Foreign Affairs 1911-16 and Secretary of State for Foreign Affairs 1916-17. For the Ten Article Agreement, see below.

[16] For Plunkett's and Monteith's time in Germany with Casement, see below.

calibre have periodically and consistently practised feats of ill-conceived greed for political pomp and power. But, in most instances, those very makeshift and clever artists very rarely suffered death as sincere soldiers of Ireland. No, quite the opposite. They pulled a tight rein when their fiery war horses were in full gallop to death or glory. On the other hand, the real live Irish separatists were isolated and left abandoned to do or die, or, as Casement himself used to say: It is not the wild oratory of some Irishmen that England fears most; it is direct action of wide-awake Irish rebels that she dreads to face in deadly combat.

9. A few other short newspaper articles by various people and at various times since 1916 go to make up the story of Casement's mission, truly a modest bibliography and one much in need of being added to.

For this reason, the present volume will, perhaps, be most welcome. It is a fresh contribution from a source hitherto untapped, a source, moreover, that can claim to be well fitted to supply "inside" information. I was Casement's military organiser and principal recruiting officer in Germany, as well as acting in the capacity of adjutant to Commandant-General Joseph Plunkett during his tour as military delegate from the headquarters of the Irish Volunteers in Dublin.[17] When General Plunkett left for Ireland in July 1915, my duty involved a fairly accurate knowledge of all the proceedings between my chief Roger Casement, the German government, Ireland and also the Irish leaders in the USA.

The narrative can justly claim to be thus invaluable as giving a picture of the Casement-Plunkett embassy and the Irishmen who volunteered for the Irish Brigade, a picture of conditions from within. The book is not – and makes no claims to be – a full and complete story of the Irish Insurrection of 1916 but only as far as German relations with Ireland are concerned, or as the original plans undertaken by Casement and General Plunkett contributed to that insurrection's making. What it can honestly claim to do is to throw light from a new angle on an outstanding episode in Irish history that will hold more interest for all the more that is learned about it.

---

[17] Joseph Plunkett (1887-1916) spent a number of months in Germany in 1915 with Casement, sent there by the Military Council of the IRB. He was a poet and editor, Director of Operations of the Irish Volunteers, a member of the IRB Supreme Council and a signatory of the 1916 Proclamation. He married Grace Gifford, an artist, in Kilmainham on the night before his execution which was carried out on 4th May 1916.

Probably any further additions to our sources of information concerning the Casement mission will be in the nature of private letters, diaries or reminiscences.

Captain Robert Monteith (Commander, A Co., First Battalion Irish Volunteers, Dublin Brigade), who came to Germany via the US in a coal bunker in October 1915 and took over my command of the Irish Brigade, may write the story of his experiences in Germany with his Irish Wild Geese and of his perilous trip with Casement in U-Boat 19 to lonely Banna Strand on the Kerry coast.[18] I recall Capt. Bob saying goodbye as he handed me back my command over his machine-gun trained, 20 teams of "rough diamond Irish rebels" as he used to call the Irishmen of the Casement contingent so affectionately in his jocular military manner. He was so well known by the Dublin Brigade of the Irish Volunteers during his term as Director of Training throughout the days of grim determination in 1914-15, with the boys in green at the parade grounds of Blackhall Place and Kimmage in Dublin.

Capt. Monteith was a truly brave Irish officer and a good Irishman to every inch of his powerful physical manliness and soldierly appearance. I doubt not but that every old Irish Volunteer alive today in Dublin or Limerick can still hear the echo of his short, sharp military command; few if any could equal Capt. Bob in those far-off dark and evil days in Ireland when her volunteers were purely volunteers in the cause of Róisín Dubh. He refused the rank of major from John Bull's High Command in Ireland at the opening stages of the World War. Instead he chose the hard road to a fame that shall hold good in the cherished memory of Ireland's true sons and daughters in the immortal pages of Irish history.

Today his name may be forgotten by most latter-day converts to soldiering in Ireland. But tomorrow the name and self-sacrificing example of Capt. Bob Monteith will ring out with vigour anew: "Young Ireland, attention! Stand to arms!"

There are not likely to be further publications of documents by any of the interested governments. For the English, the main point is that the Casement expedition was frustrated; for the Germans, it is of no interest now to investigate why the project of Casement failed or whether it might have succeeded (except in the vital interest of truth and justice); for the Americans, it is not essential to explain how the laws and security of the USA came to be endangered by the action of some of its Irish citizens whose

---

[18] Robert Monteith (1879-1956), who had fought in the British army during the Boer War, 1899-1902, did indeed write the story of his expereinces with Casement. The book, *Casement's Last Adventure*, was first published in 1932, with a second edition in 1953.

ancestors materially and financially assisted America "in the making" from 1776 right to the present day. For the Irish-Irelanders today, it may suffice in clearing up certain old scars remaining still as running wounds, and which caused a septic decay throughout the last decade of years since 1916.

Yet, it is enough when a goodly number of Irishmen now plainly see almost red when they think how the undaunted and fearless Casement and his mission to give Irish Volunteer soldiers the called-for military material was nipped in the bud from almost the main source it sprung from in November 1913.

None the less the Casement mission must sooner or later be weighed up, and assigned its appropriate place in history – in Irish history and in European. Some years have now elapsed and it has become possible to view the matter with unbiased minds. For this, what is needed is knowledge, as much knowledge as we can procure; such additional knowledge as this volume supplies may lay facts open in a highly important degree.

Meantime, while awaiting the precise assessment of the enterprise as an Irish-Ireland historical event, it is well worth our while to ponder somewhat on the men who played parts in it. Their names are not overly well known, but they are evidently men of no ordinary stamp. Regarding them just as they showed themselves, they are intrinsically entitled to a certain homage – some more, some less:

1. Roger Casement himself, a high-souled Irishman and generous-hearted patriot, who died on the Anglo-Saxon gallows.
2. Captain Karl Spindler, so painstaking and resourceful, the fitting sea-officer of a forlorn hope.
3. Commandant-General Joe Plunkett, the poet-soldier and the first Chief of Staff of Ireland's youngest volunteer army in open battle with her centuries-old enemy. He was the seventh signatory to the Proclamation of the Irish Republic in 1916 and the first officer to take over the organisation command of Casement's Irish Brigade in Germany, where he mapped carefully the well-intended plans for the reoccupation of the Irish home fortress.
4. Captain Robert Monteith, a leader of soldiers without the usual demagogue type of aggressive approach. He finally dared and outwitted an empire's mercenaries in Ireland by escaping to the US in September 1916 disguised in the cloth of a padre, though he was a Protestant, yet none more "Irish of the Irish".
5. Sergeant Joe Dowling, the redoubtable follower of Casement who succeeded in landing safely from a German

submarine on the Co. Clare coast and delivering his message which later reached the chiefs in Dublin. In the April 1918 so-called German Plot, "the Irishman in a boat" faced England's naval power and was eventually arrested through a bank official's treachery at Ennistymon, Co. Clare. Joe was sentenced to imprisonment for life and served over six years in nine different English convict jails. In 1924 he was released, a broken-down warrior who knew no surrender. It was nearly 25 years since an Irish rebel was so long incarcerated in a "felon's cell" – Tom Clarke, the Fenian and father of the 1916 Insurrection, being the last long sufferer who was released in 1898.

6. Adler Christensen, the shrewd and reliable retainer, the last, or at least the latest, Norseman to turn Irish.[19]

These are, after all, the sort of men to learn more about – to learn all we can about, indeed. For there are times in Irish history when only this sort counts for anything worthy of the name of volunteer in the cause of Irish freedom.

Above all, what I seek to achieve in these pages is a just vindication of the sacred name and Irish-Ireland character which vibrated in the all-humane soul of my chief and martyr – Roger Casement.

Michael Keogh

---

[19] Adler Christensen was a Norwegian sailor whom Casement met in New York. Casement took him with him to Germany. Some biographers paint a very unflattering picture of Christensen, for which see below.

Contents

INTRODUCTION

Descendants keep letters, diaries, memoirs and other documents faithfully because they know that in those pages lies a link with a time fast passing from memory into history.

The descendants of Michael Keogh are no exception as regards the practice of faithful document keepers. He led an exciting, adventurous and indeed at times dangerous life, about which he wrote in some detail and at various times. At the heart of that life was his devotion to Roger Casement, whom he first met in New York in 1911, and with whom he worked closely in Germany during the years 1914 to 1916 as part of Casement's project to recruit an Irish Brigade from Irish soldiers who had joined the British army to fight in the First World War, and who subsequently found themselves prisoners of war in German camps. Casement's intention was to return to Ireland with this brigade to fight for Irish freedom.

Michael Keogh wrote a detailed account of those years in Germany with Roger Casement. It had always been his intention to publish that account in full in book form – an aim he did not get around to fulfilling during the course of a busy life, although he did publish many articles and give many lectures about his experiences with Casement's Irish Brigade.

Kevin Keogh kept many of the articles his father wrote. Another son, Joseph, now deceased, kept others. But they had been deprived for more than 40 years of the longest and most detailed account their father wrote. Kevin recalls seeing his father working on that account at various times over the years. Sometimes Keogh senior would be working late into the night, drafting and redrafting, and would resume the process early the following morning. One of his daughters-in-law, Mary, said that he never went anywhere without these manuscripts, which he carried with him in a kind of briefcase.

When Michael Keogh was suffering his last illness in 1964, he was taken to James Connolly Memorial Hospital in Blanchardstown, Co. Dublin. It seems that he took the papers that contained the main account of his time in Germany with him into the hospital. His son Kevin concluded this to be the case because he remembers visiting the hospital one day and finding his father very distressed and calling out for his papers. When Kevin asked him where they had been, he replied that he had had them under his pillow and that they were no longer there.

Kevin then called a nurse who had been attending to his father and asked her if she knew anything about the papers he was talking about. In the course of their conversation, she reported that Keogh senior had had a visitor the previous night – a priest whom none of the hospital staff knew by appearance or name. He was not a hospital chaplain or local parish curate but he had called to the hospital and had asked to see Mr Keogh. For the hospital staff, there was nothing unusual about priests visiting patients.

The Keogh family had no idea who the particular priest might be and they never found out who he was but they associate the missing papers with him. They could see how distressed the disappearance of his papers had left their father and they believe that his loss of these precious documents may have hastened his death, because he died around two days after they went missing.

Just over 40 years later, in 2005, Kevin Keogh's son, also called Kevin, was doing some research into his family's history with a view to compiling a family tree. He decided to do a search on the internet and he entered the name of one of his grandfathers, Captain Michael Keogh. To his amazement he discovered that the University College Dublin Archives (UCDA) had papers belonging to his grandfather who had worked for Roger Casement in Germany during the First World War.[18]

From the UCDA site, the Keogh family learned that their father's papers had been found among the Maurice (Moss) Twomey papers, which were deposited in the archive in 1984 by a Fr Maurice Twomey.[19] The Keogh family could not say if their father knew Moss Twomey, who had been active in the IRA for many years and who ran a newsagent's and tobacconist's shop on O'Connell St in Dublin from the 1940s onwards. He died in 1978. The archivist in UCDA could see that the Michael Keogh papers had no direct or close connection with the Twomey papers and as a result filed them separately.[20]

---

[18] Interview with Michael Keogh's son, Kevin, and daughter-in-law, Mary, conducted in Dublin on 31st January 2008.

[19] Moss Twomey (1897-1978), from Fermoy, Co. Cork, was active in the 1st Southern Division of the IRA during the War of Independence. He fought on the anti-Treaty side during the civil war and became IRA Chief of Staff in 1927. The IRA was outlawed in 1936 and he was arrested and imprisoned 1936-38. Thereafter he withdrew from direct IRA activities. He ran a newsagent's and tobacconist's shop on Dublin's O'Connell Street from the 1940s. The Twomey papers are at UCDA, call number [P69].

[20] They are available at UCDA [P128] under the name Michael McKeogh. Michael Keogh used "McKeogh" and "Kehoe" as variants on his name.

Who was the mysterious priest? Why had Michael Keogh's papers disappeared? How did they come to end up among the papers of Moss Twomey? The Keogh family were glad to have the main segment of their late father's papers back but would like answers to those questions.

Roger Casement made a profound impression on Michael Keogh, an impression that did not diminish in any way with the passing of the years – the very opposite, in fact. Many years after Casement's death, Keogh's wife told her daughter-in-law that she had lived all her married life with his memory.[21] But Keogh was in no way exceptional in this regard. One of Casement's biographers has remarked that so many who met him were immediately captivated by his charisma.[22]

One who met him for the first time in Germany during the First World War was Robert Monteith. He had fought in the British army during the Boer War in South Africa from 1899 to 1902. When the Irish Volunteers were formed in 1913, his military background led to him instructing and drilling members of the new force. He was then sent by the IRB to assist in the training of the recruits to Casement's Irish Brigade at Limburg and Zossen prisoner-of-war camps in Germany. After many adventures and with extreme difficulty, he made his way to Germany via the US in the latter months of 1915.

"To meet Casement was to institute a life memory," he later recorded. This was how he recalled that first meeting: "Feeling, as I did, that I was with one of the outstanding figures in the titanic conflict of arms and brains, it was the proudest moment of my life. Here was a man who had made, and was still making history; the man who had walked through savage Africa armed only with a walking stick, whose written word had shaken the throne of Leopold II of Belgium, a man who had saved millions of lives in the Congo and Putumayo."[23]

At times, Monteith wrote with deep emotion about Casement, of which the following is a good example: "I have known no eyes more beautiful than Casement's. In his case they were truly the windows of his soul: blazing when he spoke of man's inhumanity to man, soft and wistful when pleading the cause so dear to his heart, mournful when telling the story of Ireland's centuries-old martyrdom. They were eyes that seemed to search the heart and

---

[21] Interview with Kevin and Mary Keogh, 31st January 2008.

[22] Jeffrey Dudgeon, *Roger Casement: the Black Diaries* (Belfast, 2002), p.452.

[23] As a British consul, Casement's investigations and reports exposed appalling human rights abuses of the natives of the Congo in central Africa, under Leopold II of Belgium, and of the natives of the Putumayo in South America.

read one's very soul ... A man is indeed fortunate who can say that he has clasped Casement's hand and received his kindly smile of welcome."[24]

Another who met Casement in Germany for the first time, and who has left a record of how much he esteemed him, is Dr Charles Curry. This Irish-American academic was a mathematician and physicist and a professor at Munich University. He had a summer residence in the countryside near Munich on the shores of Lake Ammersee and invited Casement to spend time there whenever he wished. Later, writing to Casement's sister Nina, he referred to her as "the sister of the man I worshipped and adored".[25]

So it can be observed that men as diverse as the adventurous, soldierly Monteith and the quieter, academic Curry both found themselves spellbound by the charismatic Casement and remained devoted to his memory for the rest of their lives. Little wonder, then, that Michael Keogh's experience should have been so similar.

His background and life, up to the time that he became so closely involved with the brigade project in Germany, would certainly have predisposed him to see eye to eye with Roger Casement. In the first chapter of the story that will be unfolded in these pages, Keogh writes about the importance of heredity. "Consciously or unconsciously, heredity plays a powerful part in our destinies and lives. If its urge is latent in one generation, it returns with cumulative force in another. Circumstances may curb it, but no power can ever eradicate it."

His father, Laurence, came from Coolgreany, Co. Wexford, a county which saw much action and many struggles on behalf of Irish freedom from British rule, especially during the 1798 rebellion. His grandfather, Michael, had fought for the rights of tenant farmers during the late 1870s and 1880s, in the period known as the Land War, and his great-grandfather had been out in 1798.

Michael himself was born in Tullow, Co. Carlow, in 1891. He attended national school there and, at the age of 14, entered the seminary school of St Patrick's Monastery on a county-council scholarship. He stayed there for two years until, in 1907, he went to visit his aunt in New York; he was to remain in the US for the next five to six years.

---

[24] Robert Monteith, *Casement's Last Adventure* (Dublin, 2nd edition, 1953), pp. 107, 80, 89-90.
[25] Dudgeon, *Roger Casement: the Black Diaries*, p .452.

He had joined the Gaelic League branch in Tullow and also joined a branch of the same organisation in New York. In the same city, he also became a member of Clan na Gael, the American wing of the Fenian organisation. "In these Irish-Ireland[26] ranks, my mind was aroused to the more serious and wider aspects of Irish nationalism, and to a clearer perception of the influence which England never ceased to exert the wide world over in pursuit of international domination," he later wrote.

A military tradition also existed in Michael Keogh's background. His granduncle was Colonel Myles Keogh who joined the Papal Zouave[27] Army when he was just 16. Four years later he went to the US where the American Civil War was raging. With previous military experience, and showing natural leadership qualities, he was immediately elected captain of the volunteer company of Irish-Americans in the New York Irish Brigade. This brigade took part in almost every major campaign during the civil war.

By the end of the war, Myles Keogh had risen to the rank of colonel – a temporary wartime rank – and he decided to make his career in the army. He joined the Seventh Cavalry, then being formed at Fort Leavenworth, Kansas, with the rank of lieutenant. The regiment had Lieutenant-Colonel George Armstrong Custer as its second-in-command. Keogh was soon promoted to captain and became Custer's favourite subordinate officer. He was to die by his side at the Battle of the Little Bighorn in Montana on 25th June 1876.[28]

In the following newspaper article which he wrote,[29] and in which he refers to his illustrious predecessor, Myles Keogh's

---

[26] The term Irish-Ireland refers to the revival of Irish cultural nationalism in the late 19th and early 20th century. It was concerned with such things as the revival of the Irish language, the education of Irish children in the national history and literature, the playing of Irish games and the use of Irish-made products to strengthen the Irish economy. The term is most associated with the journalist D.P. Moran who published *The Philosophy of Irish Ireland* in 1905.

[27] Originally, Zouave was the name given to some infantry regiments in the French army. The Papal Zouaves were formed to defend the Papal States in the late 1850s as the Italian unification movement sought to incorporate the states into a united Italy.

[28] *Irish Times*, 17th October 1983.

[29] Michael Keogh wrote a number of newspaper articles from the 1920s to the 1950s. Some of these have survived in the papers to which the editor has had access; some are inaccessible for various reasons. This particular article has no evidence on it of where it was published but bears the date of July 1952. Most of his articles seem to have been published in a British paper called the *Sunday Chronicle*. The latter title disappeared in 1955 when it was merged with the *Empire News*.

grandnephew Michael told about his own first military experiences in the US.

Only two living things escaped the Custer massacre by Sitting Bull's Sioux Indians at Little Bighorn in June 1876 – and both were part Irish. When the 10,000[30] Sioux and Cheyenne braves charged in upon General Custer and his five companies of the Seventh US Cavalry, a half-breed scout named Jack Curley – his father was Irish, his mother a Pawnee squaw – tucked an Indian blanket around him, swung up on a loose army horse, and rode safely through the Indians.

The horse was Comanche and he belonged to my granduncle, Colonel Myles Keogh, Gettysburg[31] veteran, who died that day at the Little Bighorn, standing back-to-back with "Yellow Hair" Custer. Fort Keogh in Montana is today called after him. I rode Comanche 34 years after the massacre – at Fort Riley, Kansas, when I was doing a mounted infantry course in the American army. The old horse was then 38 and living at the fort in honorary retirement.[32]

I was taking up again the fighting tradition of my family. For here I was, an eager Irish emigrant of 21, tossing aside my engineer's job in New York to go battling with Mexican guerrillas in Texas and New Mexico. In a way my uncle Jack Tynan, a leading Fenian, was to blame. In 1906, he came on a holiday to the family home in Coolgreany, Co. Wexford, from Newark, New Jersey, where he owned a newspaper. And he persuaded my parents to send me to America.

So, in March the next year, I sailed in the White Star liner, Celtic – second class, four to a cabin, fare £10. I was passing up a £50 county-council scholarship to Blackrock College in Dublin. But Captain Jack Tynan, the man who tried to blow up Westminster Bridge in London, sounded more adventurous to a country merchant's son just turned 16. Harry Lauder and Vesta Tilley, bound for their first

---

[30] The number was more likely to have been between 2,500 and 4,000. See *Irish Times*, 17th October 1983.

[31] The Battle of Gettysburg, fought in early July 1863, was the battle with the greatest number of casualties (between 46,000 and 51,000) in the American Civil War. It was a Union victory and is generally regarded as a turning point in the war.

[32] Comanche became the prize mascot of the Seventh Cavalry until his death. He was then stuffed and his remains survive today in the US Army Museum at Fort Leavenworth, Kansas. See *Irish Times*, 17th October 1983.

American tour, were on board the Celtic too.[33] I used to slip up to catch a glimpse of them in the first-class saloon.

I was 17 and still at school at Fordham College in New York when I joined the "Fighting 69th" – the 69th Irish Volunteer Regiment of the National Guard. My battalion adjutant was the future father of the 1916 Easter Rebellion, Captain Tom Clarke.[34] In this company I was already immersed in the Irish republican movement in America: I had been inducted into Clan na Gael by Clarke and O'Donovan Rossa,[35] the old Fenian.

The 69th is a sort of home guard. I went once a week for training at the 69th armoury in Manhattan. The rest of my time was spent in studying for an engineering degree, which I took out at Columbia University in 1909. A year later I was working in the New York municipal engineering department when President William Taft[36] issued a call for volunteers to patrol the frontiers of Texas and New Mexico against the Mexicans.

Mexico, land of primitive beauty and savage nature, had been in revolt ever since the French attempt to set up Maximilian the Habsburg as its ruler had failed. Three leaders were fighting for control at the moment: Huerta, Madero and Pancho Villa.[37] Three hundred of us answered

---

[33] Harry Lauder (1870-1950) was a Scottish entertainer, mainly associated with music-hall entertainment. His most well-known songs are 'Roamin' in the Gloamin', 'I Love a Lassie' and 'Keep Right on the End of the Road'. Vesta Tilley was the stage name of Matilda Alice Powles (1864-1952), an English male impersonator and vaudeville star. She was a Conservative MP from 1924 to 1931.

[34] T.J. Clarke (1857-1916) was an active Fenian who spent 15 years in prison in England. He then went to the US and returned to Ireland in 1907. He was one of the main planners of the Easter Rising, after which he was executed.

[35] Jeremiah O'Donovan Rossa (1831-1915) was one of the founders of the Fenian movement. Jailed numerous times, he was finally exiled in 1871 and went to the US where he spent the rest of his life. When he died in 1915, his body was returned to Ireland and buried in Glasnevin Cemetery.

[36] William Howard Taft (1857-1920) belonged to the Republican Party and was the 27th President of the US from 1909 to 1913.

[37] Maximilian (1832-1867) was a member of the Austrian imperial Habsburg family. With the backing of Napoleon III of France and a group of Mexican monarchists, he was proclaimed Maximilian I of Mexico in 1864. He was overthrown by Mexican republicans and executed in 1867. In 1876, Porfirio Diaz (1830-1915) overthrew the elected president and established a dictatorship that lasted until 1911, when he was overthrown in what became known as the Mexican Revolution (1910-1921) but which was more like a civil war. Opposition to Diaz was led by Francisco Madero (1873-1913), Emiliano Zapata (1879-1919) and Francisco "Pancho" Villa (1877-1923). Madero was ousted and killed in 1913 by Victoriano Huerta (1850-1916),

the call to form a frontier guard against the three armies on the United States' newest border. For New Mexico, the latest state in the Union, was formerly Indian territory and settlers were pushing into the open spaces now that the terrible Apaches[38] had been broken and driven into reservations.

The 300 frontier guards were a mixed bunch. Our major in charge of the four troops of mounted infantry was an Irish-American named Coghlin. My top sergeant was an Englishman called Napier and my quartermaster-sergeant was Kreuger, a former Prussian hussar. We rode out of Fort Riley for the Texas border after three months of tough training: riding 50 miles a day, making camp in the open, shooting with cavalry carbine and Colt revolver from both sides of the saddle at full gallop, tracking and, most important of all, learning how not to disclose one's presence while operating in strange country.

We were trained by men who had fought the Apaches to a standstill. Our uniform was olive drab green short puttees, riding breeches, open-necked shirt with sleeves rolled up and Stetson hat. We did not carry sabres but our carbines and revolvers were reinforced by a couple of Gatlin guns, the weapon that had beaten the Red Indians.

We battled with the Mexican *tamales*[39] on a border that ran along rivers, over sun-baked mountains and across prairie, scrub and treacherous desert. It was the dirtiest war of any I ever got into. The Mexicans were vicious guerrillas, armed largely with French and Spanish muskets and razor-sharp machetes with which they used to sneak up and slice the heads off our sentries at night.

The three rival armies were a rag and bobtail, living off the countryside and bringing their womenfolk with them wherever they went. They were superb light cavalry. But they had never heard of chivalry in war. Some bronco braves in the Apache reservations had joined them. And whatever feelings the three groups held towards each other, they were one in their deep hatred of the American *gringos*.[40]

---

with the connivance of the US ambassador to Mexico but without the support of President-elect Woodrow Wilson. Zapata was assassinated in 1919 and Villa in 1923. Border clashes with US forces were common during this period.

[38] The Apachean peoples fought tenaciously against the encroachments onto their lands by the Mexicans and later by white Americans. The image of them as bloodthirsty and wanton savages is a gross and misleading caricature.

[39] *Tamale* is a Mexican dish of seasoned meat and maize flour steamed or baked in maize husks. The author is not sure how the term applied to Mexican fighters.

[40] This Latin-American term refers to a white, English-speaking person.

Our headquarters were in San Antonio but my troop of 50 men, which I led with the rank of lieutenant, was based in Sam Houston,[41] the town named after the first president of the Lone Star State. We rode constant patrols along the border on the trail of guerrillas who had slashed across the frontier to burn down settlements, rob, kill and carry off arms, horses, cattle and women. We laid ambushes – and in turn were ambushed. It was a war of fast raid and reprisal. And it was fought with sickening cruelty.

One of our troop, Jack Darcy, a Galwayman, was captured with two other men while in an outpost guarding our horse corral in a ravine. I split up the troop into groups to search for them. We found them. Their limbs had been chopped off and their bodies disfigured. Then when they had died after long agony, they had been shot and their heads cut off.

Sergeant Tom Cooney, a Spanish-American veteran,[42] with eight men tracked down the Mexican party and captured two of them. He was on the point of dealing out similar treatment to them when I came up and stopped him. The two murderers were later hanged after court-martial at Fort Leavenworth.

Once I was out with a small squad of troopers when we sighted a dust trail. We gave chase. Then a peon we came across saved our lives. The dust cloud concealed Pancho Villa and more than 1,000 of his so-called *salvadores*.[43] We turned tail promptly for the American line.

The rebel leader, Madero, was an intelligent man, a real military commander. Huerta was likewise a man to merit some respect. But Pancho Villa, though he has been glorified by Hollywood, was a brutal peasant and a brigand. His men always disfigured Americans before killing them. They slaughtered helpless farmers and settlers as a pastime in between battles. Pancho Villa and guerrillas-without-mercy taught me one tactic that is necessary to the soldier who wants to stay alive: the first point of valour is to observe the laws of preservation.

I was 10 months on the frontier when we rode into an ambush and one of Pancho Villa's men knocked some of the

---

[41] Sam Houston (1793-1863) was a 19th-century American statesman and soldier and an important figure in the history of Texas.

[42] The Spanish-American War of 1898 was fought to force the Spanish to cede independence to Cuba. The Treaty of Paris, which ended the war, gave the US the former Spanish colonies of Puerto Rico, the Philippines and Guam.

[43] This Spanish word translates as "saviours".

family military tradition out of me. I was shot out of the saddle by a bullet in the abdomen. I rode out of Texas in an ambulance wagon, first to Fort Riley and then to Fort Siocum Hospital in New York. And three months later I relinquished my command and went back to my engineering job. The US government was forced in the end to send down regular troops and build blockhouses along the frontier to keep out the Mexicans.

I was just a year home from my first war when I met Roger Casement. He had come to America to meet President Taft and to press his appeal for an international commission to the Putumayo to expose the rubber scandal on the Amazon. I was introduced to Casement at a Gaelic League concert in New York. I was then secretary of the Emmet branch of the league. Patrick Pearse[44] was at that concert; he was then in America to raise funds for his school in Dublin, St Enda's. Old John Devoy[45] the Fenian – "the Old Man" as he was known and the key to revolutionary Irish activities in North America – was also present.

I shook hands with Casement for the first time on that occasion. It was a meeting that was to change my life and to lead me to many strange adventures.

Michael Keogh's narrative of his life from the time he met Casement in New York in 1911 until his return to Ireland in 1922 just as civil war threatened to explode is what constitutes the main body of this book. The central part of that narrative is concerned with the years 1914 to 1916 in Germany and the travails of Casement's brigade project. We will see from his narrative that he joined the German army in the latter stages of the Great War (by which time he had married a German woman) and that he fought on the Western Front. He gives an interesting account of an encounter with Lance-Corporal Adolf Hitler in which he says he may even have saved Hitler's life. After the war, he was caught up in the chaos that engulfed the defeated

---

[44] Patrick Pearse (1879-1916) was a teacher, barrister, poet and writer in both Irish and English. He was a member of the Gaelic League and edited its newspaper, *An Claidheamh Soluis*, from 1903 to 1909. In 1908, he founded his own school, St Enda's, in Dublin. He was a member of the IRB Military Council which planned the 1916 Rising, in which he was one of the leaders (in one document he is described as President of the Provisional Government). He was executed after the rising.

[45] John Devoy (1842-1928) was the leader of the American Fenian organisation, Clan na Gael, and editor of the *Gaelic American* newspaper. Initially supportive of Casement's mission to Germany, he afterwards turned hostile towards him and wrote negative things about him.

Germany. He was in Munich, near his wife's home area, and fought against the Munich Soviet early in 1919.

He left Germany in December 1919, following his discharge from the German army, and came back to Ireland. For the next two years, he was involved in various capacities in the War of Independence. At least one of those capacities, as we will see from his own story, entailed gun-running to the IRA from Germany.

Kevin Keogh's mother told him some details of what life was like for her and her children during the infamous Black-and-Tan era in Irish history. The British had put a price on her husband's head. In later years, Kevin recalls seeing the poster with his father's photo and the reward offered for information leading to his capture – a poster that his father kept for many years. He was constantly on the move during the 1919-21 period and his wife had frequently to pack up house and move the children in her endeavours to be along with him.

Initially she lived with Michael Keogh's parents in their house in Tullow, Co. Carlow. Any time it was raided by the Black and Tans she was subjected to extra abuse because she was German. On occasions they threatened to kill her baby by throwing him out the window if she would not give them information about her husband's whereabouts. What made it extra difficult for her in her initial years in Ireland was that she spoke very little English, although it was probably just as well that she did not understand a lot of what the Black and Tans were saying to her.

What of Michael Keogh's life after 1922? There is little or no written evidence in his papers and the information that follows has been supplied by his son, Kevin. His father joined the Irish army some time after his return from Germany but when, exactly, Kevin does not recall. However, there is a letter among his father's papers which gives the dates and places of birth of his six children. Rosaleen, the third child, was born in the Curragh army barracks in Co. Kildare on 6th December 1922, which suggests that Michael Keogh had joined the Irish army by that time. It seems that his work in the army was of an engineering rather than a combat kind. The fifth child, Kevin, was born in Arbour Hill barracks in Dublin in November 1925. Five years later, the sixth and last child, Anna Marie, was born in Nuremberg in Germany.

So by 1930, Michael Keogh had left the Irish army and had gone back to his wife's homeland to live and work. There he worked as an engineer on the U-Bahn or underground railway system in Berlin. The family lived at 35 Jüdenstrasse in the city. The Olympic Games were held in Berlin in the first half of August 1936 and he worked as an interpreter at the games because of his fluency in both English and German (he was also fluent in Irish).

We learn from his own narrative below that he left Germany and returned to Ireland in September 1936, where he spent the rest of his life. His son Kevin says that he returned to Ireland because Eamon de Valera[46] wrote to him inviting him to do so, in view of his service to the national cause. Kevin, who was 10 or 11 by 1936, remembers his father's excitement as he came in the door of their Berlin home and showed them the letter, told them they were going back to Ireland and that he had been promised a house and a job.

They duly returned to Ireland and booked into a hotel in Dublin. Eight months later they were still in the hotel with no sign of either the promised job or house. It was expensive keeping a wife and six children in a hotel for that length of time and Michael Keogh's savings became depleted as a result. The family moved to small rented accommodation around the city for some time until he managed to get a job contract, involving pipe laying, in Portlaoise, Castletown and Mountrath in Co. Laois.

When that particular contract was finished, he was idle for some six or seven months until he secured another contract in Scariff, Co. Clare. This was a much longer posting, lasting four years, and involved work on a large reservoir there. During the years of the Second World War, Michael Keogh was involved in the running of the Pigeon House power-generating station in Ringsend in Dublin. His fluency in German was a great advantage to him because many of the engineers who had run the station were German. They had been recalled to Germany by Hitler during the war and the plans and blueprints concerning the functioning of the station were in German (the machinery was all German). In fact, it would probably be no exaggeration to claim that it was largely thanks to him that the plant was kept going during the war. Following the war, he worked for some years in the sugar-beet factory in Carlow.

Now in his late 50s, his health was somewhat precarious because of an enlarged heart and he retired from regular employment. He occupied his time by writing articles and giving lectures about his adventurous young manhood. But there can be no doubt that he and his family had led somewhat of a peripatetic and uncertain existence from the time they had returned from Germany in 1936.

---

[46] De Valera entered the national movement by way of the Gaelic League. He was the most senior officer to survive the 1916 Rising. From late 1917 he was president of both Sinn Féin and the Irish Volunteers. He opposed the Treaty in late 1921/early 1922 and remained in the political wilderness for some years thereafter. He founded Fianna Fáil in 1926; six years later his party got into power and he was head of government without interruption from 1932 to 1948.

So, why the letter from de Valera that brought him back to Ireland in 1936 and why were the promises contained therein not fulfilled? Kevin Keogh has no explanation but speculates that it may have had something to do with his father's personality. He was a strongly independent person who would not tow any party line but preferred to express his untrammelled opinion on the issues of the day without fear of or favour to anyone. He had not taken sides in the civil war and would not take any political side when he came back to Ireland in the mid-1930s. It was a much polarised place politically at the time and it must have been difficult to maintain a neutral and independent line. Was he asked to run for political office for de Valera's Fianna Fáil? If so, and he refused, a dim view would have been taken. But this is no more than speculation and, like others areas of his life, will have to remain something of a mystery in the absence of written evidence.[47]

Robert Monteith's account of his time in Germany gives us some insight into the character of Michael Keogh. Monteith arrived in Germany in late October 1915 and remained until early April the following year. He described Keogh as "a quiet dispositioned man, of plump and short physique, prone to follow the line of least resistance, but possessed of the knack of getting things done". Monteith said that Keogh spoke German well and continued: "I attributed this to the fact that when out of barracks [he was] usually accompanied by a charming human dictionary, who made the study of the language a labour of love."[48]

On 2nd November 1915, Monteith wrote a letter to Roger Casement from Limburg prisoner-of-war camp. The letter contained the following paragraph: "Regarding Keogh, I am rather in doubt in this matter. I have learned that there are other attractions in Limburg for the Sergeant-Major besides recruiting, but as he might be able to help things along, I think it would be wise to send him down. I will make sure that he carries out his share of the work." Given the comment quoted from Monteith at the end of the previous paragraph above, it is likely that in the phrase "other attractions" he was referring to a woman.

The other member of Casement's Irish Brigade who had an account of his experiences in Germany published was Anthony Quinlisk.[49] Although he referred to Michael Keogh, he did not

---

[47] Interview with Kevin and Mary Keogh, 31st January 2008.

[48] Monteith, *Casement's Last Adventure*, pp. 120-21.

[49] For biographical details on Quinlisk, see Chapter 6 below. He had two articles published under the title, "The German Irish Brigade: Diary of Casement's

comment on his character. So what insights into Keogh do we get from his own narrative, which constitutes the main body of this book?

One characteristic of the man revealed is that he possessed a sardonic humour. We have already seen an example of it from his account of his first military adventures along the US-Mexican frontier in 1910-11. His granduncle, as we have see, was Captain Myles Keogh of the Seventh Cavalry who perished at the Little Bighorn, and Michael Keogh referred to himself as following in this family military tradition. But, "I was 10 months on the frontier when one of Pancho Villa's men knocked some of the family military tradition out of me. I was shot out of the saddle by a bullet in the abdomen."

Another example is when he commented that he could have escaped to America when war was declared in 1914 but instead decided to take the chance of being shipped to France with his British army regiment because he had "sufficient intuition" of making his way from there to Germany. "Admittedly, it was not a trail over which one might carry an insurance policy for life," he remarked dryly and with some understatement. Again, when he was put in charge of the camp medical room at an early stage in the prisoner-of-war camp at Limburg, he said that he was in charge of "the sick, the lame and the lazy".

While in Germany, Roger Casement kept a "Diary for John Devoy" for a few days in late September 1915. In it he considered his general treatment by the Germans as dreadful: "... again and again I got rebuffs – and so rudely administered that I got quite despondent". He still found the German "civil element" a tolerable breed but the military men he considered hostile and stupid. He felt the Germans had shown a poor understanding of how to deal with Irishmen; they could not be brought to understand that Irishmen needed work and discipline but also freedom, humour, affection and a light rein.[50]

Early on in his narrative, Michael Keogh referred to Casement's difficulties with the Germans, not so much with the diplomats but with what Keogh called "the military heads of baronial jackboot officialdom". While trying to recruit men to the Irish Brigade in Limburg in the early stages, he got little help from camp officials. He said they were "all old reserve officers and preferred a quiet life. Isolated solitude was more in their line of soldiering." But, unlike Casement, he was not about to get

---

Lieutenant," in the British magazine, *Land and Water*, on 6th November 1919 (pp 18-20) and 13th November 1919 (pp 16-17).

[50] B.L. Reid, *The Lives of Roger Casement* (New Haven and London, 1976), pp. 307-8.

despondent as a result of their rebuffs. Nor was he about to let them enjoy a quiet life. "I promised them a hot time and kept that promise."

We saw above that Robert Monteith considered Keogh a man of quiet disposition who was prone to take the line of least resistance. It was true that he took the sensible course of not causing unnecessary problems but he did not take things lying down either. He was not afraid of a fight when he considered that one had to be fought. An example would be when he was accused of desertion of his unit when he left Danzig in the spring of 1918 to join and fight with the 16th Bavarian Infantry Regiment of the German army. Although he could have stayed in Bavaria, he decided to go back to Danzig and to take on his accusers on their own ground. It was a tactic that would and did make his victory over them all the sweeter.

In his narrative, Michael Keogh does not gloss over or glamorise the horrors of warfare. This may be seen from his descriptions of his experiences at the first Battle of Mons in the very early stages of the Great War. There he referred to the German "artillery belching death at short range". The British forces found themselves facing overwhelming odds during the battle: "Scarcely had half an hour elapsed before word was passed down the extended firing line: 'Every man for himself! Save yourselves as you can!' We were in a veritable death-trap, and officers and men simply acted on their own instincts of defence. I well remember one young Gael of immense stature, well over six feet, become suddenly bereft of all reason. He stripped off his jacket, rolled up his sleeves and, armed with drawn sword in one hand and a revolver in the other, dashed forward on his own, shouting and firing at random. It was a typical and tragic incident."

Having become a prisoner of war, he then joined Casement's Irish Brigade and finally moved on to enlisting in the German army. He took part in the major offensive launched by the Germans on the Western Front in the spring of 1918. When writing about his experience of the latter, he referred to modern warfare having become a "hell on earth" and he also alluded to "the sickening horror" of the process of machine-gunning huge numbers to death and of "mowing down a retreating enemy like locusts before a hurricane on the African veldt".

The piece of prose just quoted is a good example of Michael Keogh's skill as a writer. He was capable of evoking a broad range of registers in his writing. In the following passage, he describes the terrain through which he passed as he was being transferred by train with other prisoners of war from Sennelager camp in north-west Germany to Limburg camp in the south west. It can be seen from the passage how he enlivens factual description with well-chosen adjectives, nouns and verbs that convey awe, enthusiasm and admiration but also a sense of homeliness.

The journey from Sennelager, Westphalia, is a most instructive one to all lovers of the art of landscape scenery. One traverses great stretches of the fertile plains of Westphalia, inhaling the agreeable perfumes of the extensive pine forests which bear witness to the enormous forestry resources of the empire that came into being in 1870 under the German prince of politics, Count Bismarck. We gradually arrive in a valley of industry. The Rhine-Ruhr province was a veritable network of war-and-peace commerce, the sight of Krupps at Essen a marvel for the average visitor from the Green Isle.

It was fast approaching the dusk of the evening as our transport train slowly chugged its way onwards through this roadway of modern enterprise. On each side of the permanent way, massive factory structures seemed to rise up, casting a ruddy glow upon the sky from the electric-lighted buildings which formed a vast beehive of mechanical energy and power. The hour of exchange in work between the day and night shifts told an impressive tale in itself. Great masses of tradesmen and munitions workers – men and women – thronged on each railway station platform awaiting the local passenger trains which conveyed them to a well-earned repast and the more pleasant surroundings of home and family, with a peaceful repose assisting to relieve the strain of a weary and dangerous toil among the grinding mechanisms which sent forth their deadly missiles of modern war.

In the following example, Keogh displays one of the most necessary skills of the good prose writer: the ability to vary sentence type and style to maintain the reader's interest. Mixed in with this varying of sentence structure is a range of stylistic devices such as alliteration, assonance and metaphor.

But in her insensate endeavour to extirpate the Gael, England has succeeded only in fortifying his spirit. In seeking victims, she has given us martyrs. The essence she thought to destroy flourished more richly in the frame her rapacity had emaciated. The soul, as ever, flourished even when the flesh succumbed, and its divine mission is yet to be accomplished. In homely phrase, the hero-tale was told around the fireside, while the spirit of patriot-heroism went forth as an element against which gun and gold alike have been impotent.

Further examples of his skill as a writer may be found in his moving account of the death of one of the brigade members, Private Patrick O'Holohan, on the eve of St Patrick's Day, 1916 in Zossen prisoner-of war camp, to which members of the brigade were transferred from Limburg. "St Patrick's Day 1916 brought sorrow to the brigade: Volunteer Patrick O'Holohan was carried to his grave on the shoulders of his Irish and German comrades. He had been in poor health for some time, having never recovered from the effects of the rigorous campaign of the first three months of the war." On the day before Private O'Holohan died, Michael Keogh sat at his bedside: "I asked him if he had any particular message, and I can never forget his reply. 'My dear and kind-hearted Irish mother is in heaven,' he said, 'and there I hope to join her soon. One sister is in Ireland, another married in the United States. Let them know some day, if you have the opportunity, that I died a true Irishman.'"

The following day, Keogh returned to his bedside vigil beside the dying man "Then, as the Angelus bell tolled in the village of Zossen, heralding the eve of Ireland's national festival, he peacefully closed his eyes in death ... Just as the sun prepared to sink somewhere west of the Green Isle on St Patrick's Day, Volunteer Paddy O'Holohan was borne to his final resting place with full military honours."

Roger Casement paid for the erection of a granite headstone over the grave and he also paid the cemetery committee to have the grave looked after for a period of 20 years. "Patrick O'Holohan's grave and memorial make a centre of pilgrimage for Irish exiles in Berlin each recurring St Patrick's Day," concluded Keogh's account of this sad occasion.

Finally worth addressing is the question of why Irish prisoners of war in Germany chose to join or not to join Casement's Irish Brigade. Michael Keogh never had any doubt that Roger Casement was absolutely right to go to Germany to seek aid there for Irish freedom and also that he was right to try to recruit an Irish Brigade from Irishmen who had joined the British army and subsequently found themselves prisoners of war in Germany. In his narrative, Keogh points to Wolfe Tone's going to France in the 1790s to try to get the French to send military aid to free Ireland as Casement's historical precedent for going to Germany in 1914. He also makes mention of the numerous Irish Brigades who served against Britain in wars from the 18th century onwards, especially the brigade led by John MacBride[51] that fought on the side of the Boers in the Boer War in southern Africa from 1899 to 1902.

Robert Monteith, who made his way to Germany via the US in 1915, with extreme difficulty and at considerable risk to his life, in order to join Casement's brigade was quite clear in his own mind about the purpose of the brigade and the motivation of the men who joined it. "The men who joined the brigade in Germany never received one penny from the German government. They were asked by Casement, and through him by Ireland, to fight in and for Ireland only against Ireland's sole enemy – England. They were not asked to fight their own countrymen."[52]

The historian Andreas Roth proved unusual among commentators on the brigade in that he concerned himself with why men joined rather than why they did not join. He pointed out that the vast majority of those who joined had not been connected with the Home Rule movement before the war, never mind to more radical nationalist groupings such as the IRB. Roth put forward the valid argument that it is difficult to say why exactly most of them joined because of "the scant first-hand sources" available on which one could build some conclusions.

Some who were repatriated after the war said they joined solely to see if they could get better conditions as prisoners of war. But there were a few who gave as their motivation for joining that they did so because they wanted to fight for Ireland. Most of them were probably too young (the average age of brigade members was 24) to have wives and children, so they would probably not have been worried about reprisals being taken against their families by the authorities back home in Ireland, Roth contended.

However, and he did not allude to this, it probably was the case that many would have enlisted in the British army in the first place for economic reasons, and their parents would have received financial support from the authorities while their sons were prisoners of war in Germany. If it became known that they had joined the brigade – the equivalent of desertion – that financial aid would have been discontinued.

Roth speculated that it may well have been the case that those without prior nationalist backgrounds joined "in order to escape the dullness of prison camp routine". Nor did the prospect of going back to their former civilian lives promise much for them

---

[51] John MacBride (1865-1916) had emigrated to South Africa where he raised the Irish Transvaal Brigade to fight the British when the Boer War broke out in 1899. Most members were Irish or Irish-American miners living in the Transvaal.

[52] Monteith, *Casement's Last Adventure*, p. 93.

because only a third of them had some kind of professional qualification, he argued.

Roth agreed with Monteith that no one joined the brigade as a result of sympathy with Germany. The Germans made no attempt to persuade Irish prisoners to join their army. Articles II and III of the German-Irish Agreement, signed by Casement and German Chancellor Bethmann-Hollweg,[53] on 28th December 1914, stated that the brigade was an autonomous unit and not part of the German army. Roth concluded that one of the reasons for the failure of the brigade project was because of a lack of mutual German-Irish understanding, and he quoted one brigade member as follows: "I needn't tell you the Germans knew damn all about us."[54]

But *was* the brigade project a failure and, if so, to what extent? There is no doubt that all who have written about it consider it an abject failure and they give various reasons why it failed. One Casement biographer, Geoffrey Dudgeon, argued that the first Irishmen the Germans captured were mostly regular soldiers who were not going to be easily coaxed away from their comrades, unless they did not get on with them. The war in 1914 was still popular and Belgium, the perceived reason why the British went to war in the first place, was regarded by many Irish soldiers as a small Catholic nation invaded by Protestant Germans,[55] who could be cruel in their treatment of British prisoners, especially as regards food and medical treatment.[56]

The German historian, Reinhard Doerries, has written the most detailed study of Casement's time in Germany. He believes that both Casement and the German General Staff organised attempted recruitment to the Irish Brigade extremely badly. The custom with Irish secret societies, he says, was to approach people individually but instead it was decided to call prisoners together and explain to them in public about the brigade. Doerries thinks it natural that most men were unwilling to step forward and show their nationalism before all. Others, he speculates, were probably concerned about the financial security

---

[53] For the details of the full agreement, see below, Chapter 5.

[54] Andreas Roth, "'The German soldier is not tactful': Sir Roger Casement and the Irish Brigade in Germany during the First World War," in *The Irish Sword*, vol. 19, no. 78 (Winter 1995), pp. 329-30.

[55] Belgian neutrality was guaranteed in 1839 by five European powers: Britain, France, Prussia, Austria and Russia. When the Germans invaded Belgium en route to France in early August 1914, Britain used this violation of Belgian neutrality as the reason for declaring war on Germany. War for the defence of "little Catholic Belgium" was an effective British recruiting slogan, especially in Ireland.

[56] Dudgeon, *Roger Casement: the Black Diaries*, p. 450.

of their families at home. Looking back, he finds it hard to understand why the German General Staff officers responsible for Irish affairs let Casement address all the prisoners, including those loyal to Britain, who must have regarded Casement as a traitor.

Doerries refers to the men who eventually joined the brigade (their numbers were between 55 and 60) as consisting of adventurers and republicans and others who appeared indifferent, which explains why the first two types but not the third joined up. He goes on to remark that Casement was not the type of man to organise successfully a military unit like the brigade or to instil the necessary morale and camaraderie in the men. On the other hand, he says, it should also be recalled that life for Irish prisoners of war in German camps was such that most would not have had any good reason to wish to cooperate with the Germans. Treated poorly since capture, even after they were sent inside Germany, many continued to complain of bad clothing and too little food. And neither the German military officers nor the civilian Foreign Office personnel detailed to deal with the Irish prisoners daily succeeded in forging a closer relationship with the prisoners of war.[57]

Michael Keogh's explanations for the limited numbers of men who joined the brigade agree and disagree with some of the foregoing analysis and add new perspectives as well. His narrative bears out Doerries' point that it was very difficult for men to step forward and show their nationalism in front of their comrades. Indeed, intense intimidation was practised by pro-British and West British elements among the men to prevent recruits coming forward to join the brigade. However, he would strongly disagree with Doerries' comment about Roger Casement not being the sort of man to organise such a unit or to instil the discipline and camaraderie required in the men. As far as Keogh was concerned, no fault whatsoever can be attributed to Casement. Yes, the Germans were incompetent and did not know how to deal with Irishmen; the IRB in Dublin and the Clan na Gael in the US – both of whom had a vested interest in the brigade project – also bungled and were ineffectual at times in their organisation and communication, but Casement held up his end of the bargain and did everything that was humanly possible to make a success of the brigade, Michael Keogh believed.

The sorting out of potential brigade recruits was done so badly that English-born prisoners were allowed to infiltrate the prison camp that was supposed to be for Irish prisoners only,

---

[57] Reinhard Doerries, *Prelude to the Easter Rising: Sir Roger Casement in Imperial Germany* (London, 2000), pp. 9-12, 14.

Keogh pointed out. He also told of ladies' societies, who were loyal to the British, being set up in Ireland when news got out about Limburg prisoner-of-war camp being set aside especially for Irish prisoners, with a view to persuading them to join a brigade. These ladies' societies sent large numbers of parcels to the prisoners at Limburg, parcels containing food, clothing, tobacco and even money. So, asked Keogh, why would men want to involve themselves in a risky project like the brigade when they were doing so well from this deluge of parcels from Ireland which were making their lives so much more comfortable than most of the prisoners in other German camps?

The existence of such societies is confirmed by the following anecdote that Monteith told in his book.

An amusing incident happened about New Year. A bag of mail came in. One man received two letters. They were both from the same person, Lady _____, Co. Kildare, Ireland. One was dated a week later than the other. The first informed the man that Lady _____ was pleased to adopt him as a "war child" or "war son" or "war" something or other. By doing so, the writer pledged herself to send him a parcel monthly, papers at intervals, etc. The second letter informed him that her "ladyship" had learned that he had followed that awful traitor, Sir Roger Casement, and was now in the Irish Brigade, and therefore she, more in sorrow than in anger, struck him off her exalted list of "war orphans" or "war babies" or what not. Quite a little tragedy in its way.[58]

In the final analysis, what might be worth commenting on is the fact that as many as up to 60 men joined Casement's Brigade despite all the obstacles militating against their doing so. Some indeed were no doubt adventurers; from his ultimate fate, as we shall see, Timothy Quinlisk was perhaps the best example of this particular type. Others were certainly committed republicans or at least, strong nationalists. Michael Keogh himself was among these and so was Robert Monteith. According to Keogh's list of the names of brigade members,[59] 14 of them afterwards served in the IRA during the Irish War of Independence from 1919 to 1921, and two of them were killed in action.

Why the other 40 or so men enlisted to follow Casement we shall probably never know. But, to the end of his life, Michael Keogh never expressed the least regret or doubt about his decision to follow a man he came to regard as the noblest being he had ever met or could ever hope to meet. It must say something about the quality of Roger Casement's character that

---

[58] Monteith, *Casement's Last Adventure*, p. 131.
[59] See Appendix 3 below.

he was capable of inspiring such devotion from men such as Michael Keogh and Robert Monteith.

CHAPTER 1: The Importance of Heredity

(a) My own heredity

Though the story of a dramatic phase of the last great fight for Irish independence, which I am about to unfold, draws its scenes from a strange country during the throes of the great World War; and though many events and personages were ordinarily far removed from the focus of my hopes, and alien to the impulse of my energies, the mainspring of my ambition remained singular and immutable. That was the absolute freedom of Ireland from foreign damnation and subversive influences.

Consciously or unconsciously, heredity plays a powerful part in out destinies and lives. If its urge is latent in one generation, it returns with cumulative force in another. Circumstances may curb it, but no power can ever eradicate it. I am free to confess with pride that the tradition of hostility to tyranny and injustice was a powerful factor in my national creed and inspiration. Opposition to racial abasement had ever been among those whose name I bear. It was implanted in their blood by centuries of long resistance to oppressive inroads. It had all the glamour of past heroism and the sanctity of past sufferings to vindicate it.

My father, Laurence Keogh, was the son of Michael Keogh, of Glenogue, Coolgreany, Co. Wexford, a leader almost half a century ago in the fiercest fight against ruthless landlordism (which has become an historic phase in the history of Irish agrarian agitation): the struggle made for their homes by the Coolgreany evicted tenants. He was thrown on the roadside with his young family of 10 children; his paternal homestead was razed to the ground, and his farm of 100 Irish acres was confiscated. Such too was the fate of most of his neighbours in the townlands of Glenogue, Ballyfad and Coolgreany – sacrificed that the vicarious grip of England might be secured on Ireland's throat by the destruction of her ancient peasant race.

There too in historic '98, the insurrectionary torch was first kindled by Father John Murphy, and thence, 80 years after, came the saintly historian of that glorious effort, Father Kavanagh.[60] It was ground dedicated by patriotism, from the heyday of the clans O'Toole, O'Byrne and Kavanagh, who kept the cause of freedom safe in the Wexford mountains and far beyond the Wicklow Gap.

---

[60] Patrick J. Kavanagh, *A Popular History of the Insurrection of 1798* (Dublin, 1874).

Tradition breathed of resistance to oppression in that territory and, generation after generation, domestic injustice combined with a sense of racial humiliation to fuel the sacred flame.

My kindred responded to the tocsin that rang out so fatefully from Boolavogue.[61] The story of that marvellous campaign, waged by a small minority of the nation, can be read in the glowing pages of Fr Kavanagh's history, and it were well, indeed, that it should be studied by young Ireland today. The settings of world epics may change, but the elements of heroism and barbarism are unalterable when right confronts might. It would be well that the youth of Ireland were made familiar with the great events and tragic episodes of that inspiring struggle; made to learn of the gallantry which, unorganised and only half-armed, swept British symbols and soldiery almost clear of Wexford soil, from Oulart Hill to Ferns and Gorey, from Wexford town to New Ross. It would be well too that they should know how British power, aided by native hirelings, triumphed under Cornwallis at Vinegar Hill – for defeat before such odds has lessons as pregnant of wisdom as the greatest victories.

De Ruth, the French military historian,[62] recalls a little-known incident in the student career of Fr John Murphy of Boolavogue. "The Irish," he wrote, "were under the leadership and military command of the superb tactician, Fr John Murphy, who in his young priesthood days in Paris saved the life of Major Bonaparte in the hunting field, an action which preserved for France her first Emperor Napoleon. In 1798," he adds, "Ireland with a united manpower constituted a fighting force not easily dealt with, particularly when placed on even a semi-organised basis." How richly Napoleon might have repaid that timely deed of the young Irish padre. How striking also it is how this mention of Napoleon's name links up the tragedy of Wolfe Tone's embassy to France[63] with Casement's mission to Germany 117 years later.

The history of Ireland during the 15 years preceding the insurrection of 1798 has been presented from many aspects and need form no feature of this work. It is impossible, however, to ignore the process of economic and military development which was proceeding during those years when England's preoccupation with many wars, mostly of a predatory character, kept her for a

---

[61] Fr John Murphy, already mentioned, was from Boolavogue and became one of the leaders of the 1798 rising in Wexford.

[62] The editor has been unable to trace the origin of this reference.

[63] Wolfe Tone went to France in 1796 in hope of enlisting French aid to help free Ireland. The French sent three expeditions to Ireland. Tone travelled on the last of these, was captured and sentenced to death but died (it was claimed by suicide) before the sentence could be carried out.

time inactive in opposition to Irish national aims. But she was not indifferent to the trend of events. Temporary compromise appeased the pressing danger. Grattan's Parliament was founded, and at once England set to work to render the Volunteers, who had forced that concession of an independent parliament, harmless. The seeds of disunity were sown on the fruitful grounds of jealousy and selfishness. The ranks of the Volunteers thinned, their patriotism evaporated, and at last they degenerated into county militia units commanded by alien land settlers and social parasites who adhered to the ideal of a foreign king in Ireland.

The combined policy of cajolery and corruption worked slowly but surely, and threatened the utter ruin of Irish nationality. To counter the subtle machinations of the unchanging enemy, the young soldier-diplomat, Wolfe Tone, founded the Society of United Irishmen who were pledged to unalterable hostility to the English connection and influence. In this work, he was assisted by his faithful adjutant Seán Keogh. The scheme, daring in conception and pursued with sacrificial zeal, failed partly through inertia at home and lack of enthusiasm abroad.

It remained for the fighting clansmen of Wexford and Wicklow to strike the most potent and dramatic blows in that particular war of independence. Left to fight alone, save for equally isolated risings in Connacht and Ulster, the end was inevitable. Had the other counties risen simultaneously, the history of Ireland would provide more pleasant reading and the agonies of many a penal hour would have been spared our people. Through all the gloom and squalor of the period, there nonetheless shines, with undiminished radiance, the gallantry of those who found at one and the same time a patriot grave and heroic immortality.

The memory of bloodshed and brutality with which the insurrection was finally overcome, and the orgy or rapine and robbery that followed it, could not fade among the descendants of those who had suffered in that regime of blood. Nor were they permitted to forget such things. Each succeeding generation experienced the hatred of the same imperial tyranny and added fresh names to the roll of Irish national martyrs. Whether the process was the rope, the prison cell or the famine fever, the purpose was always the same: the extermination of the native Irish race. Eviction and exile supplanted rope and bullet, and were deemed just as effective and less spectacular.

But in her insensate endeavour to extirpate the Gael, England has succeeded only in fortifying his spirit. In seeking victims, she has given us martyrs. The essence she thought to destroy flourished more richly in the frame her rapacity had emaciated. The soul, as ever, flourished even when the flesh succumbed, and its divine mission is yet to be accomplished. In homely phrase, the hero-tale was told around the fireside, while the spirit of patriot-heroism went forth as an element against which gun and gold alike have been impotent.

In the late 1870s and early 1880s, the Coolgreany farmers were cast upon the highway from their ancestral homes to depend upon the generosity of neighbours for food, warmth and shelter.[64] Such comforts were never withheld and may have appeased the patient sufferings of aged and careworn parents. What solace of hope could they afford the young? What prospect of future welfare did they promise for the children whose heritage had been wrested from them? The emigrant ships bore a tragic succession of goodly freight in those days. The Celt was again going with a vengeance; exile was the only alternative to pauperism.

Four of the Keogh family of Coolgreany sailed for the United States during this exodus. The remaining members found livelihoods at home. The Land Resettlement Act of 1897 replaced two of my uncles, Pat and Mark Keogh, in their father's home at Glenogue. As was the case with most evicted tenants, only half of the original holding was restored. This, and an improvised house, was the extent of the restitution made. As in the Penal Days,[65] the most arable land was invariably retained by some alien settler or colonist who hailed from north of the Boyne or had descended on his spoil from across the channel. The West Briton was not forgotten either, and proved as trusty an agent of the new plantation as any foreigner could.

In the peaceful churchyard of Ballyfad, a stone marks the grave of a leader of his class in the fight for the hearthstones of their sires. The inscription reads:

Michael Keogh,
Glenogue, Coolgreany, Co. Wexford.
Born, 23rd January 1819.
Died, 15th May 1898.
R.I.P.

In the old homestead at Glenogue (The Glen of Youth) can still be seen the pike-head which his father used in many a hard-fought encounter from Gorey to Vinegar Hill. These are the silent symbols of two distinct but analogous phases of our age-long

---

[64] This period of agrarian struggle in Irish history is known as the Land War. The Land League was formed by Michael Davitt in 1879 to fight for the rights of tenant farmers.

[65] The Penal Laws were laws passed by the Ascendancy Protestant-dominated Irish parliament. They applied from the late 17th century through much of the 18th century and discriminated against Catholics and non-Conformist Protestants (those who didn't conform to the established Anglican Church of Ireland). They were aimed mainly at property owners.

fight for national existence – the stone above the clay of the victim of Britain's economic war upon our people; and the weapon which outraged manhood forged to vindicate that manhood and preserve its honour unsullied. With such reminders of the past, is it strange that the spirit of revolt against the persistence of alien domination should have survived there? Is it aught but natural that in such an environment, permeated with such traditions, struggle should seem preferable to subservience and insurgency should be chosen before submission?

My boyhood was spent in the historic town of Tullow, Co. Carlow, where the patriot priest, Fr John Murphy, was done to death in '98. My education was begun in the excellent national school there, and at the age of 14 years, I qualified by a county-council scholarship to enter the seminary school of St Patrick's Monastery. There I remained for two years until, in 1907, an invitation to visit my paternal aunt, Miss Mary Keogh, in New York was accepted and new scenes and emotions presented themselves to my youthful outlook.

I soon became a member of the Gaelic League classes under the presidency of Major McCrystal in the Emmet Arcade, 59th Street and Lexington Avenue in that vibrant city, and in this way maintained the connection I had formed with the revival movement at home in the O'Growney Gaelic League branch in Tullow.[66] Under its auspices, I had felt the thrill of the new enthusiasm between the years 1903 and 1906, when I had competed in Gaelic singing and dancing at feiseanna in Carlow, Wicklow, Laois and Wexford. Not long afterwards in the US I became a member of the Clan na Gael in New York and of the Rocky Mountain O'Brien Branch of the same organisation in Denver, Colorado. In these Irish-Ireland ranks, my mind was aroused to the more serious and wider aspects of Irish nationalism, and to a clearer perception of the influence which England never ceased to exert the wide world over in pursuit of international domination.

The extent of the ramifications of the policy of our hereditary enemy was made manifest during the years 1908-10 when, to

---

[66] The "revival" referred to here is that instigated by organisations like the Gaelic Athletic Association and the Gaelic League, both founded in the later 19th century to revive an interest in Irish sports, culture and the Irish language. Fr Eugene O'Growney (1863-1899) was a founder member of the Gaelic League and Professor of Irish at Maynooth; his *Simple Lessons in Irish* contributed enormously to making Irish people familiar with their native language.

secure the success of the Entente Cordiale[67] in Europe, she managed to provoke financial crises in America. Even then, years before the murder at Sarajevo had fired the train,[68] the encirclement of Germany had been begun. The financial interests Britain possessed were ably used for the strangulation of German commerce, and Wall Street responded wholeheartedly. The situation that inspired the World War and the ammunition that prolonged and decided it were moulded by the Mammonites of America at the behest of their confreres who controlled international finance in Europe.

These insidious manoeuvres were well known to Irish nationalists in the States who could only wait to see with what hypocritical guise the long-planned *casus belli* would be presented. When at last the slogan "Defence of Small Nations"[69] was sounded, they were neither surprised nor shocked, only more deeply impressed than ever by the mendacity of that people and government against whom they had been fighting for centuries.

It would be useless to deny, however, that the pretence succeeded in deceiving a large part of an unsophisticated world. Some there were who did not need to be deceived and who simulated indignation and enthusiasm with admirable artistry. Others fell for it through sheer unthinking emotionalism. These attitudes applied to many races in America. They should not have influenced those of Irish blood. Yet they did, not only in the Republic of the West but at home, with results we can all assess now.

The campaign, once started, knew no abatement of audacity or intensity. The abuse poured out upon Napoleon and the French 100 years earlier was now directed against the German Emperor and his people. German atrocities in 1914 were translated from French outrages in 1814, and while British garrisons in Ireland were venting their savagery on our people,[70] just as in 1814 the same power was invoking the North American

---

[67] The Entente Cordiale, signed between Britain and France in 1904, put an end to centuries of intermittent conflict between these two old enemies and paved the way for the diplomatic and military cooperation that preceded the First World War.

[68] On 28th June 1914, an extreme Serb nationalist assassinated the heir to the Austo-Hungarian throne and ignited a series of events that led to the outbreak of the First World War just over a month later.

[69] When Germany invaded Belgium at the start of the First World War, Britain was able to use the violation of this small nation's sovereignty to claim it was fighting the war for the defence of small nations.

[70] Following the Howth gun running in late July 1914, where the Irish Volunteers brought ashore 1,500 guns from the continent, soldiers of the King's Own Scottish Borderers fired on a crowd on Bachelor's Walk in Dublin city, killing three people.

aborigine and his methods of warfare against the soldiers of the new republic in western Europe. It was a case of the same guile and the same guilt, the same posture of altruistic rage and ever the same selfish motives beneath.

Such were the happenings and the situation at the outbreak of the Great War that awoke the latest but not the last uprising of Irish nationalism and gave to Éire a new blood-roll of martyrs and heroes.

It would have been strange indeed if, when a world upheaval came to pass and when the shibboleth of one confederation was "the freedom of small nations", that Ireland should have remained unmoved and inert. Yet such, and worse, her attitude seemed likely to be for a long time after August 1914. Saxon wiles promised again to be successful in doping Ireland's instincts of freedom, and ere long she presented the spectacle of a nation sending its sons to fight a cause in which she didn't believe, with an ally she could not trust. The intrigues which brought about this humiliating position have long since been exposed and are now confessed. The major characters in that drama of deceit and shame have taken their rewards and are indifferent to their ignominy. Still all has not been revealed. The honour that resisted humiliation and the courage that withstood danger have had little credit done to them as yet.

In December 1911, I first met Roger Casement in the US. It was at one of the Irish-Ireland feiseanna held at Selzer's Park on 129th Street and 1st Avenue, Manhattan, in New York. He was then fresh from his victory in Putumayo in South America.[71] It was a cousin of my family (Myles Foley, hotel proprietor, 62nd Street and 2nd Avenue) who introduced the Irish patriot as a most likely and suitable honorary member for our IRB branch. Myles Foley had gone into exile many years before that from his parental home at Aughrim, Co. Wicklow, where his father had an extensive business and a farm of land.

The Parnell split[72] sowed the seed of disaster in this Irish family, hence the emigrant ship. The Irish mother of Myles Foley and my grandmother were sisters, so we used to go over the history of the Land League days in old Ireland. Although then quite early in the 20th century, he had amassed a fair amount of wealth through hard work and honest endeavour as an Irish

---

[71] Casement served as British Consul in Brazil 1906-11. In 1910-11, he revealed the appallingly cruel exploitation of native labour by white traders in the Putumayo River region of Peru and his report, published in 1912, earned him a knighthood.

[72] In 1890-91, following Parnell's involvement in the Catherine O'Shea divorce case, the Home Rule parliamentary party he led split, causing deep divisions in Irish nationalism.

exile. Nevertheless, his heart and dollars were ever at the command of the Irish-Ireland movement in New York.

Roger was always a fervent admirer of the song and dance of Gaeldom, so ere we parted friendship at the Selzer's Park feis, Myles from the Wicklow hills, although then advanced in years, was entreated to "trip the daisies" to the tune of "The Wind that Shakes the Barley" played by O'Shea, the old Celtic Park Irish piper.

It will be my endeavour in the following pages to disclose how a handful of hereditary Irish rebels took the hardest road of all, and threw themselves fearlessly across the path of British and allied militarism to show that the spirit of Irish nationalism still lives. This narrative will turn only where unavoidable upon the events and undercurrents that moved the Volunteers in Ireland prior to the rising of Easter Week 1916. With all due respect to the abilities and honesty of those who have contributed something to the history of that period, I may be permitted to say that it is still far from having secured a complete and authoritative chronicle. The surface of the waters only has been illuminated; the depths have yet to be explored and the darker recesses plumbed.

It is my purpose to deal here with the formation and vicissitudes of Roger Casement's Irish Brigade in Germany, and to refer to proceedings at home and in the United States only where such a reference is absolutely necessary. The link between the revolutionary movement in Ireland and in America was at all times closer than many suppose, much closer than some who know are now willing to admit. This was abundantly proved by the negotiations which preceded Casement's fatal expedition. The volte-face was only too clearly evident in the aftermath of that heroic attempt to retrieve Ireland's honour and preserve her devotion to the cause of liberty.

It is only fair that the Irish people should know the obstacles and discouragements that beset Roger Casement, Joe Plunkett and his compatriots in Germany and which resulted in the brigade as a whole failing to vindicate their aims and motives by a fight upon their native sod. These difficulties were not of their own making. They arose neither from unpreparedness nor hesitancy. As I hope to show, they grew out of divided councils elsewhere and lack of that initiative which is the essence of all revolutionary endeavour. I promised our Chief, Roger Casement, that, if I lived, I would endeavour to vindicate his work and our resolve; that I would relate the inner and full story of the formation of the Irish Brigade, its relations with and experiences under the German government and military authorities, so far as its primary purpose of striking a blow for Ireland's freedom was concerned.

It is regrettable that, as in the case of most Irish patriot-martyrs, we are forestalled by a shoal of foolish or malicious tales. "Diaries of Casement" were offered to the late Michael Collins during the Treaty negotiations, which were intended to poison the fount of Irish patriotism at its source in the abode of unselfishness and devotion in the patriot heart. The foul ruse failed, for Collins was too astute and knew his England too well to recognise in these clumsy concoctions the hand of the chivalrous Casement. Other publications have been equally misleading, though perhaps unconsciously. Writers in America have speculated with post-mortem sapience on the reasons why "the 1916 Rising failed" and "what might have been"! Others assert that it was owing to the demobilisation order of Eoin MacNeill.[73]

Each has a theory of his own, some no doubt the product of genuine thought, more simply the outcome of a desire to exploit a dramatic episode in Ireland's modern annals. A few more mendacious than all the rest proclaim that "the Germans let Casement down; he was duped by them; he was mad". One, whose motive was exposed by his official connection with Casement's enemies, secured unenviable notoriety by besmirching his victim's personal character. It is an old story – a traditional phase in British warfare – and the shame of it is that there were Irishmen, even pretending nationalists, prepared to accept and report the dastardly products of envenomed hatred.[74] Roger Casement had no reason to shirk an examination of his entire life, no cause to blush for his actions or motives in any phase of his existence as the friend of the Boers in South Africa in their fight for freedom; as the enemy of slavery in Africa and South America; as the succour of our own fever-stricken peasantry in west Connacht; and as the protagonist of Ireland's struggle for independence. As such he died, unrepentant and uncompromising.

---

[73] On Holy Saturday 1916, Eoin MacNeill, President of the Irish Volunteers, issued a countermanding order telling members of the organisation not to turn out for manoeuvres the following day (an order had already been sent out by the Military Council of the IRB earlier in Holy Week calling on Volunteers to turn out for such manoeuvres). MacNeill's order was published in the *Sunday Independent* the following day. The action is generally seen as limiting the extent of the rising that began on Easter Monday.

[74] It is difficult to pinpoint which specific writers or biographers are being referred to here, but a number have alluded to Casement's difficulties with the Germans and most have examined the question of his homosexuality.

It was a consciousness of his own rectitude of character that prompted him to speak as he did to me on the occasion of our last conversation, on the old Linden Tree Road outside Zossen by Berlin, a few days before his departure on the expedition which proved so tragic. *"Let all know the truth!"* was his parting injunction. That command will be obeyed to the best of my ability. It involves a simple statement of facts, explaining why Casement came to Ireland and why his brigade did not accompany him. Around these events mystery and antipathy have raised a smokescreen of inaccuracies that are unjust to the dead and the living alike.

(b) Roger Casement's heredity

Roger David Casement, Irish patriot and martyr, was born in Doyle's Cottage, Lawson Terrace, Sandycove, Co. Dublin on 1st September 1864, and not in Ballycastle, Co. Antrim, as wrongly stated wholesale elsewhere. His father, also Roger, was a born Ulsterman, a colonel in the Antrim Militia in the 1847-48 period. His mother, Ann Jephson, was a Catholic from Dublin who had her son secretly christened a Catholic at Rhyl in Wales when he was three. She died when he was nine and his father died when he was 13; he was raised by Protestant paternal relatives in Cushendall, Co. Antrim.

The Young Ireland movement of the 1840s created the forces of an almost-resurgent Irish nation which were dispersed through the enforced famine of Queen Victoria and her military mercenaries in Ireland, aided by a piously proclaimed decree exhorting the Irish peasantry to starve and die on the roadsides, to the extent of two million,[75] rather than to challenge the usurping landlords' vineyards then blockaded against a cowed and oppressed people. Wholesale pestilence followed the hungry Irishry into the death ships of emigration, to feed the shark-infested waters of the ocean with Irish corpses or fill mass graves when carried ashore in the United States and Canada.

Such scenes drove Roger Casement senior, Meagher of the Sword, Doheny, O'Mahony and many other Young Irelanders to Paris and the continent.[76] With Europe in the middle of upheaval

---

[75] It is not clear what is meant here by a "decree". In the Great Famine of 1845-49, some one million people died and another million emigrated.

[76] Thomas Francis Meagher (1823-1867), "Meagher of the Sword", was arrested and sentenced to penal servitude for life after the unsuccessful Young Ireland rising of 1848; he escaped to America in 1852 and was the founder and Brigadier-General of the Irish Brigade that fought on the Union side in the American Civil War. Michael Doheny (1805-1863) fled to the US after the 1848 rising, where he helped found the

from the Danube to the Tiber and from the Elbe to the Seine, republican forms of government were springing up from barricades overnight.[77] In Paris, those Irish exiles struck the Irish Republican tricolour of green, white and orange for the first time. It was subsequently presented, through returned exiles, in Dublin city by veterans of 1848.

The soldier Casement in Paris met the Hungarian independence leader Louis Kossuth and went with him to that south-eastern European country then in the pangs of oppression by the young Habsburg Emperor of Austria, Franz Joseph. Here the Irishman was aide-de-camp and adjutant to General Kossuth, and fought many a hard battle with his Honved Cavalry Regiment and brave Hungarians against the imperialistic Austrians. As ever with smaller nations, might prevailed and right was deprived of justice – by defeat alone. Only victory could have sustained Hungarian claims. The ultimate end saw Kossuth and Casement – with the remaining rebel forces – thrown into retreat over the Macedonian frontier and disarmed and interned by the then reigning Ottoman Turkish power.[78]

The so-called "Terrible" Abdulmecid I of Turkey refused, even under threat of immediate and terrible war, to hand over his prisoners of warfare to Kaiser Franz Joseph. (In 1915, Roger Casement junior and Joe Plunkett in Munich had the pleasure, or displeasure, of seeing from a distance in a passing crowd the same Emperor Franz Joseph, who little thought of 1848-49 and Louis Kossuth and the Irish patriot Casement of Young Ireland.) But, curiously enough, the Sultan of Turkey did grant Roger Casement senior's request to send a food ship to the starving Irish people, irrespective of the Famine Queen of England or threat of reprisal.[79]

Fenians; he wrote *The Felon's Track*. John O'Mahony (1819-1877) fled to France after the rising and thence to the US where he became a founder member and president of the Fenian organisation. He was an Irish scholar and translator.

[77] 1848 is known in European history as "the Year of Revolutions".

[78] Historians agree that Russian intervention led to the defeat of the Hungarian revolt against Austrian rule in 1848-49. Kossuth fled to Turkey and then to England and the US. He lived in exile in England and Italy for the rest of his life. Roger Casement senior's involvement with Kossuth is substantiated in the latter's memoirs. See Margaret O'Callaghan, "'With the eyes of another race, of a people once hunted themselves': Casement, colonialism and a remembered past," in Mary Daly (ed.), *Roger Casement in Irish and World History* (Dublin, 2005), p. 60.

[79] Whatever about sending a food ship, the Sultan of Turkey, whose private physician was Irish, pledged £10,000 to famine relief in Ireland but lowered that amount to £1,000 to avoid offending Queen Victoria, who herself gave only £2,000. By contrast, the Society of Friends or Quakers raised over £200,000. See Famine

Here we witness the soldierly and humane act contributed by Casement's father. In 1915, the Irish patriot remembered the Terrible Turk, much to the disgust of other less patriotic Irishmen, sitting in safety behind the Statue of Liberty and Park Row of Tammany Hall, New York.[80]

To return to Roger's childhood, after his mother's death as I have said, he, his brother Tom and only sister Agnes were sent to Co. Antrim to his father's people, where another phase of the Irish environment and Irish life awaited the patriotic youth. As can well be surmised, when young children meet such a loss of a loving mother, an unfathomable memory survives. Roger junior was a timid and reserved character in boyhood, very humane so far as the weak and oppressed were concerned. Even a bird disabled attracted his gravest sympathy and desire to protect the helpless.

When he was only 14 years of age, he ever afterwards cherished the memory of encouraging words imparted to him by John Mitchel himself prior to his last public appearance in Ireland. Mitchel placed his hand on the boy's head and asked him to be a true Irishman. He also cherished those fearless, hard-hitting words he found in the pages of Mitchel's *Jail Journal*.[81] Is it any wonder we find Casement imploring his equally timid aunt to reserve a school vacation abode or special room to plaster the walls with pictures and printed messages characterising rebel and "traitorous" Irish Fenianism? From one scene to another, we find Casement fighting against two extremes: British imperialism versus the spiritual idealism which kept Ireland's national rights for freedom soaring high despite all coercion and intrigue, the slavish attitude of West British elements stagnating then as now, and the ever easily gulled Irish masses.

Commemoration Committee, *Ireland's Famine: Commemoration and Awareness* (Dublin, 1995).

[80] One of the clauses in the agreement Casement reached with the German government in late 1914 referred to the possibility of members of the Irish Brigade fighting with the Turks, who were allies of the Germans, to help the Egyptians gain their freedom from British rule – this possibility was to apply only if the brigade couldn't be transported to Ireland to fight for Irish freedom. The clause was disliked by Clan na Gael members in the US. Tammany Hall was the Democratic Party political machine that controlled New York city politics for some 70 years, in which the Irish were particularly prominent.

[81] John Mitchel (1815-1875) was one of the fieriest of the Young Ireland leaders. After the failed 1848 rising, he was sentenced to 14 years' transportation but escaped in 1853 and settled in America. He was later a Fenian agent in Paris, returned to Ireland on being chosen as MP for Tipperary but died shortly afterwards. His *Jail Journal*, published in 1854, is one of the classics of prison literature.

Education and position at all times urge most Irish youth onwards, especially those under native Irish guardianship. His was a family producing a Young Irelander or Irish Fenian in the making with each successive generation. Eventually we see him evacuating Cambridge University with highest honours[82] and seeking a living in the higher civil service of the British people. But he never forgot he was Irish no matter where his duties took him, not even in darkest Africa where his humane soul was ever ready to advance and elevate the sordid conditions of the mere natives, though black and uncivilised in the eyes of the colonial administration conventionally administered by all European so-called civilisation.

He was in South Africa during the later stages of the Boer War, filling the post of Consul at Durban. Here the Irish patriot received his first baptism of fire which really laid bare England's perfidy in the form of Kitchener's internment camps where 20,000 Boer women and children perished.[83] The cries of defenceless women and children herded together in filthy compounds brought forth from this Irishman the most scathing condemnation of the British Empire and lust for territorial conquest. He spoke openly and undeterred against the dirty work being performed by Joey Chamberlain's Tea Party gang.[84] Of course, such tirades could not be countenanced by the British colonial administration, and the wily Foreign Office at London thought well enough to transfer Casement, with promotion, to a far-off South American republic with its capital at Rio de Janeiro.

In that free land, he could best serve as Consul-General and promulgate his democratic principles far from the madding crowd in the hub of empire, and where there was less fear of Fleet Street, London press manipulators questioning his views on open and fair-minded issues and affairs of state not in keeping with the double dealings of secret diplomacy.

---

[82] Casement did not attend Cambridge. He joined the British Foreign Service in 1882, having been a pupil at Ballymena Academy.

[83] In the later stages of the Boer War, the British army under General Kitchener used a scorched-earth policy to destroy Boer opposition. This involved the setting up of concentration camps in which large number of Boers and native Africans, including thousands of women and children, were incarcerated. Many thousands of the internees died; it is difficult to arrive at an exact figure but it is likely that it is greater than 20,000.

[84] Joseph Chamberlain was British Colonial Secretary during the Boer War and was an avowed imperialist. When the war broke out in 1899, the optimistic British referred to it as the "Tea Time War". It was to drag on until 1902.

In South America, Roger Casement found a fair field of operation as a defender of the underdog. Sir Edward Grey[85] kept a close eye on the Irishman but with little effect. The South American native Indian became his admirer and trusty friend. Soon the exiled son of an Irish rebel leader feasted fast on the progressing ideals of freedom imbuing the greatest mastermind hailing from the province of the "red hand",[86] which gave such champions in Ireland's cause as Chieftain Red Hugh[87] down to the birthplace of the United Irishmen under the leadership of Wolfe Tone.

A small narrative at this juncture may serve to illustrate how vividly he perpetrated the good example set in Ulster of the Red Branch knights.[88] The ill-famed treaty alliance of 1904, known as the Entente Cordiale, that wily-fox Grey had weaved into the net for his globe-trotting sporting master (a namesake of Neddy the Peacemaker)[89] was an endeavour to balance the manpower of Europe in the event of war, and to overbalance the all-powerful grip already held by Britain's navy as the mistress of the seven seas. It would also serve as a security against any infringement being enacted that might prove detrimental to an all-British route in commerce as monopoliser of world trade.

As was usual on an occasion such as the signing of the Entente Cordiale, the Whitehall Admiralty decided the most suitable thing to do was to send a visiting naval fleet around the world. It was done and in due course it fell to Casement as Consul-General in the capital of the South American republic to receive and entertain en fête the visiting Anglo-Saxon naval warlords. He did so, but with no small amount of discomfort, having arrived at a most critical stage in an Irishman's views of the state of Europe, fomented in the signal note couched in the term "allies".

However, the toasts were set in all the pomp of imperialism, assisted by the aspirants to honour and befitting an English

---

[85] British Foreign Secretary from 1905 to 1916.

[86] The red hand was the symbol of the great Gaelic Irish ruling family of the O'Neills of Tyrone.

[87] Red Hugh O'Donnell (1572-1602) was taoiseach or chief of the O'Donnells of Donegal. With Hugh O'Neill, he led the Nine Years War against Tudor rule in Ireland at the end of the 16th century.

[88] In Irish mythology, the Red Branch was the name of two of the three royal houses of the king of Ulster, Conchobar Mac Nessa.

[89] The reference is to Edward VII, king from 1901 to 1910. He was popularly called "Peacemaker" because of the good relations he fostered with other European countries, especially France. The Entente Cordiale was signed while Lord Lansdowne rather than Sir Edward Grey was Foreign Secretary.

colony of the packed-meat industry then infesting that particular South American capital. It came to Roger's turn to raise his glass, and by this time a sensitive feeling of unrest, approaching disgust, had settled on him in relation to his surrounding fellow Europeans. "I stood up," he said, "and in answer to Admiral Simpson, my toast was simply 'God save Ireland'. A veiled and astonished countenance was stamped on each of my hearers as loyal subjects to the British Crown figurehead. I cared not what they thought, but heard it later in the words of old Bob Beresford, the holder of the key to British naval barbarism.[90] 'That young hothead Casement needs careful watching. He is following in the footsteps of his father who showed his true colours in the time of the Young Irelanders.'"

From 1907 to 1912, Casement wrote in exile many essays on the "freedom of the seas", and in 1911 propounded for private publication and to friends in the Irish-Ireland movement at home his most prophetic treatise: "The Freedom of the Seas and Ireland in the Coming War in Europe".[91] Some of those I am sure are still to be had moulding away on the dusty shelves of the many private libraries in the homes of Irish-Ireland intellectuals.

---

[90] The reference here is probably to Lord Charles Beresford (1846-1919), known to the British public as "Charlie B". He was an MP and enthusiast for extending the British navy. He also served in the fleet and was Chief of the Channel and then of the Mediterranean Fleet. He was involved in a number of controversial incidents, such as the bombardment of Alexandria in the Egyptian War of 1882.

[91] Perhaps what is meant here is *Ireland, Germany and the Freedom of the Seas: a Possible Outcome of the War of 1914*. This pamphlet was published in New York in 1914.

CHAPTER 2: Ireland as a Factor in the World War of 1914

The culminating and critical phase of the national movement in Ireland was reached when it became apparent that Carson's Ulster followers and their British allies were determined on provoking bloodshed. They had and flaunted materials of war, smuggled in under the closed eyes of the British navy, contrary to all the laws in force in Ireland.[92] To oppose these organised forces and armaments, Redmond's Volunteers[93] possessed only wooden guns, and the preparations they professed to make to meet the impending onslaught were laughable, did not a great tragedy seem imminent. The old racial fighting spirit had been aroused by quasi-military displays, such as that in the Phoenix Park in Dublin early in 1914 of the Irish Volunteers under the command of British reserve officers, with patriotic slogans, and it would have been criminal to have left it unprovided with the means to protect and assert itself.

The situation had to be faced, and faced promptly. Shortly after the Curragh Mutiny,[94] which was fortunate inasmuch as it disclosed how widespread and powerful were the ramifications of the enemies of Irish nationality, Roger Casement, Eoin MacNeill

---

[92] Following the passage of the third Home Rule Bill through the British House of Commons in 1912, in January of the following year Edward Carson and James Craig, leaders of the Ulster unionists, formed the Ulster Volunteer Force pledged to resist Irish self-government. In April 1914, they imported 30,000 rifles to arm the force in what became known as the Larne gun running.

[93] John Redmond (1856-1918) was the leader of the Home Rule party from 1900 to 1918. His party had not organised the original setting up of the Irish Volunteers in late 1913 but, with the spread of the organisation, he demanded that his nominees be accepted onto the Provisional Committee, a demand that was accepted.

[94] To deal with the threat of the Ulster Volunteers should Home Rule be passed into law, the commander of the Curragh British army base, Sir Arthur Paget, was ordered by the War Office in London in March 1914 to prepare to march to Ulster should violence break out there. Paget understood the order as one to proceed immediately to Ulster, whereas it was really an order for precautionary deployments in the event of an outbreak of violence. On his own initiative, Paget offered his officers a choice of resignation rather than going north. Fifty-nine out of 70 officers, who were mostly Irish unionists, threatened resignation. They were not technically guilty of mutiny as they had not refused to carry out a direct order. Asquith's Liberal government backed down in the face of such a threat and the lesson was not lost on Irish nationalists.

and, I believe, The O'Rahilly[95] visited London on 12 May 1914 to interview the Irish Parliamentary Party leaders, Redmond, Dillon and Devlin,[96] to ascertain their exact attitude and policy in regard to the oncoming menace. They wanted to know what use were 100,000 trained men without some more effective equipment than dummy rifles. The views of the deputation and those of the party leaders were soon found to be vitally divergent. Finally, Redmond summed up his own attitude and, I presume, that of his colleagues, in a pronouncement to this effect: "I cannot openly arm my countrymen who claim my leadership, but if you think that by force of arms you can obtain the freedom of Ireland, you have my full permission to arm the Irish Volunteers."

This permissive and passive approach was far from what the delegation had a right to expect from a professing nationalist. It meant that the parliamentary machine would not assist them in organisation and that many, under plea of old affiliations, could cover their timidity and defend their antagonism. And this, as we all know now, did occur all over the country. Still, the deputation cannot have been altogether disappointed for they must have, even then, distrusted the unnatural blend of imperialism-cum-nationalism which the Westminster environment had involved, and which disclosed itself nakedly on the declaration of war some months later.[97]

With a nearer and clearer conception of the situation at home and the duty it imposed, the decision of the Irish Volunteer deputation was inevitable: force would have to be resisted by force if the historic Irish nation was to survive without an ignominy that would be more unendurable than destruction. That resolution was taken under grave and unfavourable circumstances and was put into immediate practice with a zeal not unmixed with foreboding.

---

[95] The O'Rahilly was a founding member of the Irish Volunteers. He was killed in the fighting during the Easter Rising.

[96] John Dillon (1851-1927) was MP for East Mayo 1885-1918; he succeeded John Redmond as leader of the Irish Parliamentary Party in 1918. His father was John Blake Dillon of the Young Irelanders and his son was James Dillon, a TD for many years and leader of Fine Gael 1959-1965. Joseph Devlin (1872-1934) was Home Rule MP for Belfast West 1906-1918, Nationalist MP for Belfast Falls 1918-22, Nationalist MP for Belfast West at Stormont 1921-29, and for Fermanagh-South Tyrone 1929-34. During the 1890s, he founded the Ancient Order of Hibernians, an organisation that developed much control within the Home Rule party.

[97] This refers to Redmond's speech at Woodenbridge, Co. Wicklow, on 20th September 1914, where he urged members of the Irish Volunteers to join the British army and fight in the war in Europe.

The men about to be involved in this perilous and patriotic exercise had diverse, collateral parts to play. To Roger Casement fell the momentous work of arming his fellow countrymen – a responsibility vouchsafed to no other Irishman since the heroic labours of Wolfe Tone and Robert Emmet.[98] Financial assistance had first to be found and he applied himself to that preliminary task with enthusiasm and success. He himself affirmed, in one of the many conversations cherished by the writer: "I gained help from Irishmen who could claim Ireland as their country only by right of their parents' nativity, and who themselves were born in the heart of London."

He made a brief trip to the continent early in May 1914 and on his return proceeded at once to the United States, which he reached through Canada via Scotland. In the second home of the Irish race he made contact with the old Fenian leaders, John Devoy and Joe McGarrity.[99] He found them willing aides in the great adventure at hand. There were risks involved which could not well be foreseen or avoided. Casement had to trust many unknown allies, the depths of whose devotion to the cause he had neither time nor means to test. Some of these, as after events proved, were unreliable – indeed beachcombers and sand-riddlers who had more uses for their pretended patriotism than the achievement of Irish freedom.

The Howth gun running materialised on Sunday, 26th July 1914. It is not necessary for me to deal at length with that daring exploit. It took place in Irish waters and upon Irish soil and its effects and sequel on Bachelor's Walk are, or should be, in the main familiar to all Irish nationalists. I might, did the occasion serve, throw some lurid light, imparted to me by Casement himself upon some details of the affair. One point I must make clear: *the material delivered at Howth was not of the actual quality selected* – the chosen and paid-for goods – approved by Rory of the Gael at the behest of a committee of three officers representing GHQ of the Irish Volunteer army, established at Wynn's Hotel, Dublin on 25th November 1913. This assertion defies contradiction. The explanation must remain for some other time. It was at that fateful meeting that Casement proposed the motto, "Let all true Irishmen today hope forever", and the flag of

---

[98] Robert Emmet (1778-1803) was a member of the United Irishmen. When the rising of 1798 was defeated, he set about planning another rising, which involved acquiring and manufacturing arms. His attempted rising in 1803 failed for various reasons and he was captured and executed.

[99] Joe McGarrity (1874-1940) was a leading member of Clan na Gael, a successful businessman and a strong supporter – including financial – of the cause of Irish independence.

the new army and era of redemption, the green, white and orange tricolour as a symbol of unity in that aspiration.

Nor need I recall the scene of wanton, panic-savagery on Bachelor's Walk later on that historic July Sunday evening when the King's Own Scottish Borderers shot down unarmed Dublin citizens in true Amritsar fashion.[100] Some at least of those heroes paid the penalty of their battue far from the scene of its cold-blooded accomplishment.

At the same moment, the hand of England's diplomacy was busy in another murder-plot, which bore its desired evil fruit in the assassinations at Sarajevo. There, in the midst of the ever-turbulent Balkans, Anglo-Russian machinations procured a Serbian emissary to press down the lever that overturned the world. The next four days brought about with cataclysmic speed the events that gave a new and fatal direction to Irish policies, grim as they had been before. The World War began and humanity was mobilised for its own destruction in the intoxication of brazen shibboleths that even the partial history of that tremendous epoch has proved to have been lies.

Within a few weeks of the slaying by O'Connell Bridge, the English masters and the Irish abettors of the valiant Borderers had the audacity to call upon the Irish people to "Remember little Belgium" and avenge the "violation" of a treaty of supposed neutrality 80 years old. They sent their heralds and envoys to call on Dublin to forget treaties broken there, and on Ireland to forget its centuries-old endurance of ravage and repression. It was then that the Irishmen who could not lend themselves to the arming of their countrymen for self-preservation and liberty appealed to those same countrymen to fight the battle of their one and only enemy on God's earth! The situation had altered fundamentally, and had there been greater loyalty to Ireland inculcated in the preceding quarter-century and less Lazarus-fawning on England preached, it might well have proved the final turning point in our national destinies, as it was unquestionably a vital stage in our racial struggle for freedom.

The warlord capitalists of Europe had found it consistent with their Christianity and, more important still to them, with their interests to provoke a war unparalleled in the history of man.[101] The guilty have never been lacking in plausible professions when

---

[100] In Amritsar in the Punjab in India, on 13 April 1919, British army soldiers under the command of General Dyer fired on an unarmed crowd of men, women and children. According to official sources, 379 were killed but private sources put the number at 1,000, with 2,000 wounded.

[101] It must be remembered that Michael Keogh was writing this well before the Second World War occurred.

such opportunities arise; nor were they wanting on this occasion. "The defence of small nations!" "War to end war!" "Militarism must be abolished so that a peaceful balance of power may be maintained!" These, and many more equally specious and false, were the pleas put forth. We know their worth today. It is outside the scope and purpose of this chronicle to discuss how far such ideals have been attained after four years of carnage and eight years of so-called peace under the Treaty of Versailles.[102]

As an Irishman, my only concern at that time was to help forward in every way Ireland's right to a full share in the new world Utopia proclaimed. That claim was neither new nor intermittent. Ireland had never relinquished her right to a place among the nations great and small. She had never ceased to struggle for the inalienable privilege of determining her own destiny. She, who had shone as the luminary of Europe in the Dark Ages of western civilisation, had surely equal claim with any to "a place in the sun" which was yet to rise.

The enemy was perturbed. The blood-clouds England had invoked threatened to overwhelm her. Gloom enshrouded its sinister metropolis. The Germans and Austrians were marching relentlessly over victims she had designed to stay their advance. She had hoped to beat the dual enemy with subsidised and doped allies, as she had succeeded in beating Napoleon a century earlier. The old scheme, brought up to date, did not at once produce the expected results. She must gird herself for the fray and discard the more congenial role of war-broker for that of combatant. She had not overlooked this possibility when she laid the explosive train fired in Bosnia,[103] but she had hoped that such a dire necessity could be evaded.

Her ever strongest arm – diplomacy as subtle as that of Satan himself – was invoked, and not in vain. Her flank, Ireland, must be secured; the vulnerable point in her armour must be repaired. Force would have precipitated her destruction, so fulsome flattery was applied. "Ireland is the one bright spot," proclaimed the arch-procurer of unrighteous advantages, Sir Edward Grey. Once again, tens of thousands of Irishmen drank the honeyed cup so readily handed to them by their leaders; and the delusion was completed when George V of the Hanover Wettins complaisantly

---

[102] The most important treaty to be signed as a result of the Paris Peace Conference that followed the First World War was the Treaty of Versailles signed with Germany. It was a punitive and controversial treaty as far as Germans were concerned, especially the "war-guilt" clause that blamed Germany exclusively for causing the war.

[103] The reference here is to the assassination at Sarajevo in Bosnia-Herzegovina.

put an ill-omened name to a designedly misleading "Act" of his wily ministers – the shelved Home Rule Bill of September 1914.[104]

The rapidly succeeding acts of treachery which followed need little narration. They were too humiliating. The Irish Parliamentary Party leaders called upon the Irish to rally to "home defence" and so relieve the strain that would otherwise fall upon the "predominant partner". The spell worked and the stampede of folly and treason to Ireland was begun. England dictated every subsequent move. "Ireland can be defended only in Flanders," was next the cry and thither the line of "home defence" was moved, with the ecstatic approval of the party national leaders. Ireland, the ancient nation and her long-suffering people, were all forgotten and bid forget everything in this whirlwind of imperialism and mirage of battles for small nations.

Yet there were some who did not, could not and would not forget. While the world was being convulsed in the throes of a titanic struggle, we will follow the fortunes of one Irishman at least who knew and loved the "Isle of Destiny" too well to forget or neglect it. He had gallant comrades as we shall see. And the story of his labours and sacrifice, however badly told here, will yet become a heroic epic of the motherland and the Inisfáil of his dreams.

When Casement left Ireland on 2nd July 1914 and two days later sailed from Glasgow on the SS Cassandra as a second-class "emigrant" en route for Montreal, how little did he think of what was before him! He chose that route to avoid publicity and possible interviews at New York, as well as the probable attentions of the British Spy Bureau, whose agents in Ireland had been so maladroitly pursuing him since the eventful meeting at Wynn's Hotel on 25th November 1913, for the establishment of the Irish Volunteer army, in which he took a prominent part. He embarked on the Cassandra at Glasgow on 4th July 1914 as "Mr R.D. Casement", his right name and initials but without the prefix his knighthood conferred. Thenceforward he forbade his compatriots to address him as Sir Roger; he especially imparted this wish to Sergeant Joe Dowling[105] and myself in December 1914 in Germany. "I am plain Roger Casement the Irishman," he wrote; "the pseudo-Anglo Saxon 'Sir' was forced on me in my absence." It was the British Foreign Office way of covering up his

---

[104] The Hanoverians became the British royal dynasty with the accession of George I in 1714. Wettin was the surname of Prince Albert and also of Queen Victoria by virtue of her marriage to him. George V was the grandson of Queen Victorian and king 1910-36. Home Rule became law in September 1914 but was postponed for the duration of the war.

[105] A prominent member of the Irish Brigade in Germany.

exposure of them in the Putumayo. But the remuneration accruing from the "title" served to assist the founding of a school in Connacht for Gaelic-speaking children. It also served well since 1911 in enabling him to augment the funds of the young Irish-Irelanders in the ranks of the Fianna,[106] foundation stone of the Young Ireland army.

The following description of his journey, which takes up from the time the patriot boarded the Cassandra, is quoted from his own diary:

> No one suspected I was Sir Roger Casement and one passenger once asked me if I was any relation of that "well-known Irish baronet". I laughed and said I believed I was a near relative and that I knew him well. With the exception of one Irish boy from Cork, the passengers were Scotch – and very largely Butter-Scotch. At least they talked it. I know no language that fills me with the sense of nausea that Glasgow or Butter-Scotch does... Voyages I have made enough but the Cassandra's was very much better than the majority. Barring the Butter-Scotch, I enjoyed myself.
>
> On Sunday morning 5th July at 7 a.m., I looked from our port and saw far south the jagged precipices and towers of Tory Island. It was, perhaps, some 12 miles off and beyond it rose in blue lines Muckish, Errigal and the Irish hills of my heart. I could almost see Cloghaneely and the shining strand of Magherahersty, whence two years before – in August 1912 – I had gone over to Tory Island with that famous party of Gaels, the fiddler, the piper and the rest.
>
> So far as I can now recall, we were 12 days on the voyage to Montreal, although it may have been only 11. My diaries had to go overboard on the later voyage from New York to Norway on the Oskar II – not so very far from Tory either, as will be told when we reach this latter more memorable journey. The only objects of interest on the Cassandra voyage to Canada were the icebergs we passed during two days, when near Newfoundland. These were the first I had ever seen, and unlike most "first sights" or much talked-of things, they more than realised all I had conceived of them. Great Artic palaces, green and gold sometimes, with a crystal sheen and a dazzling white as of concentrated snow, they sailed past us bound to their doom in the Gulf Stream. At one single point during the second day of the bergs, we sighted 17 at the same time from the ship's upper deck – from the

---

[106] The reference is to the Fianna Éireann, a movement founded in 1909 by Bulmer Hobson and Countess Markievicz as a paramilitary boy scouts organisation. Some of those who fought and died in the Easter Rising began as Fianna members.

near-at-hand "growler" sagging past to the vast domes of white (and pale white, too) outlined against the distance of the calm grey horizon.

Newfoundland's coast grew clear on our right – a pleasant coast in a fine transparent air. I now forget the towns we passed or dimly sighted, rather fishing settlements than towns, but I remember St Pierre (near Miquelon) for there we saw the town well enough where, in 1905, it had been suggested by some friend of Lord MacDonnell's[107] that I should go as Consul. The post, I think he said, was then vacant, and I was purposely idle at the time, having practically retired from the British Consular Service over the Congo red-rubber controversy. I had been so anxious to support my friend E.D. Morel[108] in his Congo fight – more with the British Foreign Office almost than with Leopold – that I had asked to be seconded (without pay) from Lisbon, whither the rather wily British Foreign Office had sent me after the publication of my Congo Report in the beginning of 1904. Lisbon had not agreed with me – still less the Foreign Office method of conducting the controversy with King Leopold of Belgium, which consisted largely in running away from their own charges and offering apologies for my report. So in December 1904, I seconded myself and so remained a freelance, devoting myself to Irish affairs alone until, in August 1906, Sir E. Grey wrote to suggest my return to the Consular Service, when I went out, first to Santos, then to Para, and finally to Rio de Janeiro en route to Putumayo.

I thought of these things as I looked at the little town, St Pierre, and wondered, as we steamed past it, what might have been the difference had I accepted the advice of Lord MacDonnell's friend and applied for St Pierre. Happily, I was then so well occupied in Ireland, trying to keep Irishmen out of the British army, and dreaming of an Ireland that might yet be free, that I gave no second thought to that after-dinner suggestion any more than to a later one of Sir Eric

---

[107] Lord Anthony MacDonnell (1844-1925) had been very involved in the British administration of India before becoming Irish Under Secretary from 1902 to 1908. He was sympathetic to Irish Home Rule.

[108] E.D. Morel (1873-1924) campaigned against slavery in the Congo Free State through newspapers such as his *West African Mail* in collaboration with Casement. In 1904, he founded the Congo Reform Association, at Casement's suggestion. He later attacked Britain's "secret diplomacy" and helped to set up the Union for Democratic Control. He was imprisoned for six months in 1917 and was elected Labour MP for Dundee in 1922.

Barrington[109] that "Stockholm was vacant and might be offered me". I was immersed in Irish-Ireland affairs all through 1905 and right up to the very day of my departure for Santos in August (or was it September?) 1906. It was those 18 months or so in Ireland, 1905/06 – when "seconded" from the Consular Service – that moulded my subsequent activities and carried me so far on the road to John Mitchel's aspirations, that everything I have since done seems but the natural up-growth from the seed then sown.

Some day I may try, if alive, to write the full story of the Congo and how I found out King Leopold; of the Putumayo and that abominable London Company, and of the "inordinate wild Irishman" who went out on both quests in the garb of a British Consular official, but with the soul of an Irish felon. If the English had only known the thoughts in my Irish heart, and the strong impulses I had obeyed when I did the things they took pride in, I wonder would their press and the scapegoat West British newspapers in Ireland have praised my "heroism" and "chivalry" as they did, or would that expatriated patriot, T.P. O'Connor[110] have referred to me at the Reading election last November as "one of the finest figures in our imperial history"? What will he and the *Westminster Gazette* and even my poor kind London *Daily News* say when the Christiania Catastrophe becomes public in England and common property with Britain's loyal supporters on John Bull's other island?[111] But I am anticipating, and must return to the Newfoundland shores and the Bay of Anticosti and the Great Gulf of St Lawrence.

We sighted the Marconi Station on the New Brunswick shore near Gaspé Bay and, next morning, were in the "Mouth of the St Lawrence", steaming close enough to the south shore, to the point where the ill-fated Empress of Ireland went down.[112] The banks of the St Lawrence River are extremely pretty and interesting and, in some respects, at a

---

[109] Sir Eric Barrington (1847-1918) was a senior figure in the British Foreign Office.

[110] T.P. O'Connor (1848-1929) was an MP for nearly half a century; he was Home Rule MP for Liverpool from 1885 to 1922, the only Irish nationalist MP to be elected outside of Ireland. With the end of the Home Rule Party, he sat as an Independent. He was also a journalist and author.

[111] Christiania is the former name of Oslo; for "the Christiania Catastrophe", see below. George Bernard Shaw wrote a play called *John Bull's Other Island* in 1904.

[112] In late May 1914, the Canadian Pacific liner, the Empress of Ireland, sank after colliding with a Norwegian collier, the Storstad, in fog on the St Lawrence River in a tragedy almost as bad as that of the Titanic; 1,012 died, eight more than perished on the Titanic.

distance *bien entendu,* recalling the vistas of the mighty Amazon I knew so well in South America. But the Amazon is a river – a vast flowing sea of fresh water – and this is a gulf of the sea right up to Quebec. Many towns, and even cities, were passed during the day and finally, late at night, we reached Quebec.

We left again very early in the morning and then began the true St Lawrence River almost at once. Up to Quebec it is a seaway, an estuary, if you will, but from the heights of Abraham it becomes a river – often vast in breadth, with many islands and distant, far-seen banks, sometimes narrowing to half a mile or a mile. Again, many towns and churches were passed, and towards 6.30 p.m. the smoke of Montreal – I say smoke advisedly for of all the filthy approaches to a beautiful site (but not city), Montreal, belching forth the blackest smoke in the world, surely takes first place. From the river, little is seen but a noisome line of zinc and corrugated horrors – grain stores – of factories and warehouses and a shrieking railway; then the "docks" with more corrugated iron abominations – and above the town the first glimpse of the St Lawrence rapids. We quickly docked, and at 8.30 p.m., terra firma once more, when I sought the Queen's Hotel. It was a hot Canadian summer's night, 16th July 1914.

Next morning I took train for New York, having written my old friend, John Devoy, to say I hoped to see him at his office on Friday, 18th July. The journey was long and hot and quite stifling. The windows of the carriages of the Yankee "cars" open only a little way up from below, and some of them will not remain open, but slide down again slowly, and have to be constantly re-hoisted. Mine was one of these; so to breathe at all, I had to put a hat-box in below the lifted sash – to the scandal of the guards and some very uninteresting passengers: the dullest-looking lot imaginable.

The scenery compensated for the want of the picturesque in the human environment. Lake Champlain we skirted for over a hundred miles, often running along the edge of cliffs and precipices above its pellucid aquamarine waters. I thought of the days when Mohicans and the Six Nations[113] had here a hunter's paradise. Poor Indians! You *had life –*

---

[113] The Six Nations, also called by the French term "Iroquois Confederacy", were a confederacy of native north-eastern North American peoples. They were the Mohawks, Oneidas, Onondagas, Cayugas, Senecas and Tuscaroras. The confederacy was a long-established democracy which influenced the founding fathers of American democracy, such as Benjamin Franklin and Thomas Jefferson.

your white destroyers only *possess things*. This is the vital distinction, I take it, between the "savage" and the civilised man. The savage *is* – the white man *has*. The one lives and moves to *be*; the other toils and dies to *have*. From the purely human point of view, the savage has the happier and purer life...

We got to New York about 8.30 a.m., after a delightful journey, from the point of view of scenery, down the Hudson River to Manhattan Island. The shores of the Hudson and the Catskill Mountains were more lovely than I had expected. I went to the Belmont Hotel in New York, as it lay just opposite the Central Railway Terminal, and from the first movement found Irish faces and Irish voices round me: the elevator boys, outdoor porters, the waiters in the bar and at cash-counters were mostly Irish born or of Irish descent, I thought. Some had even the true *brogue* still lingering round the shores of that broad estuary of smiles that takes the place of a mouth in a true Milesian face.

Strolling down Broadway in the thought of perhaps locating old points of view, like Ponds and the hotel I lived in during the end of the 1880s, a young Norwegian sailor spoke to me – and him I befriended and asked to see me next morning. I mention him here because he is destined to figure largely in this story in connection with the infamy of the British Ambassador at Christiania. His name was Eivind Adler Christensen, then 24 years old, of Moos, near Christiania. He had run away from home as the result of a severe beating for playing truant at school, and had stowed away on an English collier – this when he was 12 years old. He landed at Glasgow, and was left there; but some Norwegian sailors took him later in charge, and so he became a fireman on a succession of Norwegian steamers. When he met me he was out of work, starving almost and homeless. He was grateful for my help.

Let me interrupt the narrative here to say that in the course of one of our conversations in Germany, Casement told me it was during that sojourn in the United States in the late eighties he first met Charles Stewart Parnell, of whom he wrote, on 6th October 1891:[114]

Hush – let no whisper of the cruel strife,
Wherein he fell so bravely fighting, fall

---

[114] This was the date on which Parnell died.

Nigh these dead ears; fain would our hearts recall
Nought but proud memories of a noble life –
Of skill unmatched to lead by pathways rife
With danger and dark doubt, where slander's knife
Gleamed ever bare to wound, yet over all
He pressed triumphant on – lo, thus to fall.
Through and beyond the breach he living made
Shall Erin pass to freedom and to will
And shape her fate: there, where his limbs are laid,
No harsh reproach shall penetrate the shade;
Death's angel guards the door, and o'er the sill
A mightier voice than Death speaks: "Peace, be still."

To return to Casement's narrative:
After meeting John Devoy, on the morrow of my arrival, at the *Gaelic American* office, who took me to luncheon at Moquin's, I met shortly afterwards John Quinn and Bourke Cockran.[115] I then went to Philadelphia and saw Joe McGarrity and stayed with him overnight, returning to New York to visit Bourke Cockran at Port Washington. The Ancient Order of Hibernians being in annual session at Norfolk, Virginia, McGarrity begged me to go to their convention and address them in the name of the Irish Volunteers. I consented, if invited. The invitation came by telegraph, and as I was asked to get him too if I could, I motored down with John Quinn to Bourke Cockran's at dinner-time, and carried him off by assault to Norfolk. Our hurried return to New York to catch the 9 p.m. night train to Norfolk was a record motor-car run on these roads – and it was a foggy night. Quinn phoned up for tickets and we got the train with a bare five minutes in hand.

The journey to Norfolk was interesting during the latter stages, across wide bays, past old Point Comfort to Hampton Roads and the fair, very hot Virginian city of Norfolk. The town was all beflagged with green banners and the Stars and Stripes, no flags being anywhere shown save the Irish and American. The Hibernians were in session in a large theatre. Their president, ex-president and nominees for the presidency for the present convention's elections met us in a deputation – and in a few minutes Cockran and I were seated on the platform as guests of our countrymen, with Patrick

---

[115] John Quinn (1870-1924) was an Irish-American lawyer, art collector and important patron of Irish artists and writers. He disagreed with Casement's decision to go to Germany early in the war. William Bourke Cockran (1854-1923), from Sligo, was a Democrat member of the House of Representatives and a lawyer.

Egan[116] alongside us. I was asked to speak first and gave an address, on the spur of the moment, on the situation in Ireland, particularly from the Irish Volunteer standpoint. I avoided purely political references and to some extent I eulogised the example set by the Ulstermen, to the evident content of the great majority of those broad-minded Irish exiles.

In Cork city, in January 1914, Casement, it will be remembered, asked his hearers to copy the example set by the Ulstermen. He went further by calling on all to admire rather than ridicule the direct action of their northern countrymen. This only irritated the narrow minded, the so-called Nationalists, and even a few Irish-Ireland politicians, all of whom seemed anxious to make capital out of a very frank and honest conclusion.

But to return once again to the patriot's own telling of the events:

It was a shirt-sleeves and fan audience. Cockran followed me with an oration, and Egan spoke too. Then we returned to our hotel and spent the rest of the day motoring out to Ocean View Beach, until it was time to return. On the way back, I got off at Philadelphia and stayed with McGarrity. During the period of waiting for Sunday, 26th July 1914 (the day I had arranged with Erskine Childers and his brave American wife that the two yachts should arrive at Howth, and the Dublin Volunteers should march out to meet them and get the rifles) I got a letter from my staunch old Fenian friend, Tom Clarke, telling me all was well and that "our friends were on the sea".

The threatening situation in Europe, following the cowardly murder of Austrian Archduke Ferdinand and his consort, and the ultimatum to Serbia, gave me cause for some anxiety. At other times, I should have been even more anxious, but the fears for the landing of the guns at Howth swallowed up all other fears for the time. I had told only John Devoy and Joe McGarrity of the scheme planned before I left Ireland. It was timed for the forenoon of Sunday, 26th July. That Sunday I spent at McGarrity's in great anxiety and on tenterhooks. It was a very hot day. At 7 p.m., Joe and I walked down the fields in front of his house until full twilight fell and darkness came.

We lay on the grass and talked of Ireland – and often, watch in hand, said: "Now it is midnight in Dublin; now 1 a.m. – soon something must come over the cables." About 9

---

[116] Patrick Egan (1841-1919) was a Land Leaguer and supporter of Home Rule. He went to the US in 1881, joined the Republican Party and later the Democrats. He was US Minister to Chile from 1889-93.

p.m., one of the sub-editors of a Philadelphia paper I need not name rang up Joe over the phone and told him a news-message had come in to say that a landing of rifles for the Irish Volunteers had been effected near Dublin that day, that the British troops had been called out to disarm the Volunteers and had fired on them, killing several persons and securing the rifles. Joe flew down to the Hibernia Club. Later on, a message came from him to his wife to tell me that the guns had not been captured by the troops but remained with the Volunteers.

We hardly slept that night. Joe returned about 2 a.m. (on Monday morning); he had already taken the steps necessary to have a great protest meeting (against the British army murderers of innocent boys and girls at Bachelor's Walk, Dublin), to be held the following Sunday, 2nd August 1914, in one of the big theatres of Philadelphia, and had announced me as the chief speaker! So, whether I liked it or not, I was now in for it up to my neck. I would have wished to keep quiet (as bigger stakes were still in progress and Scotland Yard, London, were hot on my track since I had beaten them at their own game, and the Irish Party were at bay for the first time in 20 years), but, from every national point of view, it was necessary this meeting should be held and, if held, that it should lack no support I could give it. So I reluctantly agreed to a step already taken in my name.

The next day, Monday 27th July, I was interviewed by some of the Philadelphia papers – and photographed – and the interview appeared in full in all the evening papers, particularly *The Bulletin*. In this interview, I spoke very strongly of the lawless action of the British authorities in Ireland, culminating in the murder of women and children in the streets of Dublin, and then put the blame fair and square on the shoulders of the British Prime Minister, Mr Asquith. The interview gave general satisfaction to the Irish exiles in the USA, while I learned it had greatly incensed the Anglo-American loyalists, some of whom wrote stupidly irate letters to my host. From this on to Sunday 2nd August, McGarrity was busy, and more than busy, with the arrangements for the monster Sunday meeting of Irish citizens in Philadelphia. I was a passive agent in his hands. He did everything.

Before leaving New York for Christiania, on the way to Germany, Casement, on 17th September 1914, addressed the following Open Letter to the Irish race:

As an Irishman and one who had been identified with the Irish Volunteer movement since it began, I feel it my duty to protest against the claim now put forward by the British government that, because that government has agreed with its political opponents to "place the nucleus of a Home Rule Bill on the statute book" and to defer its operation until after the war and until an "Amending Bill" to profoundly modify its provisions has been introduced and passed,[117] Irishmen in return should enlist in the British army and aid the Allied, Asiatic[118] and European powers in a war against a people who have never wronged Ireland. The British Liberal party has been publicly pledged for 28 years to give self-government to Ireland. It has not yet fulfilled that pledge. Instead, it now offers to sell, at a very high price, a wholly hypothetical and indefinite form of partial internal control of certain specified Irish services if, in return for this promissory note (payable after death), the Irish people will contribute their blood, their honour and their manhood in a war that in no wise concerns them. Ireland has no quarrel with the German people or just cause of offence against them.

I will not pronounce an opinion upon the British standpoint in this war beyond saying that the public profession under which it was begun, namely to defend the violated neutrality of Belgium, is being daily controverted by the official spokesmen of Great Britain. The London *Times*, in its issue of 14th September 1914, declared that Great Britain would not consent to peace on any terms that did not involve the "dismantling of the German navy" and the permanent impairment of Germany's place in the world as a great sea-faring nation. That may or may not be a worthy end for British statesmanship to set before it and a warrant for the use of British arms against Germany, but it is no warrant for Irish honour or Irish commonsense to be involved in this conflict. There is no gain, moral or material, Irishman can draw from assailing Germany. The destruction of the German navy or the sweeping of German commerce from the seas will bring no profit to a people whose own commerce was long since swept from land and seas.

Ireland has no blood to give to any land or to any cause but that of Ireland. Our duty as a Christian people is to abstain from bloodshed; and out duty as Irishmen is to give our lives for Ireland.

Ireland needs all her sons. In the space of 68 years, her population has fallen by far over 4,000,000 souls and, in

---

[117] This refers to an addendum to the Home Rule Act which stated that it would not come into effect until some provision had been made for part of Ulster.

[118] In the First World War, Japan was an Anglo-French ally.

every particular of national life, she shows a steady decline of vitality. Were the Home Rule Bill all that is claimed for it, and were it freely given today to come into operation tomorrow, instead of being offered for sale on terms of exchange that only a fool would accept, it would be the duty of Irishmen to save their strength and manhood for the trying tasks before them: to build up a depleted population and the fabric of a ruined national life.

Ireland has suffered at the hands of British administrators a more prolonged series of evils deliberately inflicted than any other community of civilised men. Today, when no margin of vital strength remains for vital tasks at home, when its fertile fields are reduced by acts designed to producing animals and not men, the remnant of our people are being urged to lay down their lives on foreign fields, in order that great and inordinately wealthy communities may grow greater and richer by the destruction of a rival's trade and industry. Had this war the highest moral aim in view, as its originators claim for it, it would still be the duty of Irishmen to keep out of it.

If Irish blood is to be "the seal that will bring all Ireland together in one nation and in liberties equal and common to all", then let that blood be shed in Ireland, where alone it can be righteously shed to secure those liberties.

It was not Germany that destroyed the national liberties of the Irish people, and we cannot recover the national life struck down in our own land by carrying fire and sword into another land. *The cause of Ireland is greater than the cause of any party, higher than the worth of any man, richer in its poverty than all the riches of the British Empire.* If we sell it now, we are unworthy of the name of Irishmen. If today we barter that cause in a sordid bargain, we shall prove ourselves a people unworthy of freedom – *a dwindling race of cravens from whose veins the blood of manhood has been drained.*

If to now fight is our duty, then let us fight on that soil where so many generations of slain Irishmen lie in honour and fame. Let our graves be in that patriot grass whence alone the corpse of Irish nationality can spring to life. Ireland will be false to her history, to every consideration of honour, good faith and self-interest if she now willingly responds to the call of the British government to send her brave sons and faithful hearts to fight in a cause that has no glint of chivalry or gleam of generosity in all its line of battle. If this be a war for "small nationalities", as its planners term it, then let it begin, for one small nationality, Ireland, at home.

Speaking as one of those who helped to found the Irish Volunteers, I say, in their name, that no Irishman fit to bear arms in the cause of his country's freedom can join the allied millions now attacking Germany in a war that at the best concerns Ireland not at all and that can only add fresh burdens and establish a new drain on its manhood, in the interest of another community, upon a people that has already been bled to the verge of death.

CHAPTER 3: At War and a Prisoner of War

It is noteworthy that in 1912, and two years prior to the World War, the Irish patriot was preparing in secret with a few Irishmen at home and in the USA – members of the still existing Irish Revolutionary Brotherhood. This organisation dates back over 120 years and served as one of the successors to the United Irishmen Society of 1791-98.[119] Its chief ideal and determination in Ireland's affairs was always a complete separatist policy. Its membership in the USA carried with it this outlook on the most broadminded and democratic basis. The members, though limited in number, were for the most part Irishmen of letters and high character. It cannot be said to have been a secret Irish society or with a distinct political code. It was not bound by any secret oath but all members were pledged as Irishmen born or by descent to swear allegiance to the furthering of Irish national freedom.

Not a few of the brotherhood were Irishmen of affluence and influence in the States. Some were born in America of Irish parents who, in the dark past of Ireland's sad history, were forced into exile, the peasant homestead and land of their forefathers having been confiscated by the West British and Anglo-Saxon dry-land pirates in evening dress in Ireland.

In 1908 in New York, when the author first made acquaintance with the Irish Revolutionary Brotherhood, it comprised a few direct descendants of the United Irishmen of 1798. One, John Hope, was a great grandnephew of Jimmy Hope, the staunch Irish patriot and former Ulster friend of Wolfe Tone. Myles Byrne, the Park Row, New York cabinet and furniture maker could prove his claim to direct descent from the Irish insurgent leader Billy Byrne of Ballymanus, whose rebel cavalry routed the ill-famed Huntergown's mounted Yeomanry at the famed Tubberneering and Ballyellis battles in counties Wexford and Wicklow during the insurrection of 1798. The descendants of the Young Irelander period of Irish history were also represented. And those from the Fenian period of 1865-68 were there too in person and sincerity, though few in number.

It is well to state that no connection or combination of the brotherhood sought interference from any other association in America. It put up the shutters against any dictatorship from

---

[119] See below where Michael Keogh distinguishes between the Irish Revolutionary Brotherhood and the much better-known Irish Republican Brotherhood.

scions of the secret Irish societies, and against tyranny evolving from such archives of intrigue, those clinging on with pugnacious tenacity to the Irish-American coat-tails of Tammany Hall, New York.

During the winter of 1908 and with the Entente Cordiale of Europe completely in the bosom of America's Wall Street finance ring, I had the occasion of first listening to the forcible and plain truth spoken by the Irish patriot, James Connolly.[120] The great socialist democratic leader was invited to lecture to the members of the Sheares Brothers[121] Club of the Irish Revolutionary Brotherhood, known for short as the IRB but not to be confused with the Irish Republican Brotherhood, also known as the IRB. The Irish Revolutionary Brotherhood in the USA did not have the numbers of the much younger and oath-bound secret Irish society of the Republican Brotherhood. In New York city, with its almost overwhelming Irish population, there was but one club (Sheares Brothers) of the Irish Revolutionary Brotherhood consisting of 50-odd members. The club president was Martin Sheares from rebel Cork and a direct descendant of the illustrious brothers whose name he bore. These patriots of 1798 fame were executed in the prison yard at Arbour Hill Barracks, Dublin. All members of the Sheares Brothers Club were obliged to be descendants of Irishmen who had proved worthy in the cause of Irish freedom at some period in the insurrectionary movement in Ireland or America.

In 1908 at this aforementioned meeting and lecture by our worthy fellow countryman James Connolly, the speaker's subject was "Robert Emmet, the Irish Patriot, and the Insurrection of 1803". Connolly's argument was that Emmet's nationalism was compatible with what socialism then stood for. The 1916 leader imparted the impression most vividly on each Sheares Brothers comrade that Emmet was Ireland's first great "socialist democrat", a fact more easily understood when we examine closely Emmet's declaration of Irish independence in 1803. Connolly was made an honorary member of the Sheares Brothers Club in those seemingly far-off days of 1908. He was then in the initial grips of

---

[120] James Connolly (1868-1916) was the founder of the Irish Socialist Republican Party and the Independent Labour Party, a joint organiser of the Irish Transport and General Workers Union with James Larkin, editor of *The Workers Republic* and author of *Labour in Irish History*, among other publications. He was one of the leaders of the 1916 Rising and was executed afterwards; he is generally regarded as the greatest intellectual force behind Irish socialism.

[121] Henry (1753-1798) and John Sheares (1766-1798) were two leading members of the United Irishmen. They were executed after the rising and their bodies are buried in the crypt of St Michan's Church in Dublin.

the pending great strike and gallant stand made by the workers of the New York Metropolitan Railways and Street Car Company.

I recall his earnest appeal for unrestrained assistance on behalf of our countrymen then about to stand out for their just rights as exiled workers of Ireland. The appeal did not need to be stressed for most of us were fellow workers, each in his own sphere or classification. Many of the Sheares Brothers fraternity were Irishmen of some worldly means and, at the close of the lecture, a voluntary subscription amounted to some $200, with the promise of more to follow to assist the sorely stricken families of Irish railway workers in New York.

It is the Irish exile who is ever ready to assist, with his hard-earned dollars, Irishmen and Irish causes at home and abroad. Yet how little thanks they receive at times from Irish hearts who so easily forget. It is the millions of Irish exiles in America who have come to Ireland's rescue at all times of trouble and tribulation in her life-and-death struggle with perfidious Albion. It was so in the convict-ship days prior to and after the 1798 Insurrection, and in the Great Famine days of 1845-49 when America's Irish population opened their purses and homes to hundreds of thousands of hunger-stricken Irish exiles. Right down the decades of oppression and evil in Ireland by the Anglo-Saxon hordes, it was the open doorway in Uncle Sam's second Irish home that received the victims of John Bull.

Irish-American dollars minted the slogan "Irish independence" in 1916 and with the funeral cortege of one of Erin's greatest and noblest exile sons was formed the bodyguard of Irish freedom in 1915 with the national funeral oration over the venerable corpse of O'Donovan Rossa at Glasnevin Cemetery in Dublin. Patrick Pearse sounded the Easter Week trumpet in his historic graveside oration.[122]

In the autumn of that fateful and historic year, 1914, accompanied by another Irishman, I sailed from New York to Ireland. Our purpose was to enlist in Irish regiments of the British army in the same spirit and with the same aim as inspired the earlier soldier-Fenians, such as John Boyle O'Reilly, John Devoy and Colour-Sergeant McCarthy.[123] That aim needs no

---

[122] At O'Donovan Rossa's graveside, Patrick Pearse gave his famous oration which included the following: "They think that they have pacified Ireland. They think that they have purchased half of us and intimidated the other half. They think that they have foreseen everything, think that they have provided against everything; but, the fools, the fools, the fools! — they have left us our Fenian dead, and while Ireland holds these graves, Ireland unfree shall never be at peace."

[123] John Boyle O'Reilly (1841-1890) was a member of the Fenians who joined the British army in Ireland and recruited many Fenians into his regiment. Colour-

elaboration. My companion, being a southerner, elected to join the Munster Fusiliers. I enlisted in the 18th Foot, the Royal Regiment of Ireland, a title dating from the inglorious days of King James II and the Boyne.

I was at once drafted to the depot at Clonmel for training. There I spent a reasonable time learning the rudiments of the soldier's trade – a discreet course but entirely superfluous as I had already served my time in the United States where I had trained with the National Guard in their summer camp near Fort Riley, Kansas, and seen service in 1911 down El Paso way during the Huerta insurrection in Mexico.[124] This formed an exciting and instructive break in the monotony of my life as a mining engineer in Texas – the most severe and beneficial training a soldier of fortune could have, fighting often as lone a hand as any *gringo*, quick and sharp with Winchester or Colt.

During the first two weeks of training, I passed the educational test, obtaining a first-class certificate – rather an exceptional achievement for an Irish ranker in Britain's service. The examining officer, I remember, was Captain Butler, son of General William Butler, who showed up the Chamberlain "Tea Party" game in the initial stages of the Boer War.[125] He congratulated me on my success, convinced, no doubt, that His Majesty had secured the making of an efficient soldier. Six years later I met this Irish gentleman in a curious way in Cologne, which I was at the time (September 1919) visiting incognito. We encountered in the vicinity of the Catholic Cathedral and he at once recognised me as an Irishman. A good linguist, he said he had been greatly interested in the German sermon he had just heard. As a loyal British officer, he would, I am certain, have been equally interested in my mission and the special passport in my possession. But he was none the wiser of the meeting. This was well, for had else transpired, some few Irish soldiers' kit-bags with false bottoms would have been ransacked and many a good German Mauser would never have had the opportunity of paying

---

Sergeant Charles McCarthy was also a Fenian who joined the British army. Following a punitive term in British prisons, he died shortly after his release in 1878, at the age of 44.

[124] The Huerta insurrection did not break out until 1913. Perhaps what is meant is the Madero rebellion that began in 1910.

[125] Lieutenant-General Sir William Francis Butler (1838-1910) was acting High Commissioner in South Africa in the late 1890s. He expressed views on the probability of war that were not to the liking of the British government and he was ordered home. Joseph Chamberlain was the Colonial Secretary at the time and the optimistic British referred to the Boer War, when it broke out in 1899, as the "Tea Time War". It was to drag on until 1902.

back in kind the gentle deeds on the Black and Tans in Ireland in 1920-21.

To return to Clonmel. My presence did not seem to please some sergeant instructors there and, in the autumn of 1913, I found myself with the 2nd Battalion of the regiment in the South Raglan Barracks, Devonport. I was joined here by a wild Irish "bronco-buster" from the States – a lad of the Rocky Mountain O'Brien type. Matters progressed quietly at Devonport, but the thoughts of the better elements among the Irish soldiers were constantly turning to developments in Ireland and the prospects of a conflict between north and south. This brooding often found expression in words and these did not pass unheeded. I soon found myself under the furtive watching of the West British type of comrade among whom I was timorously referred to as "the Irish Yankee spy". Nothing overt happened, however.

The climax of tension was reached early in April 1914 when British army officers in the Curragh openly flouted the weakling Asquith, declared they would not proceed to the north, and would tolerate civil war. This introduced politics into military ranks with a vengeance and the army authorities were gravely perturbed regarding its probable effect upon the Irish troops. Orders were promptly issued prohibiting all barrack-room discussions of the situation in Ireland. The edict was futile; the determination was daily and openly expressed: "Certainly we will go to Ulster."

I challenged the infringement of freedom of speech under the order once too often. I was tried by court-martial for what the prosecuting officer termed "a crime of a highly seditious nature", and I spent 28 days in the military prison. This imprisonment silenced me effectively for that period, but it riveted more keenly than ever the attention of my Irish comrades on the laudable character of the protest I had made. I have often wondered since how my continuance as a soldier was countenanced thereafter. I suppose my outburst was attributed to the waywardness of the Irish temperament. Talk, instead of being suppressed, spread, even to the officers' mess, in which there were many young Catholic officers, and free fights and all their outward symbols followed each carouse in those exalted precincts.

After my release from my month's imprisonment in the summer of 1914, I could have skipped back to the United States two days subsequent to the declaration of war on an American schooner from Falmouth, where portion of our regiment had been temporarily stationed some time before our embarkation for Boulogne. Instead, I gave my younger Irish-American comrade, Patrick Roche, the option. So, with a sufficient intuition of my own chances to break through somewhere in France, I determined to try to reach the Germany. Admittedly, it was not a trail over which one might carry an insurance policy for life. Rather it was what John Boyle O'Reilly once termed "an Irish soldier's cruel path to Calvary on the Anglo-Saxon fiery cross". If such a road was good enough in the Fenian days for Trooper Boyle O'Reilly, Sergeant-Major McCarthy, Sergeant Darragh, Corporal Chambers, Pat Keating and the Civil War veteran, Captain James Murphy, there seemed no reason why I should quail before its hardships. The Fenian movement had been half my schoolbook; for my grandmother on the maternal family tree was a rebellious O'Boyle from Royal Meath, near blood relation to the mother of Boyle O'Reilly, and it was my grandmother's teaching and the example of her Fenian cousin that most influenced my course of life until I had the privilege of finding myself identified with Roger Casement, whom I first met in New York in 1911.

I have already referred to our embarkation for Boulogne, from Southampton, immediately after the declaration of war. On Saturday evening, 22nd August, we met the foremost German Uhlan[126] patrols near Mons. An Irish trooper of the 4th Irish Dragoon Guards was the first "British" soldier to fall victim to a well-aimed German bullet. At midnight, I happened to be one of the most extreme outposts, with four trusty scouts, each a Boer War veteran. McNamara, my right-hand man, passed the casual remark at sun up: "Now, my hardy lads, ere the sun you see has set in the west, many a good Irish mother's son will have bitten the dust." Too true and more the pity! Irishmen have ever been compelled by force of circumstances to fight everyone's battle but their own.

By noon on the memorable Sunday of 23rd August 1914 a critical situation had developed. I found myself fulfilling the duties of acting commander in charge of a section of regimental scouts attached to the 8th Infantry Brigade, 2nd Army Corps. The extreme right flank of a 20-mile front was composed of the British Expeditionary Force,[127] consisting of eight infantry brigades, four war-strength infantry battalions to the brigade. One outstanding and significant fact deserves attention. Each British brigade of

---

[126] The German Uhlan regiments were cavalry regiments. After seeing cavalry action in the early weeks of the First World War, they were either dismounted to serve as riflemen in the trenches of the Western Front or moved to the Eastern Front where the more primitive conditions made it possible for horse cavalry to be still effective. All 26 German Uhlan regiments were disbanded at the end of the war.

[127] When the war broke out, the British Expeditionary Force was sent to Belgium under the command of General Sir John French (afterwards Lord Lieutenant of Ireland, 1918-21). It suffered heavy casualties at the first Battle of Mons but helped to halt the German advance at the first Battle of the Marne.

infantry was made up of three English or Scottish regiments and one Irish regiment, the Irish to the frontal line of attack, the Scots and Anglo-Saxons bringing up the rear: as ever in Britain's wars, the brave Irish to the front, the boys of the bulldog breed in the wake, to gloat over the fruits of our fighting. And fronting us were the Germans: Germans facing us, Germans to the right of us, Germans on our left flank, Germans concealed in masses in the surrounding groves and wooded landscape, their artillery belching death at short range from the effective camouflage afforded by the timber-knitted ground.

Scarcely had half an hour elapsed before word was passed down the extended firing line: "Every man for himself! Save yourselves as you can!" We were in a veritable death-trap, and officers and men simply acted on their own instincts of defence. Forthwith, the British became non-combatants, stampeding herds before a withering onslaught. The Irish, being in the breach, suffered most, and were it not for their keenness and initiative in taking advantage of every inch of cover, it is not too much to say that not one Irishman of the 18th Regiment would have survived the experiences of that desperate hour at Mons. I well remember one young Gael of immense stature, well over six feet, become suddenly bereft of all reason. He stripped off his jacket, rolled up his sleeves and, armed with drawn sword in one hand and a revolver in the other, dashed forward on his own, shouting and firing at random. It was a typical and tragic incident.

The Germans made good use of cover; brains and tactics moved in unison so far as they were concerned. The British commanders, on the other hand, were in a fog, merely groping in the dark, except in a very few instances. Summing up the situation at Mons, Lovat Frazer, the English war critic, truly wrote that the English expeditionary forces were composed of "lions led by asses". At what a cost of human life: 500 Irishmen of one battalion lay dead and wounded or prisoners of war within the space of a few hours. Every foot of earth round Mons told its own weird story. I stuck it out until late in the evening when, completely at bay, outflanked front and rear, it was a case of "Hande Hoch!" which meant "Put them up and quick at that!"

The one thought that remained uppermost in my mind through this inferno was that in war time, England's enemy was Ireland's friend; therefore there was less reason why I should throw away my life for the British Empire than fall into the hands of those most likely to cripple that empire of tyranny. In a word, we made the best of a bad job, submitting philosophically to the fortunes of war. Four days later, I found myself, along with some 250 other soldiers – Irish, English and Scottish – in Sennelager

Camp, Westphalia, Germany. En route I paid a visit on shanks' mare to Halle, Waterloo, Louvain and Liege in Belgium. I was now a passive spectator in the historic cockpit of Europe.

The life of a prisoner of war in the Fatherland during the first months of the World War has often been described and its rigours greatly exaggerated. No further explanation of the hardships which prisoners endured is needed than the fact that they were swarming into Germany. The numbers increasing daily, the provision of housing facilities became more and more impossible. In many cases one had to await pot luck – first come, first served. Camping out, anyway, meant a second heaven compared to the prisoner-of-war mode of life. This situation did not apply to all. Here, as elsewhere, the old proverb held good: "The first in the field generally makes the best hunting." One fact must be borne in mind. After three months' warfare, Germany had to feed and house close on half a million Russians, about 100,000 French (white and coloured colonials), approximately 10,000 British – in other words, about one-fifth of John Bull's expeditionary army in France.

Napoleon never could boast of such an army. The Little Corporal's military temperament would scarcely have endured such a medley of soldier material as constituted the Allies troops now stowed away behind the barbed-wire fences of the Germans. I do not intend unnecessarily to revive memories of prison-camp life in the land of soldiers. The position can be explained in a few words. As well as hundreds of thousands of prisoners of war – approaching a million after the first three months – Germany had also to support an army in the field of almost five million men. For this achievement alone, the German people deserved more sympathy and respect than they were accorded by a purchased pro-Ally press. The rabid attacks hurled against them justified the anger of an honest, industrial race, worthily striving to extend and protect their commercial interests, and envied by England accordingly.

In Sennelager, I made the acquaintance of a German sergeant, an old globe-trotter and well-known journalist in German-American circles. He acted as an interpreter, being fluently conversant with important European languages. He spoke English like a native; Gaelic he professed to know slightly, and occasionally gave vent to his feelings in the words: "Fág an bealach, a spáilpín!" In his better moods, and particularly after reading of another big capture on the Western Front, he would exclaim for my benefit: "Go saoraidh Dia Éire agus an Ghearmáin!" In order to ensure this true German against danger of victimisation should his business necessitate visiting England, I will simply call him Hans. He understood Ireland's position; the

Irish race he thoroughly knew and appreciated. Extensive travels in the British Isles and the United States enabled him to grip the essential facts of Irish history and the characteristics of the Irish people. The only things that puzzled him then were Carson and Redmond – pro-British recruiting ringmasters in the Ireland of Parnell and Mitchel.

I was daily in the company of Hans, who frequently took me out of camp to the towns of Sennelager and Paderborn, some 10 miles distant by rail. A suit of "civvies" enabled us to develop our combined ideas in security. Early in November 1914, he gave me a cutting from a German daily newspaper referring to the coming of Roger Casement to the Fatherland, and describing in detail at attempt on Roger's life by His Brittanic Majesty's Minister-Extraordinary at Christiania, the one-time intriguing assistant of Kitchener in Egypt.[128]

---

[128] On 24th August 1914, a Clan na Gael delegation led by Devoy met the German ambassador to the US, Count Bernstorff. They asked the Germans to supply arms and enough good officers to begin the overthrow of British rule in Ireland. On 25th August, a proclamation "To His Imperial Majesty, the German Emperor" was issued (written entirely by Casement) and signed by 44 people, mainly the Clan na Gael executive. It stated: "We feel that the German people are in truth fighting for European civilisation at its best ... We recognise that Germany did not seek this war, but that it was forced upon her ... We wholeheartedly hope for the success of the German people in this unequal struggle forced upon them." Trying to persuade the Kaiser of Ireland's importance, Casement continued: "We ... draw Your Majesty's attention to the part that Ireland necessarily... must play in this conflict ... The British claim to control the seas of the world rests chiefly on an unnamed factor. That factor is Ireland ... Ireland must be freed from British control."

Regarding Casement's decision to go to Germany, there is no reliable evidence of the origins of the plan to send him there. But, whatever its origin, he quickly showed his agreement with it. In early October, he and the Clan na Gael leaders met and agreed that he should go to Germany via Norway. The German embassy in Washington helped in the preparations and Bernstorff wrote a letter of recommendation for Casement to the German Chancellor, Bethmann Hollweg.

Beardless, Casement travelled on the Oscar II as James Landy (the real Landy had disembarked shortly before departure and left his cabin to Casement). He was accompanied by Adler Christensen. In retrospect, we can see it was a mistake for Casement to have taken the Norwegian sailor with him. It is not very important whether the British minister in Norway, Mansfeldt de Carbonnel Findlay, tried to bribe Christensen into committing treason in Christiania (by kidnapping or even killing Casement) or whether Christensen made himself available for British schemes (as a number of historians and Casement biographers have stated). More curious was Casement's waste of time and energy pursuing the Christensen affair after having arrived in Germany, all the more so as he knew the German government soon did not trust Christensen.

On the last leg of the voyage, from Christiania to Berlin which he reached on 31st October, Casement was accompanied by Richard Meyer, a representative of the

I endeavoured to get into immediate touch with Casement through a brother of Hans who was in the newspaper business in Berlin. I succeeded and wrote him definitely on some matters which materially assisted him in negotiating the 10 articles of the agreement contained in the Irish-German Treaty.[129] In all our subsequent correspondence and intercourse, Roger gave me to understand that I was to go slowly, to be cautious in all dealings with both well-meaning friends in Germany and the ever-alert tools of the enemy in khaki. His reasons he explained in private conversation. The German government officials were proceeding carefully, taking "protective measures in a half-hearted manner". Undoubtedly, many high German officials were out the whole way to help Casement as the envoy sent to place Ireland's true position before the German people and government. I must emphatically state here that Casement's dealings were always through German diplomatic channels. He completely barred recourse to military heads of baronial jackboot officialdom. The latter retaliated by petty meanness and incompetence. Throughout, a majority was dead against his most explicit wishes. The outcome, whether success or failure, often depended on one deciding vote.

In his personal interview with the German Prime Minister, Herr Bethmann Hollweg, on 2nd November 1914,[130] Casement went all out for a full-count policy of goodwill towards Ireland and her people. A most important case in point arose early: how far was Germany willing in the immediate future to assist the Irish Volunteer force in Ireland, in the event of success for German arms in breaking through and making feasible an expedition to Erin? The failure of von Cluck's drive to Paris, however, foiled all hopes of occupying the Channel Ports of Calais and Boulogne.[131] The flooding of the Belgian canals did the rest. So the Prime Minister, through the mouths of his military advisers, pointed out

---

German Foreign Office. He became one of the more important functionaries given the job of attending to Casement and Irish matters. Among other roles he played, he was the interpreter during Casement's difficult negotiations with the Germans. See Doerries, *Prelude to the Easter Rising*, pp. 2-7.

[129] For which, see below.

[130] On this date, Casement met Arthur Zimmermann, the Under Secretary of State for Foreign Affairs, and not Chancellor Bethmann Hollweg.

[131] Alexander von Cluck (1846-1934) commanded the German 1st Army on the outbreak of war. He was fulfilling effectively the Schlieffen Plan to encircle Paris when General von Bulow's 2nd Army, whose advance was stalled, called for help from him. By turning aside to help von Bulow, he allowed the French and British to counterattack. Because of the failure to take Paris, the rather unfair phrase, "dumb cluck", developed.

that owing to certain plans falling through, the questions stressed by Casement (though of a most desirable nature) could not be immediately entertained. In fact, great doubt and lack of confidence prevailed among the general staff and army authorities. However, important questions were decided before the termination of a lengthy interview.

One fact the Irish patriot made clear: on no account should German naval or air attacks be directed on Ireland. The proceedings of certain personages in Germany were also given close examination; one in particular, Mr Gerard, American Ambassador in Berlin who, to put it at its mildest, was more than sympathetic towards Britain.[132] Roger plainly told Herr Hollweg to be on guard against this enemy within the gates in the guise of American neutrality. The warning went unheeded but Herr Hollweg and his government would have done well if Roger's timely advice were taken.

Germany and its people had, in the United States, a most secret enemy from the very day of the declaration of war. From the outset, Wall Street and the pro-Anglo-Saxon fanatics were secretly at war with the Central European powers: indirectly by disguised financial support, directly by openly delivering war material in ammunition-passenger ships, of which it will suffice to mention the Lusitania. In the course of the two weeks prior to her sailing from New York, in May 1915, it is well known that the Cunard Shipping Office warned multimillionaires and aristocrats not to travel on the ship. It mattered not about the smaller fry. And it was only a matter of time until direct action, through American military intervention in Europe, would counterbalance the influence of superior tactics on the Western Front – a step which eventually did turn the tide in favour of the Allies. But the phlegmatic Germans could not then appreciate the sound doctrine of Casement.

I will venture still further. In many high German diplomatic circles Casement incurred animosity for voicing this honest opinion. "Let the Yankees do their best," the German militarists said. I have met such Germans in every walk of life. But all admitted afterwards the unwisdom of the *Gross Kopfer*, or big Heads of Affairs, in not acting on the advice of *"Der ehrlicher Irlander"*, the honourable Irishman who had said: "Declare war on the Yankee dollar-hunters. Make them taste the bitterness of drastic warfare on the high seas, ere they have organised their

---

[132] James W. Gerard (1867-1951) was appointed American Ambassador to Germany in 1913. He was extremely hostile to the country and its people and to German-Americans as well. He was recalled from Berlin when the US declared war on Germany in 1917.

stupendous military and naval resources; the German people will then be in a position to demand honourable terms of peace." This was in the early summer of 1915, at the commencement of the German submarine campaign,[133] and over two years before the American entrance on the Allied side.

On the other hand, mark well what a prominent US army general staff chief said after the armistice of 1918:

> If the Germans could have held out with a deadly defensive warfare for even six months longer, in all probability the prolongation of the extreme sacrifice of American lives and the American people's indifference to European affairs involving such a heavy loss of life, might easily have evoked a national outcry against the further participation of American arms on the Western Front. The awful losses suffered by the American army in the last six months of the war had to be withheld from the knowledge of the general public in America.

What would have been the case if America was forced to an issue in 1915?

This contrast is quoted only to provide food for thought. Perhaps some unbiased military critic will answer. The chances are most people may say the conclusions I have arrived at spring from pro-German sympathy. Let me assure those who may happen to think this way that my dominant feeling through the war was pro-Irish, which connoted anti-English; other sympathies were secondary. The revelations made a month after the return of Ambassador Gerard to "God's own country" proved that the Casement mission to Germany was a pet aversion with this Anglo-Yankee cousin. His book, *The Kaiser and Germany*,[134] revealed the bias of a supposed neutral ambassador in Germany for the first three years of the war, 1914-17.

In Sennelager prisoner-of-war camp, I was kept constantly apprised of events by means of a cipher message from the Chief through Hans. My medium of despatch became, at times, desirous of learning the Irish code – a very simple device based on the words of the Irish ballad, "The Wearing of the Green", and which, turned into figures, baffled the best efforts of the all-powerful German Secret Service to decipher its tone of melody. Our little game of military chess took a decided turn towards the end of November 1914. It happened with such unexpectedness

---

[133] In February 1915, the seas around the British Isles were declared a war zone by the German government and any ship found there faced sinking without warning; unrestricted submarine warfare had begun for the first time in history.

[134] Following his return to the US, Gerard wrote *My Four Years in Germany*, published in 1917, and *Face to Face with Kaiserism*, published the following year.

that, had a German high explosive or a "Jack Johnson"[135] burst in the midst of Sennelager camp, the effect could not have been half so astounding in the eyes of some 20,000 "Froggies" and 10,000 "Tommies" who found a temporary abode within its many compounds. Fifteen hundred Irish soldiers may be included in this rough calculation.

An English-speaking German officer stood up in the centre of the main Irish compound. He made a very flattering speech, skilfully directed to reach the ears of ever Irishman there worth his salt. His words, however, were too pointed – another typical German blunder. Hans admitted this and denounced such blockhead tactics. This officer seemed familiar with Ireland's history, Irish soldiers' former exploits on the continent, the "Wild Geese" who fell from Dunkirk to Belgrade and MacBride's Irish Brigade with the gallant Boers in South Africa.[136] He said:

Irish soldiers in the history of wars throughout the world have made a name for themselves of which they may be justly proud. The first military leader of importance to negotiate a crossing over the lofty Alps was an Irish chieftain, King Daithi, at the head of his trusty Irish soldiers.

This was greeted with prolonged cheering, due, I suppose, to the fact that most of the Irish soldiers then listening never knew of Daithi's death in the attempt. He then pointed out the many unsuccessful attempts at insurrection in their beloved Inisfáil and ended up thus:

By the command of Kaiser Wilhelm II, all Irish soldiers, now prisoners of war, will be assembled in one distinct camp, be treated better, have more freedom, better food and clothing and suitable games. It is hoped, moreover, that before this war has ended, Ireland will have gained full independence and burst the chains of slavery with which a savage enemy, England, has bound the Irish people for nigh 800 years. The yoke will be broken at last and with the help of Germany. God save Ireland!

The officer had a mixed reception, not unnatural to expect, with so many West British Irishmen present. Immediately, the German officer asked to see myself. On meeting him, I inquired why he had not approached me before he spoke so openly. Casement, he said, asked him to see me. "Have you not made a mistake in not taking me into your confidence from the outset?" I

---

[135] The reference may be to the American boxer, Jack Johnson (1878-1946), who was heavyweight champion of the world 1908-15.

[136] John MacBride (1865-1916) had emigrated to South Africa where he raised the Irish Transvaal Brigade to fight the British when the Boer War broke out in 1899. Most members were Irish or Irish-American miners living in the Transvaal.

remarked, feeling assured his instructions were to this effect. A few days later he admitted it. Propaganda became a raging topic. The anti-Irish spirit forged ahead. One rusty old sergeant-major said rather heatedly in Cockney dialect, though a native of "Southern Ireland":

"I know Jerry's game. I was in the South African war. I remember Major MacBride's disloyal approaches to British soldiers and Irishmen – he may be there right now playing the same old gag."

One Irish soldier within hearing choked him off in words to this effect:

"Well, and if MacBride did so, he was a long sight a better Irishman than you are, or ever will be. MacBride, as an Irishman, had the courage of his convictions; you, as an Irishman, can only be termed a poor specimen. You had the pound of Rooty too long in your possession; you may live to go back to 'Blighty' and get the 'Rooty Medal', but that's all the good it will do you in the end. In the years to come, twopence will buy a medal, even a Mons Star, at Johnny Fox's store in Bride Street in dear old Dublin."[137]

Another Irish lad shouted "Up Dublin!" Yet another Dublin Fusilier exclaimed: "Yes, and if we get a King's Own Scottish Borderer in our midst, it's God help him!" This last Dublin lad of 19 summers could not forget his little girl-cousin shot down in cold blood a few months back in the massacre of Bachelor's Walk. O'Curry was one of the first Irishmen to join the Irish Brigade; the hope he cherished was to be given an opportunity of "revenge for those who died in Dublin town".

It was denied him, but there was one consolation: the "Dubs" did get some of their own back against the King's Own Scottish Borderers at St Quentin early in the World War. A safe estimate would be man for man in lieu of the Dublin citizens so cold-bloodedly shot at Bachelor's Walk on 26th July 1914 by the King's Own Scottish Borderers, better known as Pontius Pilate's Bodyguard.

The particular British warrant officer who referred to Major MacBride, the gallant Irish patriot of South African and Easter Week fame, had worked hard against Irish propaganda and

---

[137] The editor cannot explain the "Rooty" reference. "Blighty" was British-English slang for Britain and the word derived from Hindustani and Arabic. Its use was common in the latter days of the British Empire in India as a term of endearment for home. In the First World War, "dear old Blighty" was a common phrase to express the longing for home of soldiers in the trenches. The "Mons Star" was issued to members of the British Expeditionary Force who took part in and survived the first Battle of Mons.

Casement's endeavours in Germany, both at Sennelager and Limburg an der Lahn camps. It was at the latter, in May 1915, and within hearing of "Joe Peters" (Joe Plunkett) that he spoke those ill-meant words to Sgt Joe Dowling and myself: "Keogh and Dowling, if ever I get the chance of finding you in the British Isles, I'll have both of you hung high and dry in the Tower of London." A grand type of Irishman to bear an honoured name! Well, as the old German proverb goes: "*Gott bewahre*" – "God to shield".

To sum up the situation all those years ago at Sennelager, Westphalia: No extra or special facilities were to be accepted by "Irishmen" in Germany who were urged to "stand fast as true British soldiers". But the efforts of the NCOs and pro-British element met a reverse thanks to the astuteness of my worthy ally, "Hans". I only wished to play "Gretchen" to his "Hansel" in this irksome opera.

In the course of events from mid-November to mid-December 1914, the Irishmen in Sennelager were placed in a separate portion of the camp devoid of all barbed-wire entanglements and with ample space to play a game of football, which they did to their hearts' content. The Catholic church in the German barracks was open daily for the benefit of the Irish Catholic soldiers. On the last Sunday in November, according to my diaries, the Bishop of Paderborn visited the camp of the Irish legion in the khaki of the Anglo-Saxon. It was a special Holy Communion Sunday for them, and they greatly enjoyed a special sermon in English, which exhorted all Irishmen present to stand fast to their centuries-old Catholicity and the undying faith of their martyred forefathers, which had been preserved by their life-blood.

The bishop, now Cardinal Schulte of Cologne, imparted the Papal Benediction to all present during the three Masses. He then bade them farewell and hoped they would find more healthy surroundings in the new Irish camp, where two Irish priests would minister to their spiritual welfare. Many more than Catholics had attended these services from ulterior motives and at the instigation of certain NCOs, but they were soon eliminated, much to the chagrin of the pro-British element.

On 17th December of the same year, some 1,500 Irish soldiers were conveyed by rail to Limburg an der Lahn in the province of Hesse-Nassau. This was not until the Catholics had been sifted out, a task which proved difficult, with so many "spotters" around. The Germans failed to grasp the necessity for religious discrimination. "Was not one Irishman as good as another, religion notwithstanding?" they asked, and pointed to their own country where no such distinctions operated. But I referred them to the time of the Prussian-Austrian War of 1866, when the

Catholic southern states of Germany, Bavaria and Wurttemberg, fought on the side of Catholic Austria. The Prussians proved the victors, and hence the amalgamation of all the German states, each with its own ruler, under the one Imperial Kaiser and King of Prussia. Then was founded the *Kaisereich* or German Empire, a combination of at least 10 small kingdoms within the fold of one large Kaiserdom. "Yes, but we are nevertheless all Germans," they would argue. I agreed, and had to point out, as best I could, that the people of Ireland for the past seven centuries were in most part not all Irish; the last tribe of Milesians had long since ceased to maintain its identity.

In demonstrating the explicit honesty of Roger Casement in all his attitudes towards his fellow-Irishmen, then prisoners of war in Germany, I must record the serious injunctions he placed on me in regard to my negotiation in Sennelager camp during the winter of 1914. "On no account," he said, "encourage Germans to promote any form of recruitment among Irish prisoners." The reason was obvious: the unfortunate Irishmen then there had experienced all the horrors of war and the intensified rigours and hardships of the battlefield. They suffered from reactionary deficiencies of both body and mind. Their lives as prisoners of war in the overflowing camps were not conducive to a normal perception of right and wrong. They were deprived of the one thing mankind most enjoys – freedom. Their plight blunted their best human instincts and clouded their moral judgement.

The remedy lay in their removal to other quarters. Let the Irishmen be transferred to the special Irish camp at Limburg an der Lahn, where they can enjoy more personal freedom, fulfil ordinary camp duties and fatigues, maintain discipline and sanitary conditions, Casement urged. They would then, he believed, get back to their everyday soldier routine, secure better food, and be afforded facilities for congenial Irish recreation such as games and concerts. This, combined with isolation from the many other nationalities abounding in the different camps, and the presence of two Irish priests from Rome to administer to their spiritual wants, should soon attract them to the idea of an Irish Brigade in Germany for the voluntary service of Ireland – in Ireland.

I am certain that there are at present in our midst some hundreds of men who have been prisoners of war in Germany who can bear me out in these statements. There are, too, many who, from prejudiced motives, or through blind allegiance to the Crown of England, would malign the labours and the memory of the illustrious and patriotic Roger Casement. For myself, I feel I can say with truth that, had he given me a free hand to recruit for the Irish Brigade in November and December of 1914 in

Sennelager camp, I could have procured at least 25 per cent of the 1,500 Irish prisoners encamped there. It took me some time to fathom exactly what he desired in that direction, but I am now satisfied that I obeyed my Chief to the last letter of his commands.

CHAPTER 4: The Beginning of Casement's Mission in Germany

Rory of the Gael arrived in Berlin on the last day of October 1914, in company with Richard Meyer. Adler Christensen, a faithful Norwegian,[138] was his companion during their dangerous ocean journey from New York to Norway on the SS Oscar II. They had been held up for two days at Kirkwall, to the north of Scotland, by the British cruiser Emerald. It is a story in itself how this Celt, disguised, and with a passport as an American citizen, outwitted England's navy. Rory often laughed in describing to me his role as a full-blown Yankee from "God's own country".

"Keogh, I can assure you the hardest thing I found was in expressing myself, or at least attempting to do so, with the usual American nasal effect. Adler said I was an absolute frost in the language of guessing and calculating but, apart from all that, was I not supposed to be an ex-Yale 'Varsity man and a magnate of industry from the New England states? Those Pilgrims' descendants do not guess. They calculate quickly, and in large figures of the almighty dollar.

"My blood almost reached freezing point when I saw four poor German merchant sailors, who were married to Norwegians and domiciled for years in Norway, taken off a *neutral* ship as prisoners of war by the British pirates on the second and last day of our enforced sojourn in a Hebrides port. The British naval

---

[138] A number of Casement's biographers have questioned just how faithful Christensen was. See especially, B.L. Reid, *The Lives of Roger Casement*, pp 211-18, where it is stated that Christensen tried to betray Casement to the British Minister in Christiania for a price. Reid describes Christensen as "a mean little adventurer who loved to line his pockets by petty intrigue … a liar by instinct and habit". See also, Jeffrey Dudgeon, *Roger Casement: the Black Diaries*, where Christensen is described (p. 437) as "a psychopath, entirely self-interested but not averse to becoming emotionally involved in whatever scheme he had in progress. He had the mind and outlook of a double or triple agent but at times had difficulty deciding which way to jump." Dudgeon also argues (pp 439-47), much more significantly, that Christensen became the means by which the British found out about Casement's homosexuality, which they were to use with devastating effect against him later. It was, says Dudgeon, as a result of Christensen's revelations to Findlay (the British Minister in Christiania) that British intelligence decided to open a file on Casement's homosexual activities, "not knowing when it might come in useful." See also Christopher Andrew, "Casement and British Intelligence," in Daly (ed.), *Roger Casement in World and Irish History*, pp 76-7.

officers could find none other to cart away for, of course, we were all neutrals or American citizens, and proud of it too. Some were born Germans, who had spent years in the USA, and were going home to fight for *Gott* and *Vaterland*. These were frightened even to speak to me, suspecting I was not an American, but the only one I feared was the third officer of the steamer, an Englishman. His presence showed the naval policy of Britain – a watchdog on neutral shipping. He tried to get on intimate terms with me during the trip but there was 'nothing doing'; just the commonplace salutations. Scotland Yard and I were sparring for a knock-out since the Howth gun running.

"I wondered how that report of McGarrity went in his *Irish Press* of Philadelphia: 'Roger Casement gone to western states and coast for a recuperation course after a hard political platform campaign,' and then the jumping on and off the New York-Philadelphia Express the same day. Joe McGarrity proved a good barber, and a pair of horn-rimmed attractors did the rest. I was on board the Oscar II at Hoboken the same night, having come by motor from your former home in Newark, New Jersey.

"I was compelled by human instinct to try to make the lot of the four German sailors as comfortable as possible during their future internment somewhere in Britain. In the state dining saloon of the Oscar II, I called on all present, as US citizens and neutrals, to subscribe a few dollars for the benefit of those German sailors who, unfortunately, were about to become prisoners of war. In all, I got in or about $200. This I gave to the British captain, who handed it over to the German merchant sailors. We weighed anchor at the end of the second day and cleared north east for Christiania. Thence to Berlin."

Once in the German capital, Casement lost no time. Here, from his diary, are his initial thoughts and impressions:

> The German Foreign Office, No. 76 Wilhelmstrasse, is an old-fashioned, white, very plain house of the time of Frederick the Great[139] or earlier. You have a sentry at a wooden gateway door; he rings the bell and the door opens. We went upstairs and a servant man took our coats, hats and sticks – so different from the London Foreign Office where I have been so often chez moi!
>
> The waiting-room we were shown into was a fine salon, well furnished and large, with fine oil paintings of King

---

[139] Frederick the Great (1712-1786) won military fame for himself and Prussia and transformed Prussia into an economically strong and politically reformed state. However, he was responsible for the partition of Poland.

Frederick William III and the old Emperor Wilhelm.[140] Meyer
[Richard, brother of Dr Kuno Meyer][141] told me I was to be
received first by the Under Secretary of State, Herr von
Zimmermann, and then by Count Georg von Wedel, the
"head of the English Department". Meyer left me alone a few
minutes. Some officers came and went, cavalry men in grey
uniform.

Strong thoughts were mine as I sat on a big sofa in this
centre of policy of the German Empire. No regrets, no fears. I
thought of Ireland, my land I should almost certainly never
see again. Only a miracle of victory could ever bring me to
her shores. That I hardly expect – can only hope for. But,
victory or defeat, it is all for Ireland, and she cannot suffer
from what I do. I may – I must – suffer, and even those near
and dear to me, but my country Ireland can only gain from
my treason.

Whatever comes, that must be so. If I win all, it is a
national resurrection – a free Ireland, a world nation after
centuries of slavery. A people lost in the Middle Ages re-found
to Europe. If I fail – if Germany be defeated – still the blow
struck today for Ireland must change the course of British
policy towards that country. Things will never again be quite
the same. The "Irish Question" will have been lifted from the
mire and mud and petty strife of British domestic politics
into an international atmosphere.

That, at least, I shall have achieved.

England and her "galloping"[142] statesmen can never again
play with "the Irish Question"; she will have to face the issue
once and for all. With the clear issue thus raised by me, she
will have to deal – straight to death's agony. She must either
face a discontented conspiring Ireland – or bind it closer by a

---

[140] Frederick William III (1770-1840) was King of Prussia from 1797 to 1840. He
was not a very effective ruler but did secure an expansion of Prussian territory at the
Congress of Vienna in 1815, thanks to his help in defeating Napoleon. The "old
Emperor Wilhelm" was William I (1797-1888), the first ruler of a united Germany
(and the first to use the title "Kaiser" or Emperor). His son, William II, was ruler of
Germany when war broke out in 1914.

[141] Doerries, *Prelude to the Easter Rising*, p. 7, says that contrary to the available
published information, Richard Meyer, who worked in the German Foreign Office,
was not a brother of Kuno Meyer, for whom see fn 152 below.

[142] In British public-school parlance, a "galloper" was a younger boy whose job it
was to assist a prefect or older boy – to act as his gofer. The term was applied
disparagingly to F.E. Smith (Galloper Smith), an English Conservative MP who
worked closely with Edward Carson in the Irish unionist campaign against Home
Rule from 1912 to 1914.

grant for fuller liberties. Coercion she cannot again resume. Laissez-faire must go for ever. "Home Rule" must become indeed home rule – and even if all my hopes are doomed to rank failure abroad, at least I shall have given more to Ireland by one bold deed of open treason than Redmond and Co., after years of talk and spouting treason, have gained from England.

England does not mind the "treason" of the orthodox Irish "patriot". She took the true measure of that long ago. She fears only the Irishman who acts, not him who talks; she recognises only action and respects only deeds. Those Irishmen have killed England with their mouth times out of number – I am going to hit her with my clenched hand. It is a blow of sincere enmity based on a wholly impersonal disregard of consequences to myself. Sure alone that it is in truth a blow for Ireland, I should be a traitor to her did I not act as I am doing. I have often said, and said it without the slightest concealment, that if ever the chance came to strike a blow for Ireland, I'd do it.

Well, that chance has come.

I am not responsible for it. The crime is not mine. It is England's own doing. Grey, Asquith[143], Neddy Carson and their galloping Smith are the real traitors. They have surely betrayed their respective countries, and England's true interests, to glut the greedy jealousy of the Pan-British commercial mind. Germany's greatest sin has been her efficiency. They chose to build up a league of enmity against the German people. They failed to assail themselves but, having triumphed in their tortuous, ignoble, secret diplomacy, they joyfully hurried to the encounter when, at last, they thought sure of their prey.

For them, that so-called Liberal Administration, I have nothing but unmeasured contempt, a scorn I cannot express; and for the "governing classes" too of the pirate British realm. For the people themselves and for many individual Englishmen, I have only deep sorrow, regret, pity and affection. But as Wilfred Blunt[144] said to me in Sussex at Newbuilding in May 1914, when I lunched with him and that lovely girl (the great granddaughter of Ireland's soldier-patriot

---

[143] Herbert Asquith (1852-1928) was Prime Minister in the Liberal government that ruled Britain from 1908 to 1916.
[144] Wilfred Scawen Blunt (1840-1922), a British poet and writer, opposed British imperialism and supported Irish causes.

of 1798, Lord Edward Fitzgerald[145]), the time has come for the break-up of the British Empire.

In the name of Lord Edward's great-granddaughter we entwine what little romance there can be recorded surrounding Casement. He was greatly attached to the personality and sublime characteristics portrayed in the direct descendant of one of Ireland's bravest sons. Casement himself told me, in a rather pensive manner, that at one time the ardent desire of doing something worthy of her great grandfather's love of Ireland had gripped the mind of this Cailín Deas. "I would like to help you in any project, no matter how dangerous, for Erin's sake," she said to Roger.

But little did this beautiful daughter of Ireland's beloved Geraldine ever dream of having to witness Casement's long and weary three days' trial for his life in London in June 1916 – or still more sad – of being present at his cruel and criminal sentence to death on the feast of SS Peter and Paul, 29th June 1916. How sorrowful must the ordeal have been to her as she waved a last farewell to Roger in the Anglo-Saxon prison dock. Yet it is recorded how he consoled with a smile of faith and sincerity as he took a parting glimpse of his very few friends and boldly marched to his doom.

The good priest who prepared him for his last journey on behalf of his own dear Erin truly sums up the end: Casement's earthly love, next to God, was Róisín Dubh or Dark Rosaleen. But to return to his diary of his introduction to Germany in November 1914:

Even as Wilfred Blunt said he hoped to live to *see* it, so I hope to be able to *do* something to bring the end of British rule nearer – at least in Ireland. That empire is a monstrosity. The world will be better, the more sincere, the less hypocritical for a British defeat in Ireland.

Many thoughts like these were with me as I waited in that room in Berlin. When I was shown into Herr Zimmermann's Cabinet, I met a fair-haired, very good-natured face and a warm and close handshake. I liked the man at once. He was warm hearted as well as warm handed. He congratulated me warmly on my safe arrival and spoke of the Christiania episode in fitting terms. He asked me long about it and I described the whole incident, and his comment was my own: "Dastardly," he said, "but it is what they [the

---

[145] Lord Edward Fitzgerald (1763-1798) was fifth son of the Duke of Leinster. He became a leader of the United Irishmen, was betrayed by an informer, and died from wounds sustained while resisting arrest.

British] do and have always done when their interests are at stake. They stick at nothing – even hitting below the belt."

I had written a hasty memorandum in the morning in my bedroom – giving a fresh point and drawing in outline the form of declaration I thought the German government might be prepared to issue in defence of Irish rights. The memorandum briefly recited the cruel calumnies the British government and their West British agents were spreading through Ireland in order to defame Germany and induce the Irish youth to enlist in their army of plunderers, under the pretence that it was a war to protect Belgium and the "small nationalities", and went on to show that the German government could quite legitimately defend itself from these atrocious charges of evil intent towards Ireland by making a formal declaration of its attitude towards my country.

I read the declaration I suggested to Herr Zimmermann, Under Secretary of State for Foreign Affairs. He agreed with every paragraph and sentence and, when I had done, took the whole paper from me and said: "I accept it entirely."

After an interview more cheering and full of a spirit of goodwill than I had ever hoped for, I was taken by Richard Meyer to Count von Wedel[146]. Here I found a charming personality – a man of upright build, frank, straight brown eyes and a perfect English accent. Our talk was long and friendly. I told him I had left the memorandum and form of proposed declaration for Ireland's case with the Under Secretary of State, and we talked of the Irish soldiers in Germany and the line of action that I hoped to follow there. It is this step that appeals greatly to the Germans, I can see. They perceive its full "moral" value to link their cause with Ireland's. Meyer said to me yesterday: "If you do that, it is worth 10 army corps to us!" If only I could hope the same to be said for Ireland's Volunteers.

I made it plain beyond all misconception to Count von Wedel that my efforts with the Irish soldiers must be strictly defined as an effort to strike a blow for Ireland – not an attempt merely to hit England. I described the character of the Irishman and of the Irish soldier, and pointed out that any Irishman might commit treason against England, *for the sake of Ireland*, but would not do anything mean or treacherous. He would put his neck in the noose, as I had

---

[146] Count Georg von Wedel (1868-1950) was the head of the English section of the German Foreign Office and a close friend of Chancellor Bethmann Hollweg. Casement first met him on 2nd November and he was to prove helpful to Casement throughout his stay in Germany.

done, for love of Ireland; he would not *desert to an enemy* or forsake his own colours merely to assail England. In fact, he must have an active cause, not a negative.

If, thus, Germany made the declaration I sought as to the fortunes and future of Ireland in the event of a German victory, I had little or no doubt that scores, perhaps, hundreds of the Irish prisoners of war would follow me. "So," said von Wedel, "it is clearly the declaration first of all." He then discussed with Meyer and myself the steps for my safety in Berlin, "not alone from the British, but from our own people". He proposed going at once with Meyer to the Chief of Secret Police and explaining things, and took me back in his taxi as far as the Continental Hotel where I got out. Later in the day, Meyer returned with a card issued by the Chief of the Political Police, saying that Mr Hammond of New York was not to be molested.

This card I am to carry always and it will ensure me in case of any street trouble or enquiry. Adler is to have no paper as, being a Norwegian, he is not an "offensive neutral personage". We both, however, are going to wear little American flags in our button-holes – and this evening Adler bought them. I went for a walk after dinner, Adler taking me up to the Kaiser's Palace and round it and then back down Unter den Linden again.

We saw the fine buildings of that quarter – so many of them royal or imperial in origin and more than one pertaining to the royal house.[147] Berlin is not imposing, I think, from the glimpse I had of it today, but it is fine. It is extraordinarily well kept and clean, and while the buildings are not lofty, they are massive and well built. Unter den Linden is, frankly, disappointing. It is not a fine thoroughfare and the shops do not impress me – neither do the linden trees. The latter are short and add little to the intended character of the street so far as I can see – but then I saw them at the beginning of winter.

There are too few people visible also. The street is wide and rather empty of any human throng. The cross-street, Friedrichstrasse, is, on the contrary, full of life, and I presume the true Berlin is rather this street than Unter den Linden. The Spree is a very insignificant river in the city – one crosses it before reaching the Kaiser's Palace and again, a branch of it, on the other side.

---

[147] The German royal family was the Hohenzollerns, originally rulers of Brandenburg and Prussia.

Now I am fairly launched on Berlin – and today sees me take up a definite position as the accredited Irish Race Ambassador "incognito" in the name of "Mr Hammond of New York" – not to be molested!.

His presence in Germany soon resulted in considerable press notice. The German government's official declaration of his presence appeared prominently in large type in the centre of the front page of several Berlin newspapers, such as the *Midday Gazette*, the *Berliner Tageblatt* and the government's official *North German Gazette* of Berlin.

Accompanying it was an article headed "*Sir Roger's Aktion – zu seinem Berliner Besuche*" ("Sir Roger's Action and His Visit to Berlin"). It bore the subheading: "*Deutsche Sympathie – Erklarung fur Ireland*" ("German Sympathy – Declaration for Ireland"). The article was a thoroughgoing description of Roger's self-sacrificing work as an Irish friend of the poor "black man", the underdog of red-rubber slavery in the Belgian Congo in 1903; of the intrepid honesty of his great endeavour to rend the chains of iron which bound the meek and tortured Indian of the Putumayo in 1909-10. It was also a eulogy of the "Irishman" who wrote openly for four years prior to the World War a virtual prophecy in the essays "The Freedom of the Seas", "In the Coming War" and "The Crime [by England] against Europe", and the volume "Ireland, Germany and the Freedom of the Seas" published in September 1914 through the Irish Press Bureau in New York and Philadelphia.

Subjoined is a translation of the "Declaration for Ireland", published at Berlin on 20th November 1914, when Casement was actually on a visit to the German Army Headquarters of the General Staff at Charleville, France. (It was his first visit to the Western Front; at the end of May 1915, he paid another visit with Commandant-General Joseph Plunkett, Military Delegate from the Irish Volunteer Army Headquarters in Dublin.)

"IRELAND AND THE WORLD WAR
Statement by the German Foreign Office

20th November 1914 – Berlin
The well-known champion of Irish freedom, Sir Roger Casement, who arrived in Berlin from the United States of America, has been received with welcome at the German Foreign Office. Sir Roger Casement pointed out that statements were being published in Ireland – with the authority of the British government apparently behind them – to the effect that a German victory would inflict great loss upon the Irish people, whose homes, churches, priests and lands would be at the mercy of an invading army actuated

only by motives of pillage and conquest. Recent utterances of Mr Redmond on his recruiting tour in Ireland, and many pronouncements of Ireland's West British press to the above effect have been widely circulated, Sir Roger pointed out, and have caused natural apprehension among Irishmen as to the German attitude towards Ireland in the event of a German victory in the present World War."

Sir Roger sought a convincing statement of German intentions which might reassure his countrymen all over the world, and particularly in Ireland and America, in view of these disquieting misrepresentations emanating from responsible British quarters. In reply, the Secretary of State at the Foreign Office[148], by order of the German Imperial Chancellor, made the following official declaration:

The German government repudiates the evil intentions in the British statements referred to by Sir Roger Casement, and takes this opportunity to give a categoric assurance that the German Government desires only the welfare of the Irish people, their country and their institutions. The Imperial German Government formally declares that under no circumstances would Germany invade Ireland with a view to its conquest or the overthrow of any native institutions in that country. Should the fortune of this great war, that was not Germany's seeking, ever bring in its course German troops to the shores of Ireland, they would land there, not as an army of invaders to pillage and destroy, but as the forces of a government that is inspired by goodwill towards a country and a people for whom Germany and its people desire only true national prosperity and complete national liberty.

This very plain declaration by the German government was well received by the Irish in America, by other friends of Irish freedom abroad, and by all who were not willing pawns of the British Empire in Ireland.[149]

---

[148] Gottlieb von Jagow (1863-1935) was Secretary of State at the German Foreign Office from 1913 to 1916.

[149] One of Casement's biographers, Jeffrey Dudgeon, commenting on the declaration, said that within three weeks of his arrival in Germany, Casement had achieved his greatest diplomatic advance. The declaration was much appreciated in Irish-America, Devoy writing to Casement that it was everything "that could be expected in the present military and naval situation". The German embassy in Washington reported on 5th December that it had "made a splendid impression". See Dudgeon, *Roger Casement: the Black Diaries*, pp 448-49. Reinhard Doerries argues that what may have been the most important target for Casement was an official German government declaration in favour of Irish independence. "Later authors,

On 30th November 1914, Casement went to the German Foreign Office where Count von Wedel introduced him to the two Irish priests who had arrived from Rome. The priests were Fathers O'Gorman and Crotty, who said to Count von Wedel prior to meeting Roger that they knew "who he was" but did not know him personally. No, they did not, but Casement hoped their views might become as his before they departed. Von Wedel gave Roger to understand that the priests' instructions from Rome were to abstain from politics! Good, if they keep to that! Roger met the two chaplains and found Fr O'Gorman a professing nationalist, while Fr Crotty, the Dominican, seemed all that could be desired. Both assured him that they would not be "agents of the British government" but would confine themselves strictly to their religious concerns with the Irish soldiers at the camp at Limburg an der Lahn.

The priests, as I said, were to be "entirely non-political". The question was: would they be? Anyway, Rome made sure of their neutrality by securing the spiritual assistance of two priests seemingly the reverse of each other as far as real Irish nationality was concerned. While conversing with his newly found Irish friends, Count von Wedel showed them the notice in the London *Daily Mail*, for 21st November 1914, of the pro-German demonstration at the inaugural meeting of the Medical School of the National University of Ireland in Dublin. This tit-bit profoundly impressed the Irish priests just arrived from Rome and then in the very centre of Germany.[150]

Meanwhile, within the "hub" of officialdom at the Foreign Office on Wilhelmstrasse, who should appear but Casement's old friend from the Congo, Count Blucher, great-grandson of the

---

possibly under the influence of the memoirs of John Devoy, haven't emphasised this part of Casement's mission" and instead have given greater significance to his other aims, e.g., support for rebellion in Ireland, propaganda in Germany to win public support for eventual German action in Ireland, and the formation of an Irish Brigade. See Doerries, *Prelude to the Easter Rising*, p. 7.

[150] The idea of getting Irish priests to minister to the Irish prisoners of war had been thought about at an early stage. The German representative in Rome wrote to Berlin on 20th November 1914 that two priests there, the Augustinian Canice O'Gorman and the Dominican Thomas Crotty, were willing to go to Germany. Because they were not aware of the idea of establishing an Irish Brigade, their work with the men was to be purely spiritual. Fr O'Gorman stayed in Germany for only about six weeks. Fr Crotty stayed much longer but didn't support the brigade project and this displeased the Germans. Another priest, the Irish-American Fr John Nicholson of Philadelphia, came to Germany via Clan na Gael and the German Embassy in Washington. He was strongly in favour of the brigade project. See Andreas Roth, "'The German soldier is not tactful'," *The Irish Sword*, vol. 19, no. 78, pp. 316-19.

German victor at Waterloo a century previously, when Wellington was literally pulled out of the Napoleon fires by the more effective Prussian guns?[151] Blucher of 1914 said that Mr Gay, the US Consul-General, had first discussed with him the "pamphlet from New York" on Ireland, Germany and the Freedom of the Seas. Gay thought it actually came from America, whereas Casement had posted it to him only a few days previously through Kuno Meyer's "overseas" US mail-bag.[152] Serbia and the fall of its capital city, Belgrade, were next discussed by this Irish-German assembly. Things looked very black for Serbia then, and there was but little pity for her fate.

Her case was different from that of Belgium – although Casement pointed out that the publication of the "Anglo-Belgian Military Conventions" of 1906 entirely upset the Belgian *pose* of neutrality. She was no more neutral than France or England. Belgium deliberately allied herself with England eight years prior to the World War, and England in 1912 dared to inform Belgium that she (England) would land troops in Belgium "to defend Belgian neutrality" in case of a war between England and Germany – whether Belgium consented or not! This was the masterpiece of the 1906-12 diplomatic correspondence and the height of the neutrality of poor little Belgium in 1914. The cockpit of Europe at England's bidding, and for the avenging of which Irishmen were politically sent out to die on the cruel cross of Anglo-Saxon perfidy somewhere in Flanders.

In 1920-21, Irishmen were murdered by criminal hirelings, Black and Tans and native dupes of Dublin Castle, because the Irish Republican Army dared to fight for Ireland as a small nation on her native soil. Now that three-fourths of Erin, under a threat of immediate war, is forced to declare that portion a Dominion within the Commonwealth of Nations known as the British Empire, where will England order Irishmen to go fight for the

---

[151] Count Gebhard Blucher was a German friend of Casement from his days in Africa. He was the great-great grandson of Marshal Blucher, without whom the outcome of Waterloo might have been very different. His wife was English and the couple lived in England until the outbreak of the war. She later published a memoir, *An English Wife in Berlin*, in which she records meetings with Casement during his time in Berlin. See *Casement in Germany: A Guide to the Roger Casement Papers in Clare County Archives*.

[152] Kuno Meyer (1858-1919), from Hamburg, was a great Celtic scholar; he lectured in Teutonic and Celtic languages at the University of Liverpool from 1884 and became Professor of Celtic Languages at the Royal Irish Academy from 1904 to 1914. In the latter year he went to the US and returned to Germany in 1917.

empire in its next great war?[153] It behoves all Irishmen to remember the POSE of Belgium's neutrality in 1914, and to heed Casement's historic slogan of that year: "Irishmen have no right to fight for anyone except in the great fight in Ireland for Irish freedom." *Agus go saoraidh Dia Éire!*

---

[153] From 1922 to 1949, the Irish Free State remained within the British Commonwealth but could not be involved – without her consent – in any war in which Britain was involved, as was seen from her stance of neutrality during the Second World War.

CHAPTER 5: The German-Irish Treaty

Once in the German capital, Casement lost no time. On 2nd November he had an interview with Herr Zimmermann of the German Foreign Office and Count von Wedel, head of the English section of the same establishment. Having discussed Irish affairs in general, he placed before his auditors some important facts. The most immediate and important question was: Would German military tactics on the Western Front be adequate to occupying the Channel ports of Boulogne and Calais? The answer was: Possibly, but with great difficulty and heavy losses. The first Battle of Ypres was a failure, owing to the flooding of the canals by the Belgians.

Casement, the Irish Race Ambassador, stressed this particular phase of the Western Front operations and its vital relation to success, in the hope of securing freedom for Ireland through united German-Irish action. General von Moltke,[154] Chief of the General Staff and of Operations, made one mistake in ordering the drive to Paris in August 1914. The Channel ports should then have been the objective. Casement held this view from the beginning of the war; so did the Irish and the Germans in the United States. Was it yet too late to repair it in November 1914?

The second consideration was: If German arms succeeded in landing in Ireland through a naval victory or possession of the Channel ports, were they prepared to come as friends and as an army of deliverance for the complete freedom of Ireland? This attitude was made perfectly clear by Germany. They would be forceful mediators for Irish independence against the common enemy.[155]

---

[154] Helmuth von Moltke (1848-1916) was Chief of the German General Staff from 1906 to 1914. Some have blamed him for the German failure to capture Paris; others have exonerated him. But the capture of Paris was the aim of both the Schlieffen (his predecessor) and Moltke Plans, not the taking of the Channel ports.

[155] Doerries stated that the self-confidence and illusions of victory of the Germans at this stage were so powerful that it may well be that some Berlin officials believed it realistic to launch an attack on Britain and Ireland. He pointed out that there are records of official groups in Germany actually planning and pursuing adventurous attempts of this kind in other parts of the world, e.g., an invasion of India, military incursions into Canada and an alliance with Mexico against the US, so that the relatively modest plan in relation to Ireland is not surprising. See Doerries, *Prelude to the Easter Rising*, p. 8.

Casement's third consideration was that in all future air attacks or submarine raids, Irish interests – the fishing industry and Irish shipping – were to be immune. In case of the military camps and concentration areas for the manufacture of war material in Irish coastal towns and cities, no destructive air raids were to be made, as they would only involve innocent Irish lives and run counter to German-Irish plans at home and in America. This was agreed to. Immediately following this interview, an official statement by the German government and the newspapers of Berlin and all over Germany announced the German-Irish alliance, accompanied by a declaration of goodwill towards Ireland.

The following is a copy of the original contract of 10 articles arranged at Berlin, on 12th November 1914,[156] between the Irish Envoy to Germany and the German government. The signatories were Roger Casement on the Irish side and for the German government, Herr Zimmermann, Under Secretary of State:

I

"With a view to securing the national freedom of Ireland with the moral and material assistance of the Imperial German Government, an Irish Brigade shall be formed from among the Irish soldiers now prisoners of war in Germany, or other natives of Ireland. The object of the Irish Brigade shall be to fight solely the cause of Ireland, and under no circumstances shall it be employed or directed to any German end.

II

"The Irish Brigade shall be formed and shall fight under the Irish flag alone. The Irishmen shall wear a special distinctively Irish uniform, as soon as Irishmen can be got for the purpose either from Ireland or the United States of America. The brigade shall have only Irish officers. Until such time as Irish officers can be secured, however, German officers will be appointed with the approval of Roger Casement to have disciplinary control of the men, but no military operation shall be ordered or conducted by the German officers of the Irish Brigade during such time as the men are under their control.

---

[156] This date is not correct. Following a long wait, Casement got to meet the German Chancellor, Bethmann Hollweg, on 18th December to discuss a formal, written agreement between Germany and Ireland. Casement drafted this agreement over the next number of days, discussing it with the Germans again on 23rd December and signing it with them on 28th. See Reid, *Lives of Roger Casement*, pp 240-44; Doerries, *Prelude to Easter Rising*, p. 9; Roth, "'The German soldier is not tactful,'" *The Irish Sword*, vol.19, no. 78, p. 301.

III

"The Irish Brigade shall be clothed, fed and efficiently equipped with arms and ammunition by the Imperial German Government on the clear understanding that these are furnished as a free gift to aid the cause of Irish independence.

IV

"It is distinctly understood, and is hereby formally declared by the parties to this agreement, that the Irish Brigade shall consist only of volunteers in the cause of Irish national freedom and, as such, no member of the Irish Brigade shall receive pay or monetary reward of any kind from the Imperial German Government during the period for which he shall bear arms in the Irish Brigade.

V

"The Imperial German Government undertakes in certain circumstances to send the Irish Brigade to Ireland with efficient military support, and with an ample supply of arms and ammunition to equip the Irish Volunteers in Ireland who may be willing to join them in the attempt to recover Irish freedom by force of arms.

VI

"The certain circumstances hereby understood are the following: In the event of a German naval victory affording the means of reaching the coast of Ireland, the Imperial German Government pledges itself to dispatch the Irish Brigade and a supporting force of German officers and men in German transports with the necessary naval protection to effect a landing on the Irish coast.

VII

"The opportunity to land in Ireland can only arise if the fortune of war should grant the German navy a victory that would open, with reasonable prospects of success, the sea route to Ireland. Should the German navy not succeed in this effort, the Irish Brigade shall be employed in Germany or elsewhere solely in such a way as Roger Casement may approve as being in strict conformity with Article II. In this event, it might be possible to employ the Irish Brigade in Egypt to help the Egyptian people to recover their freedom by driving the British out of Egypt.

VIII

"In the event of the Irish Brigade volunteering for this service, the German Government undertakes to make arrangements with the Austro-Hungarian Government for its transportation through that empire to Constantinople, and to provide with the Turkish Government for the recognition and acceptance of the Irish Brigade as a volunteer corps attached to the Turkish-Egyptian army in the effort to expel the British from Egypt.

IX

"In the event of the World War coming to an end without the object of the Irish Brigade having been effected – namely, its landing in Ireland – the German Government undertakes to send each Irishman member of the Irish Brigade, who may so desire it, to the United States of America with the necessary means to land in that country, in conformity with the United States immigration laws.

X

"In the event of the Irish Brigade landing in Ireland and military operations in that country resulting in the overthrow of British authority and the erection of an independent Irish government in Ireland, the Imperial German Government will give the Irish independence of such a government, so established, it fullest moral support and, both by public recognition and by general goodwill, contribute with sincerity to the establishment of an independent government in Ireland."[157]

On reading Article VI, it will be seen that on the fortune of war and a German naval victory depended a successful landing in Ireland. In forcing events contrary to this clause, an unwise procedure was adopted by the Irish in the United States. The Irish at home had no option but to agree; the piper was being paid by our Irish-American comrades. They called the tune, and the music proved altogether out of harmony with their hopes.

The German naval authorities could not possibly have taken action sooner than they did: in the middle of May 1916 and some

---

[157] Doerries saw the treaty as a substantial success for Casement but held that it contained provisions he should have realised would be clearly unacceptable to some of the leaders of the IRB and Clan na Gael. Article VII was one such provision because the idea of the Irish Brigade being used to help the Egyptians against the British made possible a type of deployment of the brigade which the rest of the treaty seemed designed to prevent, e.g., Article I stipulated that the brigade was to fight "solely in the cause of Ireland", and the volunteers were to have their own uniform and fight only under the Irish flag. The most important parts of the treaty, Doerries argues, were those dealing with German support through war material and personnel if there was a landing in Ireland.

In the winter of 1914/15, the treaty had considerable meaning for Ireland but, continues Doerries, it and the German declaration which preceded it had consequences such as Casement's overestimation of his own popularity and of the extent of his initial successes. Some of the other leaders of the nationalist movement may also have become jealous. In fact, the IRB did not ratify the treaty and its publication seems to have been a rather limited effort. The hesitation of the German General Staff and Foreign Office to give the treaty wide publicity seems understandable because they wanted to be sure that a brigade would actually come into existence. See Doerries, *Prelude to the Easter Rising*, pp 9-10.

three weeks after the rising in Dublin. Admiral von Scheer, the victor of Jutland,[158] told me, even as late as 17th March 1922, that the perpetual Dogger Bank fogs and misty weather off the Jutland Isles would not permit action on their part sooner – and such difficulties as this are unfortunately not understood in time to make arrangements accordingly.

Any Irishman who understands inner Irish history knows what happened prior to the Fenian Rising of 1867: premature action and disunity ruined all chances of success. Earlier still the same evil manifested itself and it is even today a menace to national aspirations. Irishmen in Ireland must in the end always suffer. Ireland's confreres in the Land of Bustle and Muddle across the ocean remain in security behind the torchlight of the Statue of Liberty. The reimbursement for losses can always be made good by virtue of American citizenship.

On Christmas Eve 1914, Casement and myself sat in the little guest room of the *Alte Poste Hotel* (Old Post Hotel) with Herr Ziernberg, the kindly hotel owner, who helped to while away a lonely festival. Stories were told of the bravery and sad plight of fathers in the trenches, knee-deep by times in the life blood of fellow Christians. And the Babe of Bethlehem was again to revisit the world that night. "Peace on earth and good will to men"! The Blessed Saviour would find some comfort at least in the penitent hearts of countless poor soldiers who lay dying on the battlefields of war-stricken Europe, and His Divine Pity would be aroused by the mother's prayer of devoted trust in the almighty hand of God to protect and guard her soldier son, as by the wife's tearful intercession beseeching the Holy Mother of Jesus to petition God that their bread-winner would at least be spared yet another Christmas feast day.

Roger seemed to take greatly to heart the thought of his fellow men in the agonies of death on this particular night. He spoke little, and it was only the strains of singing by the children in the Catholic convent close by ("Stille Nacht, Heilige Nacht" – "Silent night, holy night") that brought fitting radiance to his manly countenance. In this world of probation, the sinful lust for human blood exhibits itself in all the horrors of warfare. Its devastation of sacred life, because of the unequal division of gold, did not seem to play a major part in the thoughts of the Irish patriot. He seemed rather to dwell on the consoling fact that at all times

---

[158] Reinhardt Scheer (1863-1928) became Commander in Chief of the German High Seas Fleet in January 1916. The naval Battle of Jutland occurred at the end of May 1916. It was a technical victory for the Germans in that they inflicted more damage than the British but neither the Kaiser nor Scheer were willing again to risk the High Seas Fleet in major battle and British naval dominance continued.

there existed a world of compensation far beyond the "Great Divide" and a heavenly reward for services rendered.

CHAPTER 6: The Irish Brigade: the Early Stages

In December 1914, Irish prisoners of war began to be gradually transferred from various camps, such as Sennelager (whereas I was held myself) and Doebritz, to Limburg. A summary of my impressions of the environs of Limburg camp will most appropriately introduce its activities.

The journey from Sennelager, Westphalia, is a most instructive one to all lovers of the art of landscape scenery. One traverses great stretches of the fertile plains of Westphalia, inhaling the agreeable perfumes of the extensive pine forests which bear witness to the enormous forestry resources of the empire that came into being in 1870 under the German prince of politics, Count Bismarck.[159] We gradually arrive in a valley of industry. The Rhine-Ruhr province was a veritable network of war-and-peace commerce, the sight of Krupps at Essen a marvel for the average visitor from the Green Isle.

It was fast approaching the dusk of the evening as our transport train slowly chugged its way onwards through this roadway of modern enterprise. On each side of the permanent way, massive factory structures seemed to rise up, casting a ruddy glow upon the sky from the electric-lighted buildings which formed a vast beehive of mechanical energy and power. The hour of exchange in work between the day and night shifts told an impressive tale in itself. Great masses of tradesmen and munitions workers – men and women – thronged on each railway station platform awaiting the local passenger trains which conveyed them to a well-earned repast and the more pleasant surroundings of home and family, with a peaceful repose assisting to relieve the strain of a weary and dangerous toil among the grinding mechanisms which sent forth their deadly missiles of modern war.

One heard and saw many strange sounds and sights on those German railway platforms in those early days of the World War. The wounded soldiers in field grey reclined against the seats on the passenger platforms. The Red Cross trains discharged their stretcher cases, with here and there a pitiful moan from the badly wounded, the doctor and Red Cross sister superintending the safe

---

[159] Otto von Bismarck (1815-1898) is generally regarded as having engineered the unification of Germany. He was Chancellor of the unified Germany from 1871 to 1890.

conveyance of the dangerously stricken. The soothing atmosphere of being once more in the Fatherland seemed to give fresh hopes to those unfortunate victims of hatred, blood-lust and conquest.

It all emphasised the immortal words of the poet: "Man's inhumanity to man makes countless thousands mourn."[160] It made real the horrible alternative arising from a determination to dominate and direct the Old World's commerce and monopolise its gold. Such scenes are not easily forgotten when witnessed hundreds of miles away from the seat of war. On the battlefield, one does not heed so much the horrifying sights encountered. Intensified warfare helps only to make each individual antagonist "see red"; in other words, the primitive instinct of the savage beast then becomes the dominating factor with combatant mankind – latterly known as, or rather exploited in terms of "the civilised defenders of humane Christianity".

Here let us pause for a moment and recall what the Irish patriot and martyr, Rory Casement, pronounced as the difference between "civilisation" and the supposedly "uncivilised". He wrote the following in his diary of what came into his mind when skirting the borders of Lake Champlain in the United States:

I thought of the days when Mohicans and the Six Nations had here a hunters' paradise. Poor Indians! You had life. Your white destroyers only possess things. That is the vital distinction, I take it, between the "savage" and the civilised man. The savage *is* – the white man *has*; the one *lives* and *moves to be*, the other *toils* and *dies to have*. From the purely human point of view, the savage has the happier and purer life.

How realistically did this Irishman of humane feeling conceive a simple basic contrast that was cruelly exemplified in the World War. "The defenders of civilisation" were to fly literally at each other's throats in a seething mass of mutual destruction, indeed of wanton self-destruction.[161]

---

[160] The poet is Robbie Burns (1759-1796) and the poem is entitled 'Man was Made to Mourn'.

[161] It is interesting that Captain Robert Monteith, who arrived in Germany from Dublin at the end of October 1915 and who returned to Ireland with Casement in a German U-boat just before the Easter Rising the following year, makes a very similar observation about Casement's attitude to civilisation to the one Michael Keogh makes here. "Sir Roger never seemed to me to be at home in what we are pleased to call European civilisation. The pettiness of men counted great, the greed, cunning and selfishness of governments had ever his condemnation. That those placed in power by peoples should so abuse their authority as to force millions of physically fit into the shambles of war was to him the culminating madness in the history of the world. From such horrors his thoughts ever turned to Africa, the

In actuating such slaughter en masse, the politicians of Europe saw this conflict as "the war to end all wars". Time alone will tell if such an unworthy pretence will have borne good fruit. As an Irishman of commonplace knowledge and varied experience during a seven-year war sojourn in Central Europe, I am not greatly optimistic about the "civilised" white race, as we know it today, or about the fate of old Europe either.

However, I must not allow meditations on a tottering Europe to encumber the story of the flight of a "Wild Goose" flock over the well-beaten tracks of the Rhine Valley on that cold December night in 1914. The midnight hour had not struck when we entered the Lahn Valley at Coblenz, some 50 miles from our destination, Limburg. The night being very dark, one could not enjoy the surrounding country, which I had the opportunity of seeing on another occasion. The only comparison I can make is to be found in the trip from Bray to Woodenbridge in the "Garden of Ireland". One outstanding difference is that the hillsides on both banks of the River Lahn abound with vineyards and are dotted with peaceful hamlets of flourishing wine-making and garden-farming country folk.

The rumbling train at last reached the Catholic pro-cathedral town of Limburg, snugly slumbering in the lower reaches of the Lahn Valley, with its lofty spire of the holy edifice which has borne the name of St Killian's Cathedral since the year 840. It sentinelled the surrounding vale for miles, with its 300 feet of masonry towering heavenwards. The light of daybreak on 19th December 1914 was casting its varied tinge on the centuries-old landmark of Christianity when I first beheld it. The fruitful seed of Irish Catholic missionary labours had taken firm root in the Lahn valley.

Fifteen hundred Irish soldiers marched that morning over the cobble-paved streets of this old-fashioned, south-German town, and the bracing mid-winter atmosphere seemed to quicken their sprightly march towards the camp situated about a mile from the town. The new location for the Irishmen stood on the hill south of Limburg, the slopes of which had seen many a bloody fray. The most noted of its battles was that between a combined army of German and Austrian troops and a French force under General

---

enticing lure of its noble forests, the beauties of the Umfolosi, the Vaal and the Limpopo rivers, and the vast expanse of the rolling veldt. The memories of the simple ways and kindly nature of the native tribes whom we, in our ignorance, call savages, were ever with him. Nature and nature's children were to him an unceasing source of pleasure. See Monteith, *Casement's Last Adventure*, p. 91.

Jourdan[162] in 1797. The latter was a descendant of the Irish Wild Geese. In this battle, the French were defeated and a monument stands to this day marking the event on the hill opposite that on which the Irish camp lay during the World War. The approach to it is marked by an everlasting memorial to the Saviour of all mankind in the form of the Stations of the Cross of Calvary.

The Irish soldiers' camp at Limburg in the 20th century is best remembered by the surrounding population by reason of the little cemetery lying peacefully on the slope overlooking the Lahn, where some 100 Irishmen await in silent reverie "the last call". A fine Celtic cross was erected to their memory at the instigation of the much-beloved and holy Irish sagart, Very Rev. Father Crotty, chaplain to prisoners of war at Limburg – now Rev. Prior at St Saviour's, Waterford.[163] Fr Crotty was strictly neutral as far as Irish politics were concerned in Germany. He adhered rigidly to his spiritual duties and to the mission entrusted to him by the Holy Father, but he was nevertheless a great admirer of the self-sacrificing Irish patriot, Roger Casement. Fr Crotty came a long train journey in 1916, shortly before Casement returned to Ireland, to say adieu to a good friend and honourable mediator on behalf of Catholic Ireland and independent rights for all Irishmen, irrespective of denomination.

It was two o'clock in the morning of 19th December 1914 when approximately 1,500 Irishmen marched into Camp Limburg. What a change awaited them there: fine wooden huts, each with two rooms to house 50 men, well ventilated and comfortable in every respect, and beds on wooden trestles with sufficient blankets. On that wintry December morning, after a tedious, 18-hour train journey, I slept the sleep of the just. The only troubling thought that did recur was: What would the morning reveille bring in the way of camp news?

I found that some 300 other Irish soldiers had already been mustered from different camps throughout Germany and had been there for the past two weeks. Having scouted around the different lines, I came across a lot of old faces I knew. They were principally from Doebritz near Berlin and Neustadt an der Aisch.

The whole topic of conversation centred on the recent visit of an individual called Casement, a supposed Irishman from

---

[162] Jean Baptiste Jourdan (1762-1833) enlisted in the French army and fought in America at 16. He distinguished himself as a commander of the French revolutionary army in Belgium. He was made a Marshal of the Empire by Napoleon in 1804 and awarded the Grand Eagle of the Legion of Honour the following year. After the restoration of the monarchy, Louis XVIII made him a Count of the Empire.
[163] This cross has recently been restored and reconsecrated by the people of the nearby town of Dietkirchen. See *Irish Times*, 19th November 2007.

Ireland, in connection with the Irish Volunteers at home. A few termed this tall and dark mystery-man "a damned Boer"; others of a more virile West British tinge said, in most vehement utterance, that he was some "bloody Fenian". He had come into the camp on his own without German escort and talked to the Irishmen in a casual way.[164] A few young Irish lads paid attention to what he had to say regarding the project in hand – the formation of an Irish Brigade. He told those to take the names of any soldier willing to join the voluntary service of Ireland. They promised in all good faith to do so but the majority, headed by a few wise customers and NCOs, soon checked their efforts by threats of the rope in the Tower of London.

A note was handed to me by a German civilian who floated around on his own. This gentleman proved to be a professor of languages and a former friend of the late Dr Kuno Meyer, the renowned Gaelic scholar. The note was from Roger and stated I should proceed carefully. "A bad lot, indeed," he wrote. "Young men with a fair education, those most likely to know the history of their own country, will make the best candidates," was his advice. "On no account can married soldiers be taken into consideration, as their acceptance would involve in course of time their dependants' allowances being stopped by the Downing Street gang. Keep an eye on Mr Kelly, the civilian interpreter transferred from the civilian internment camp of Ruhlheben, Berlin, a Berlin University student hailing from Co. Kerry. He volunteered his services when I visited Ruhlheben Camp and speaks German fluently. He is best used in that capacity. His instructions are to watch out for Irishmen of intelligent character. On the whole, the situation is yet in its infancy."

He anxiously proceeded to say that he waited the arrival of an Irish priest from the USA. "Joe McGarrity's choice was stopped by the British authorities. The bearer of this note, a German professor, will in the meantime see that any proposals made by you will be carried out as far as the camp officials are concerned.

---

[164] According to Reid, Casement first visited Limburg camp on 4th December 1914 and over succeeding days until 9th December; he was pretty disillusioned with his reception and with what he saw of the Irish prisoners of war there. See Reid, *Lives of Roger Casement*, pp 244-50. Roth says that on his first visit to the camp, Casement spoke to about 20 non-commissioned officers (NCOs) and explained his aims to them. He tried to persuade them that Home Rule was merely British trickery and pointed out how Irish-Americans were anti-British. But what he said proved unsuccessful and no one came forward to join the brigade. He then withdrew, leaving some pamphlets and newspapers behind. See Roth, "'The German soldier is not tactful'", *The Irish Sword*, vol.19, no. 78, pp 315-16.

I intend going into the exact position when the opportunity arises in a few days."

The beginning of a hard task was then my daily routine. Professor Schiemann[165] made due report of my progress to him in the solving of the more difficult problems. In the course of the first week, the days immediately before Christmas, I confined myself to scrutinising carefully almost every room in the camp. It did not require much acumen on my part to learn who was who. The names of John Kavanagh, Timothy Quinlisk and John McGranaghan were given to me by Professor Schiemann as those most active in securing names of candidates from the first batch of 300 prisoners. A Sergeant McMurrough of the Leinster Regiment promised Roger to assist also in the project but, if he did so, the professor said it was only to spy on the "Casement programme". Quinlisk was to be seen frequently in his company. The camp seemed well aware of the character of this 20th-century McMurrough; even in Limburg an der Lahn one could imagine what the 1170 McMurrough looked like.[166]

Tim Quinlisk was a corporal in the 18th Foot, or as historians would call them, the Royal Regiment of Ireland, a title gained as the first regiment of the line in King James II's time. I knew Quinlisk in the regiment, the Old Corps of which I was also a member. Tim we all knew as Don Quixote, or Don for short. A well-educated youth of 20 summers, he was a past pupil of De La Salle Intermediate Schools, Waterford – a fluent speaker of French with a fair knowledge of Gaelic. He had a few failings, a main one of which was a youthful inconsistency in Irish-Ireland ideals, due no doubt to the constitutional environs of the "party stronghold" – Waterford city.[167] These gleanings from his schooldays had left an impression not easily erased.

---

[165] Professor Theodor Schiemann (1847-1921) was Professor of History at the University of Berlin and was active during the war as a propagandist and political agent. He was fairly familiar with the contemporary political scene in Ireland. See Ó Síocháin, *Roger Casement: Imperialist, Rebel, Revolutionary*, fn. 7, p.596.

[166] The reference is to Dermot McMurrough (1110-1171), the King of Leinster who is famous, or infamous, in Irish history for seeking Norman help and thus opening the way for the Norman invasion of Ireland. Casement described Sergeant McMurrough as "a rogue" (Brian Inglis, *Roger Casement* [London, 1974], p. 300) and said he joined the British army because of "some serious defalcation" (Reid, *Lives of Roger Casement*, p. 249). McMurrough changed his mind and did not take any further part in the brigade project, according to Quinlisk, for whom see fn. 168 below.

[167] The party in question is the Irish Parliamentary Party. Waterford city was the constituency of the party leader, John Redmond.

Once on the occasion of a barrack-room episode of an Irish national character, which wound up with blows being struck, I was impelled to administer the KO to Don Q. Thenceforward he gave the "Yankee Fenian", as he was wont to describe me, a wide berth. Tim ever afterwards seemed to treat me with a certain marked respect, akin to the most secretive fear. He was a very impetuous young Irishman, easily led where the pitfalls of worldly design should have been apparent. At times his better instincts as an Irishman well-versed in the history of his native land prevailed. They were apt to fade out quickly, just as the mood prompted or in the immediate atmosphere of West Britonism.[168]

The Irish regiments of the British army gave ample support to everything anti-Irish. Within a few days, Don Quinlisk sought me out at Limburg camp. He told me all without my asking, especially respecting Sergeant McMurrough and their dealings with Roger. Of course, my only chance was to play a lone hand. I did so and told him what I already knew concerning the McMurrough affair. Sean Kavanagh, South Irish Horse and afterwards sergeant in the Irish Brigade, had put me on the right track in this matter. Who my informant was did not reach Quinlisk's ears, however. This was also my chief difficulty with the "wise ones" and senior NCOs among the old and new arrivals. They would not be made confidants.

A great amount of apathy prevailed in regard to Roger's mission and the forming of an Irish Brigade from the ranks. Secret cliques sprang up in every hut. The guiding lights were the NCOs, sergeant-majors, sergeants and corporals. Their spokesmen and touts could be seen all over the camp; here and there a group gathered together listening attentively to defensive tactics being proposed. For the most part, those would-be directors of prisoner-of-war strategy were so-called Irishmen with pronounced English, Scottish or Welsh accents. Once in a while

---

[168] Far from being of nationalist background, Quinlisk came from a family that had provided members to the Royal Irish Constabulary for three generations. Casement considered him a "rogue" as well. Monteith regarded him as a womaniser. See Roth, "'The German soldier is not tactful,'" *The Irish Sword*, vol. 19, no. 78, pp 327-8. Quinlisk wrote his own account of his experiences with the brigade, which was published under the title, "The German Irish Brigade: Diary of Casement's Lieutenant" in the British magazine, *Land and Water*, on 6th November 1919 (pp 18-20) and 13th November 1919 (pp 16-17). He returned to Ireland after the war. During the War of Independence he attempted to betray Michael Collins to the British and was shot dead in Cork city by the IRA in February 1920. See John Borgonovo, *Spies, Informers and the 'Anti-Sinn Féin Society': the Intelligence War in Cork City 1920-21* (Dublin, 2007), pp 76-7, 139. Borgonovo describes Quinlisk as "an adventurer", which is probably an accurate assessment.

an outburst of loyalty would grip the hearers and one heard "Good old Jock!" or "Stick it to him, Taffy!" or "Up Blighty!" while again a south Munster accent would be re-echoed with shouts of "Go on de Munsters!" or "Up Cork and the Molly Maguires!"[169]

As the Irish blood of gallant old Wexford coursed through my veins, I forgot for the moment the century-old horrors enacted by the North Cork Militia in Wexford in 1798.[170] County Cork has given of its best to the cause of Ireland in all periods of her sad history. I joined in, whenever the occasion arose, with "Up rebel Cork!" and challenged the pro-British dictator of Irish soldiers' doctrine, with the pronounced Cockney or Liverpool accent, as to his right to lecture Irishmen, natives of Ireland. Being an Englishman, or in some cases Scotsman, the answer was generally incoherent or complete silence.

How did all those non-Irish soldiers come to be in an Irish camp, meant for natives of Ireland only? It is easily explained. They got in under false pretences, but not with the Sennelager contingent, then four-fifths of the Limburg camp. I had personally seen to that part of the vital problem. The total of non-Irish Catholic soldiers who came with the 1,500 from Sennelager could easily have been counted on the fingers of one hand. It took about a month, and no small amount of energy, to weed out the chaff from the corn. The nominal rolls were revised again and again in the course of the few weeks between 15th November and 18th December – a procedure much to the displeasure of certain German officers and NCOs. Hans, the old Sennelager standfast, had served well as an antidote to the poison. His pen proved a redoubtable flail in continually drawing red lines through disguised names by which it was sought to undermine the character of the Irish camp.

Sean Kavanagh related to me what had actually happened in Doebritz camp in November. Late one night, all Irishmen were ordered to parade outside on the main compound. Some high-standing German officers addressed them, saying: "All Irish soldiers are now to be transferred to a distinctively Irish prisoner-of-war camp and to be   treated better on account of your nationality. Moreover, a great Irishman will meet you there and speak to you on matters of grave importance regarding the future

---

[169] The Molly Maguires referred to here were members of the Ancient Order of Hibernians and supporters of Redmond's Irish Parliamentary Party who were opposed by William O'Brien MP and his All for Ireland League in Cork politics during the first two decades of the 20th century. See Joseph O'Brien, *William O'Brien and the Course of Irish Politics* (California, 1976).

[170] The North Cork Militia was composed mainly of Catholics and fought against the United Irishmen. They were responsible for some atrocities in Wexford during 1798.

history of your beloved Ireland." They were told to hold themselves in readiness with a view to being drafted to this special Irish camp. That night about 100 Irishmen paraded. The next morning a list of Irishmen was called for, and the number seemed to have doubled. It was over 200! Every native of Great Britain claimed Irish nationality for obvious reasons: better treatment and conditions.

Perhaps the thought of more food proved irresistible to the ever-greedy Anglo-Saxon. I will vouch for this much. The first on the bee-line at cookhouse bugle call in the prisoner-of-war camps proved very seldom natives of Ireland, especially at Sennelager camp where some 900 Gordon Highlanders were prisoners. The famous Gordons put them up en masse on the Cambrai Road, a surrender which entailed a libel action after the armistice between the two colonels in charge of the regiment.[171] It was not proved conclusively who chucked in the sponge to "Jerry". In any event, at Mons the "Gordons so gay" stepped into the trenches made by the 18th Irish Regiment the night before. An open slaughter field devoid of head cover proved good enough for the Irish at the front.

In Sennelager camp later, the Gay Gordons[172] seemed to dominate the personnel of the cookhouse, ration stores and camp police. The black-and-white sausage ration was very small by the time it was finally dished out to the needy Irish prisoners. Many bitter fights were witnessed. The spirit of one particular Irish soldier remains vividly in my mind. This Irishman is, I believe, still a sergeant in the Irish national army. He was also a member of Casement's Irish Brigade. Mac gave a sound hammering to a British sergeant at Sennelager who was caught red-handed cutting the sausage ration systematically, thus decreasing the meagre portion of daily subsistence issued by the German quartermaster.

Poor Mac was made to toe the line for having proved a whiteman at the behest of the senior British NCO, Sergeant-Major Bub-Bub Wells of Manchester, a protégé of the Hibernian Schools, Phoenix Park, Dublin.[173] Bub-Bub served as the

---

[171] The 1st Battalion of the Gordon Highlanders was part of the original British Expeditionary Force sent to France in August 1914. At the Battle of Mons, they were forced to surrender and sat out the rest of war as prisoners. The editor has been unable to trace the reference to the libel action mentioned.

[172] This name of a popular traditional Scottish country dance was given to the regiment.

[173] The reference is to the Royal Hibernian Military School (1765-1924) which was set up originally to cater for orphans of soldiers and then to support families who were experiencing difficulties because the fathers were serving abroad.

disciplinary adviser on the British side of the camp. This Irishman had to endure the cruel punishment of being tied bodily to a tree for two to three hours daily for a period extending over a whole week. In sunshine or rain, brave Mac stuck it. How did Bub-Bub fare at the end of the war? It is related on sound authority that he was tried by court martial for many similar malpractices to the above but, instead of punishment, the War Office thought well to reward this typical British NCO by a Distinguished Conduct Medal. Military discipline should prevail at all costs.

I soon clearly saw that to succeed I must get down to business in reality. Professor Schiemann, my learned and much-travelled friend, was prepared to meet all plans put forward but, as events turned out, he was not the deciding factor. The camp officials were all old reserve officers and preferred a quiet life. Isolated solitude was more in their line of soldiering. However, I promised them a hot time and kept that promise.

It was arranged that I should take charge of the camp medical room. In this way I acted in the capacity of NCO in charge of the sick, the lame and the lazy. Camp medical reports were in my hands every morning; consequently my duty took me into every room or NCOs' bunk throughout the compound. The next thing I sought was nominal roll and history sheets of every individual in this little cosmopolitan town, encircled by barbed-wire fences and the ever-apparent electrified death wire dividing the outer and inner entanglements.

After a time, Professor Schiemann seemed to give up the effort altogether. He termed Roger's endeavours with such a mob of corner-boys "an Irish nightmare". He was not far wrong, but I was determined the lay the "ghosts" at all costs. It seems to me now like a passing brain fever. I was in the midst of a host of enemies. There were many friends too but very few I cared to trust. The best inclined were wavering, presumably unwilling to jeopardise their actual status as prisoners of war. My readers will admit that the position lacked a certain amount of hope – not to speak of confidence – as a result.

The great Christmas festival was celebrated by the majority in the camp in true Catholic and Christian spirit. Reverend Fathers Crotty and O'Gorman had left no stone unturned in securing the fulfilment of this duty to God, the Redeemer of all mankind. They secured the assistance of German English-speaking Catholic priests in order to facilitate the Irishmen attending the holy sacraments of Penance and Communion. The Christmas holidays passed over quietly.

I had the privilege of interviewing Roger in the little town of Limburg over the Christmas period. He seemed rather optimistic.

The propaganda used against us by our fellow countrymen was no mystery to him. The type of Irishmen then in camp was the usual one found in the British army, the distinction to be made being small in the extreme. However, what could one expect? They had been accustomed to pro-Britishism from infancy. Submission to mere human laws had become with them a second nature. Devilish methods of conquest, famine and rapine during 700 years of alien occupation had usurped and sapped all ideals of life among a poor, half-starved population. The lowly working class of Ireland has ever swelled the rank and file of the British army. No alternative remained except the exile ship. Pity is the only mode of discretion with which one can prove sincerity. Ignore them and we only incur their wrath in its worst form of denationalisation.

Quinlisk told me that owing to his offering to procure names and in general to promote the interests of the brigade, Sergeant McMurrough tried to draw him into a net of intrigue against my plans. Quinlisk cut the bonds of partnership with McMurrough and gave me timely warning. By doing so he had placed his two feet on the trapdoor which covers the empty space. It would have required very little energy on the part of McMurrough and his confederates to have placed the rope around his neck on the termination of war. I decided to bring him out of the camp when fit time arrived and, in the meantime, to try to put some common sense into his youthful Irish head. No other course remained open to me. My utmost endeavours were devoted to making an Irishman out of an already hardened young Irish soldier of the British army. One thing stood in the favour of Don Q: he was sufficiently endowed with intelligence and educational qualifications.

During the week or so following Christmas, I had ample opportunity to locate undesirables – Englishmen born and others. In this work I found my best proofs in the completed camp nominal rolls for Companies 4, 5 and 6, then better known as the yellow, white and red bands because members of each company were supplied with arm bands in coloured cloth and each soldier was allocated a number. The entry against each soldier's name on the camp roll told place of birth, age, whether married or single and religion. All men in the camp were supposed to be Catholics. A surprise awaited me in the large number who distinctly gave as their birthplaces London, Liverpool, Birmingham, Glasgow, Cardiff etc.

This was another farcical and serious blunder on the part of the Germans at Doebritz, whence the first 300 supposed Irishmen came in the first week of December. Fully one-third of that assignment, externally labelled "Irish goods" was purely Anglo-

Saxon, born and bred and mostly answering to such names as Cregg, Chippendale and Longworth. Those in themselves – without any evidence of English birth – told the tale. It was doubtful if ever a drop of Celtic blood coursed through the veins of their West British and Anglo-Saxon ancestors. The cloak of an adopted religion had been assumed for the purpose of getting to the special Irish Catholic prisoner-of-war camp. It was a well-played game in one sense, but a cowardly one on the other hand.

Of course the Irish soldiers were not asked to do any menial work, only the necessary work of their own camp, termed "barrack fatigues" in military language and directed towards a code of disciplinary sanitation – the routine of a soldier in the army. Physical drill was to be indulged in simply for the promotion of good discipline and health in general. All those privileges caught the gluttonous Anglo-Saxon eye, especially on mere mention of food improvements.[174]

The food question, from the German side, remained much the same as in other camps, but one thing did actually happen early in the New Year. As soon as the English War Office learned of the concentration of Irish prisoners at Limburg, Downing Street roped in the material assistance of the "Irish Society Ladies Association", composed of the type of Lady Lovejoy of the winter fox-hunting castle, somewhere in impoverished Erin, with full purses for summer residence on the Riviera. These were the noble defenders of the easily duped Irish lads who were, at the end of hostilities, to return to the mud-wall cabins and village hovels reeking with tubercular diseases, there to eke out an existence on the dole. A temporary war pension might augment their meagre resources. In many cases, few years had elapsed before they became a burden on the Irish taxpayer or, in the end, met the fate of Patrick Sheehan – an Irish workhouse coffin in the strangers' plot.[175]

The second week of the New Year of 1915 brought a change in the Irish camp of St Killian's cathedral town, Limburg an der

---

[174] In his account of his experience of the brigade, Quinlisk wrote: "English Tommies had contrived to smuggle themselves in with the Irish as they were being shifted from their original camps, hoping thereby to get better treatment than the ordinary prisoners of war." See "The German Irish Brigade: Diary of Casement's Lieutenant" in *Land and Water*, 6 November 1919, p. 18.

[175] What is being referred to here is the traditional, anti-recruiting ballad, 'Patrick Sheehan', which was written by Charles Kickham, a leader of the Fenian movement. The song tells how the eponymous young man is forced by eviction and near starvation to join the English army. He is blinded in the Crimean War and wanders as a beggar on the streets of Dublin when his nine months' pension runs out.

Lahn. The arrival of an Irish priest from the USA was duly announced in the midst of the Irish soldiers in the person of Rev. John T. Nicholson from Philadelphia. The Rev. Dr O'Gorman OP then returned to the Irish College in Rome. Before going, he gave a farewell sermon at Sunday Mass. He exhorted his hearers as Irish Catholic soldiers, despite all that might take place in the future and during the prolongation of the war, and irrespective of their status as soldiers of a belligerent country in that cruel World War then gnawing at the very heart and Christian life of Europe, to endeavour to cast out all thoughts of hatred and racial ill-will or malice. The best way to attain such an attitude, he said, would be by remaining true and loyal adherents to the teachings of the Catholic Church and the faith of their Irish forefathers.

I do not want my readers, at least those of them who profess the Catholic faith, to think that I give the credit due to the learned Irish sagart in this inadequate summary of his address. Dr O'Gorman had come to the Fatherland after the war had been four months in progress. In that time, the Allied press had aroused terrible animosity against the German people. It had made just and God-fearing men ask themselves could it be possibly true, even as wartime press propaganda of a hostile press. Legal authority tells us to learn both sides of a story before passing judgment, but an Irishman's solution could just as easily be applied in this particular instance: "If you would like to know me, come and live with me."

It is recorded in all fairness to Dr O'Gorman that he came to Germany with views not altogether favourable to its people. Hardly two months had passed when his sojourn in the midst of the German people was terminated, and this illustrious son of the Gael and Doctor of Divinity proceeded to the Irish College in Rome. The fundamental lesson he had learned as an eye witness was that the German people were defending their homeland against the would-be invaders representing the white, black and yellow races comprising the Allied armies of Europe, Asia and Africa. The United States might well be added because Wall Street had, from the declaration of war, willingly supplied the most needful of all assets – gold dust and silver bullets. In short, Dr O'Gorman departed with a pronounced esteem for the German people, and while not exactly pro-German was most assuredly anti-British.

Rev. John T. Nicholson, who had just arrived in Limburg, was a pro-Irish sagart, sent by the leaders of the Irish-Ireland movement in the US to assist as best he could in the spiritual welfare of the Irishmen in the camp. As an Irishman, he was absolutely free to hold and give vent to his feelings in the cause of Irish nationality. The views Fr Nicholson held were pointedly extreme, in the spirit of Irish Fenianism, and just and fair in the light of Ireland's history for 700 years. In assisting Casement and aiding with the work of forming an Irish Brigade, he acted in the consciousness that it was quite lawful for Irishmen to sever their allegiance to a foreign king. This brave Irish sagart, from the second home of all true Irishmen, made no secret of his honest opinion among the Irish soldiers at Limburg camp. He could be seen daily voicing sound arguments on behalf of Ireland's right to independence and urging the Irish soldiers to join Roger Casement in the vanguard of Irish freedom.

His return for this labour was little indeed; nothing but sheer ill-will was shown him, not alone as an Irish-Irelander but as an Irish Catholic priest. Many supposed Catholic Irishmen in the camp termed God's anointed "an impostor". Some remarked, "A priest! Not at all, he is only using disguised methods" and some even went so far as to declare, "This Fenian from America should not be allowed to say Mass." Others had the temerity to suggest a policy of refusing to hear Mass when said by Fr Nicholson. The propaganda went on apace thanks to the great numbers of non-Catholics present in the supposedly Irish Catholic soldiers' camp. They in turn were greatly assisted by actual Catholics who were prejudiced against him.

But those concerned in this vile and mean project had not taken into consideration the presence of Fr Crotty. He came to hear of the true situation and, in very stern language, preached a sermon not easily forgotten by the 2,000 Irish soldiers then in Limburg camp. "Fellow countrymen," he said, "in my capacity as a Catholic priest, endeavouring to minister to your spiritual welfare as soldiers of the Divine Saviour, I am ashamed to say that many of the Irishmen at present in your midst are undoubtedly unworthy of the name. It can be assumed on valid authority that some who are among you are not Irish, much less Catholics. In that case, let them throw off the garments of falsehood and depart in peace. I do not wish to have to speak on this matter again; if I do, I shall be forced to take more drastic measures. In such an event, I shall leave the camp and return to Rome."

Fr Crotty concluded by asking if Fr Nicholson were not a Catholic priest, did they imagine he would allow him to officiate at the holy altar of God. "It is for the Almighty and the Redeemer of all mankind to forgive such unjustifiable offences against a minister of the holy Catholic religion. The feeling of Irish nationality manifested by Fr Nicholson in promoting the formation of an Irish Brigade is merely a matter apart from his official duties as a Catholic priest and assistant camp chaplain. If any Irishman wishes to join the brigade he can do so; the willpower to do so is his own. On this particular subject I say to you as a Catholic priest: I do not tell you to join the Irish Brigade; neither do I tell you not to join. All I demand of you is adherence to the faith sealed with the blood of countless martyrs in defence of Catholic Christianity throughout the annals of Ireland's history. In following the teachings of Irish Catholic childhood, as taught at the knees of Irish motherhood, you cannot deviate from the principle at stake while due reverence and respect towards the vicars of Christ's true church on this earth are assured."

Of Rev. Fr Crotty can it be truly said that he never once transgressed his status of neutrality. At all times he stood firmly by his spiritual mission, as entrusted to him by the Holy Father in Rome. He did not promote feelings against Casement and the Irish Brigade; neither did he seek to advance the formation of or recruitment to the brigade. In the end he made enemies on both sides, so much so that on more than one occasion Casement himself had to step into the breach on the side of fair play. In November 1915, while I was on a special mission for the Chief, it was necessary that I also should declare on the side of neutrality in order to vindicate the good name of one of the most honourable and generous-hearted Irishmen it had been my lot to know and respect as a priest of God.

Fr Crotty remarked to me on that particular occasion, as we passed the beautiful mission house gardens attached to his temporary home with the kindly German priests of the Palatine Order in Limburg: "To think that those thankless 'Irishmen' in the camp, who pride themselves as fellow countrymen and fellow Catholics, have placed doubt and mistrust in me. The shameful and lying reports that have deceived them will not end in Germany." I was disgusted but shortly afterwards felt elated that Rory helped to stamp out all misgivings. Later on, Fr Crotty thanked me heartily for my part in assisting him against some German mischief-makers who in turn were prompted by intriguing West British Irishmen then abounding in Limburg camp. In 1919, after the World War was over, a German priest told me that the English authorities confined Fr Crotty in prison for some time on his return from Germany on a visit to his native land.

I relate the many events happening in Germany during my sojourn there just as I found them to be true and fearing not what displeasure they may cause. Friend and foe I treat alike. It is the best policy and let the decision remain an open one: "A clean win or an honourable defeat."[176]

---

[176] Quinlisk wrote that Fr Crotty was "the cause of preventing many men from joining the Irish Brigade". See "The German Irish Brigade: Diary of Casement's

Matters took a different turn, both for the Irish-Ireland cause and its opponents, after the arrival of Fr Nicholson in Limburg camp in mid-January 1915. All were now on the qui vive. The anti-Irish elements were organising strongly. It was at this juncture that I met Joe Dowling, better known afterwards as "the Irishman in the boat" of the second so-called German-Irish plot.[177] Sergeant Joe Dowling of the Irish Brigade defied Lloyd George and the English government, and Mr Larry Ginnell MP made hash of the Welsh Wizard's supposed documentary "proof".[178] Silence was Joe's motto. It proved a golden rule and won the day; yet at what a sacrifice. He endured six years' detention in nine English prisons. It was 25 years since any Irishman eked out a longer existence behind cell bars. The last Irishman to hold the record was the redoubtable Fenian fighter, Tom Clarke. Joe's favourite quotation was: "A felon's cap is the noblest crown an Irishman can wear."

With Joe Dowling yet another in the vanguard, the little band of "Irish traitors to the English Crown" seemed complete. It was essential to work in earnest. Secret meetings followed, with the gallant sagart from the Wild West in the most honoured seat when plans were discussed. It was a council of seven: Keogh, Dowling, Kavanagh, O'Toole, Quinlisk, McGranaghan and the good priest. Matters progressed slowly on the whole because the opposition was strongly fortified. Yet there was no thought of retreat, despite the overwhelming West British legions.

Lieutenant" in *Land and Water*, 6 November 1919, p. 18. Roth points out that because of his lack of enthusiasm for the brigade project, Fr Crotty was criticised by the Germans. One German interpreter for the Limburg Irish even suspected he was a British spy. The War Ministry tried to get him recalled to Rome but failed. Casement supported and defended Fr Crotty. See Roth, "'The German soldier is not tactful,'" *The Irish Sword*, vol. 19, no. 78, pp 316-18. Doerries believed Casement found the priest "a valuable helper". See Doerries, *Prelude to the Easter Rising*, p. 11.

[177] The Germans put Dowling ashore from a U-boat on the Clare coast in the spring of 1918 with a view to his making contact with the Irish Volunteers but he was quickly arrested. His arrival coincided with the widespread and successful resistance to the possible British introduction of conscription into Ireland and the British government used Dowling as an excuse to proclaim a "German Plot" and arrest large numbers of Sinn Féin and Volunteer leaders and activists.

[178] Because of his skill as a politician, and his deviousness, David Lloyd George (1863-1945), British Prime Minister 1916-22, was known as "the Welsh wizard". Lawrence Ginnell (1854-1923) was MP for Westmeath. He was ejected from the House of Commons for accusing the British government of murder after the 1916 Rising executions. He was the first Irish Parliamentary Party MP to join Sinn Féin and he was elected to the Dáil in 1918.

Towards the end of January 1915, the common enemy in Limburg camp and at home were strengthening the fortifications of resistance. The superb defence position was gained very simply indeed by Kelly, the young Irishman from Kerry already mentioned. He had been interned as a British subject in Ruhlheben camp which Casement visited first on beginning his recruitment of the brigade. Rory went there first because the Irish internees there, as civilians, would own no supposed oath of allegiance to an Anglo-Saxon king. There were only a few Irishmen present at Ruhlheben then with Kelly. Rory had him transferred to act as interpreter and to follow instructions in recruiting any young intelligent Irish soldiers who might happen to be in Limburg camp.

Kelly was quartered with an Irish monk captured in Belgium who supervised the parcel and post deliveries of the camp. Sean Kavanagh kept contact with him. He was continually asking about the attitudes of the Irish people at home towards Albion prior to the war. I disliked Kelly from the beginning and my views turned out to be correct, but my tasks fortunately kept me isolated from him. He informed Casement that they were engaged in a lost cause without the remotest chance. The result was that Roger had him released and transferred on exchange of prisoners to Holland. Thence he quickly got to England.

In a few weeks, the *Cork Examiner* was smuggled into camp in a food parcel. It contained Kelly's interview with the leaders of the Irish Party, the Casement plot against the empire, and the attempt to inveigle Irish soldiers from their true allegiance to the king etc. He said Roger gave him only verbal exchanges to the leaders of the Irish Volunteers. Kelly had turned traitor to Ireland, the land that gave him birth. He jeopardised the Irish Envoy's position in the eyes of German officialdom. The Chief's only crime was his implicit faith in an Irishman. Kelly, if he lives today to read my exposure of his true character, is at full liberty to refute it, it being immaterial what methods he may take.[179]

---

[179] Roth says that Kelly (whose first name was Bryan) did make incriminating statements about Casement to the English authorities in Dublin but that he insisted that these were not to be used against Casement in the event of a trial. Kelly seems to have regretted his actions in later years. Evidence for this is provided by Roth in a quotation from an article from *Irish Times*, 5 January 1992. The quotation is in Irish and the following is the editor's own translation: "It seems now from the research that... Kelly felt despondent and contrite when he realised what he himself had done with regard to Casement." See Roth, "'The German soldier is not tactful,'" *The Irish Sword*; vol. 19, no. 78, p. 323 and fn. 80. For a biographical note on Kelly, see Ó Síocháin, *Roger Casement: Imperialist, Rebel, Revolutionary*, fn. 63, pp. 600-01.

The result was immediately seen in Limburg. Money, cheques, crates of food and clothing parcels were send out for distribution among "the brave Irish regiments" at Limburg camp, the donors being the British government and the Irish Ladies Society. Roger was somewhat nonplussed at what was no more than Anglo-Saxon blood money – wholesale bribery. "Why should we join Casement?" the corrupt and the corrupting asked. Seven and eight bob a week pocket money, plenty of food parcels from Blighty, no work, football and concerts galore – the lives of privileged idlers. These were the visions that arose before their eyes.

The Germans were powerless to stop anything coming to prisoners of war as it would be a breach of international law according to the Geneva and Hague Red Cross Conventions. If the German military authorities prevented or interfered with such privileges, reprisals on their prisoners in the camps of the enemy would be the result. I still had a trump card to play although certain NCOs in the camp got strong on the game of countering. At least, so they surmised.

It was after a meeting at which Fr Nicholson presided that I was approached by Company Sergeant-Major T. Croke, 2nd Battalion, 18th Royal Irish Regiment, Company Sergeant-Major Brown, Munster Fusiliers and Quartermaster Sergeant McEvoy, Munsters. They warned me what would happen after the war if I did not cease negotiations with "that Fenian priest", Fr Nicholson. With me out of the way, they thought that they saw a clear coast line. Dowling was the only other dangerous party to be dealt with. CSM Croke knew my repute in the regiment for the damned Irish-American Fenian policy. "The strongest rope in London is already being made for you, Keogh, and for Dowling also," he said.

I informed them as Irishmen that no compromise would be forthcoming on my side and that I thought the same could be said for my compatriot Joe Dowling. And I warned them to be less antagonistic in their denunciations of the Catholic priest, Fr Nicholson, knowing full well the foul sources that poisoned the lesser minds in the camp. I adopted a safety-first attitude as to my personal security against any attacks because forewarned was to be forearmed. It was not a bulky parcel to carry. The calibre was .32.

Nothing of importance happened until the St Patrick's Day festival of 1915. Mass was celebrated in the open field, on a beautiful day of sunshine. I saw Roger on the eve of Ireland's premier feast day when he introduced to me a fighter in the cause of Young Ireland. This was a courier who had come from the Devoy camp in the US; he went under the name of Mr Kelly but his real name was John Kenny. I cut loose with my Irish-

American friend and he saw I could not possibly succeed from within this den of pro-Britishers, so we decided to place certain plans before Roger and the German government.

The new plan of campaign being worked out, Joe Dowling and myself left Limburg camp for Berlin on 23 March 1915, and John Kenny, IRB courier, left for Dublin.[180] Next I will explain exactly what happened with the arrival from Erin of Joe Plunkett, Commandant General and Irish Volunteer army delegate between Ireland and the Central Powers during 1915-16.

---

[180] On 20th March 1915, Casement wrote to Count von Wedel complaining that from the latest report he had received from Limburg, nothing had been done to carry out the understanding he had reached with General Exner (in command of Limburg camp), early the previous January, that English-born and pro-English men in the camp should be separated from the others. "Seemingly no change of any kind has been made in this direction." He also requested von Wedel to have "sergeants" Keogh and Quinlisk brought to Berlin (he was ill at the time and staying there). Of them he wrote: "Both are friends. Could they be brought to Berlin to see me and return quickly to Limburg? The sooner this could be done the better... No one inside the camp need know why they disappear for a day or two. If the men can be brought to Berlin *at once* [Casement's emphasis], it may tend to expedite matters considerably."

Next day he wrote again to von Wedel: "I receive again bad news from Limburg in a letter from Father Nicholson; I am being forced to the conviction that unless a complete change of method towards the men is adopted, it is entirely useless to continue further effort... I need quote but one sentence from Fr Nicholson's letter to show how hopeless it is to expect any good result from my efforts unless a complete change occurs: 'I have had to complain recently of the German guards striking the prisoners. This should be absolutely stopped, not only on account of our cause but of the serious situation that might arise... When a desperate man is aggravated, he does not think much of the consequences of his act.' I must associate myself very closely with Fr Nicholson's protest. It is to my mind not only an act of ill will, but an act of cowardice, for armed men to strike unarmed men under their guard; and unless I receive clear assurance that it shall be instantly stopped, I shall be compelled to desist from all further effort." Cited in Doerries, *Prelude to the Easter Rising*, pp 99-101. For more on Fr Nicholson, see Appendix I.

CHAPTER 7: Joe Plunkett in Germany

Roger Casement and I returned to Limburg from Berlin at the beginning of February 1915,[181] with a new arrival from the States in the person of an old colleague of mine of the 69th Irish Volunteer Regiment, the USA's National Guard Army, and also of the IRB, to which we both belonged for five or six years before the outbreak of war. This was Major J.T. Ryan. He was a born American of Irish descent and was well known subsequently as president of the Irish Self-Determination League in the US during the War of Independence from 1919 to 1921.

We decided then that there was very little use in trying to recruit by way of the slow process of the prisoner-of-war camp underground movement, and it was decided to take some of the already joined Irishmen out of the camp and get them into a separate, special Irish Brigade uniform as quickly as possible. Sergeant Dowling, Quartermaster Sergeant Quinlisk and Sergeant Kavanagh were the first to be taken from the prisoner-of-war camp. These were now outside the camp and we had two specially constructed hutments as the Irish Brigade headquarters outside the Limburg prisoner-of-war camp proper.

While we were at work on this project, Casement told me that we were going to a have a new arrival – an Irish Volunteer officer – from Ireland itself. I knew Casement very well personally and I knew it was the first time for three months that he felt that we were on the right road. The name of the new arrival from Ireland was none other than Commandant Joseph Mary Plunkett. He arrived on 25th February 1915[182] via the USA, France, Spain, Italy and Berne, where he had sojourned for a short time with his future uncle-in-law, Gerald Barry-Gifford.

Joseph Plunkett had wired through the German ambassador in Switzerland to the German government his desire to visit

---

[181] Michael Keogh is probably two months out here. From what he said at the end of the previous chapter, it was more likely the beginning of April.

[182] Both Quinlisk (*Land and Water*, 6th November 1919, p. 20) and Roth (*The Irish Sword*, vol. 19, no. 78, p. 320) give April as the month of Joseph Plunkett's arrival in Germany. Roth mistakenly calls him "Count Plunkett", which was his father's title. Reid gives the date of the arrival as "sometime about 20th April". See Reid, *The Lives of Roger Casement*, p. 296. Ó Síocháin has recently confirmed that the date was 20th April. See Ó Síocháin, *Roger Casement: Imperialist, Rebel, Revolutionary*, p. 416.

Germany and to confer with the other Irish leader – Roger Casement – being in full confidence with Casement with regards to any of these matters which would be of diplomatic importance. It was necessary to maintain great secrecy regarding all our activities, and any information regarding the arrival of men such as Plunkett could not be publicised, even to our own Irishmen, in case the British secret service would come to know. Joe Plunkett, or "Joe Peters" as we were to know him, came incognito as an American citizen, furnished with an American passport. Roger Casement confided in me and told me no one in the camp should know it was Joe Plunkett because he had to return to Ireland later on.

The German authorities, both government and military, asked Casement before they gave permission to Commandant Plunkett to enter Germany to check that his credentials and his knowledge of Irish affairs were sufficient to allow him to enter the country. Of course, Casement knew Plunkett well as co-editor with Thomas MacDonagh[183] of the *Irish Review* and as a writer in *The Republic* and other Dublin pre-1914 insurrectionary papers.[184] After an assurance from Casement, the German government permitted Plunkett to enter Germany.

There was more than one reason for these elaborate precautions. Casement feared the British the most among the Allied diplomatic and military authorities. The principal difficulty was that the exchange of wounded prisoners even from Limburg to Holland and Switzerland went on. The Limburg Irish camp had become the main target of the British secret service. Every opposition was put in the way of our recruiting in the camp. Within the camp itself, the various English-born and other British nationalities of NCOs and men had taken it on themselves to leave no stone unturned to create a feeling among the remainder of the Irishmen that after the war they would be treated as enemies of the British Crown. This anti-Irish propaganda had

---

[183] Thomas MacDonagh (1878-1916) was a playwright, poet and lecturer in English at University College Dublin. He was Director of Training of the Irish Volunteers and a member of the Military Council of the IRB that planned the 1916 Rising. He was a signatory of the 1916 Proclamation and was executed in Kilmainham on 3rd May 1916.

[184] The *Irish Review* was a monthly publication founded in 1911. It covered literature, the arts and the sciences in Ireland and its outlook was strongly nationalist. As well as Plunkett and MacDonagh, other editors were Padraic Colum and James Stephens. *The Republic* was a short-lived weekly publication founded in 1906 in Belfast by Bulmer Hobson and Denis McCullough. It was the organ of their Dungannon Clubs which merged into Sinn Féin in 1907. In the same year, the publication merged with *The Peasant*, owned and edited by W.P. Ryan.

come to a head and after a conference with Roger, Commandant Plunkett, Fr Nicholson, Captain Boehm[185] and myself, it was decided that we could not succeed until all these hostile elements had been removed from the camp. This was done.

The German camp authorities had made very grave mistakes in the first instance in allowing these in. I may add that some of the German military authorities were not very helpful to any of the pro-Irish military men concerned with the Casement project.[186] The General Staff in Berlin had delegated Captain Boehm and myself to go through the complete 2,500 nominal roll of the camp and check up on the lists. We unearthed about 150 culprits and they were removed in a very short space of time to Gessen prisoner-of-war camp in Nassau province.[187] Captain Boehm, Commandant Plunkett and I specially supervised the

---

[185] Captain Boehm was a confidential agent of the German admiralty. He had returned from the US where he had been an active secret-service agent and for a short time took part in seeking recruits for the Irish Brigade. His activities were so promising that both the military-intelligence department (Section IIIb) and Foreign Affairs wanted him transferred to them. But the naval authorities refused the request because they considered his work in the US more important. See Roth, "'The German soldier is not tactful,'" *The Irish Sword*, vol. 19, no. 78, p. 323.

[186] Roth points out that some of the German agencies involved with the brigade project became disillusioned with Casement very early on. In particular, General Staff Officer Nadolny, of Section IIIb, soon lost interest in the setting up of a brigade. As early as 2nd April 1915, he expressed doubt "whether a continuation of the propaganda action among the Irish prisoners of war is worthwhile". See Roth, *op. cit.*, p. 320.

Doerries argues that Casement never managed to establish a close relationship with his hosts and that from early 1915 onwards things got worse. The German government had no specific interest in the Irish nationalist movement. Instead they hoped to use unrest in Ireland to tie down a bigger number of British troops. They also hoped to hinder the British recruiting campaign in Ireland by giving the formation of the Irish Brigade in Germany widespread publicity. As it became clear that Casement's attempts among the Irish POWs were not having the desired results, both the General Staff and the Foreign Office lost some interest. See Doerries, *Prelude to the Easter Rising*, p. 12.

[187] On 6th April 1915, Casement sent von Wedel a letter with a list of 66 men in Limburg who were either English or pro-English and hostile to the attempt to form a brigade. "I would beg that this list might be given to the competent military authorities and I would urge that action to remove all these men *at once* [Casement's emphasis] be taken. Their removal will have a salutary effect, as they have been terrorising the well disposed among the Irish soldiers. This is the first, the immediate step called for; and when this is done we may be able to begin a much more hopeful effort with the remainder ... The three Corporals [Keogh and Quinlisk were two of the three although in a previous letter Casement had referred to them as "sergeants"] now in Berlin, whom I saw only today, should be kept here pending the removal of this batch of 'undesirables'." See Doerries, *Prelude to the Easter Rising*, p. 108.

immediate project of the general welfare of the Irish prisoners of war. By the end of April 1915, we had the camp in a pretty good state. The elements against the Irish insurrectionary movement were removed and the remainder of the men in the camp were satisfied that they were good riddance.

I should like to mention that besides the weekly allowance of camp money issued to the prisoners of war from the West British Irish Ladies' Society, many branches of the Red Cross society in Ireland had sent parcels and more than the usual amount of foodstuffs to be distributed among the special Limburg Irish camp. This was overstepping the rule in other prisoner-of-war camps. Press accounts arrived from Ireland through the *Independent* and the *Cork Examiner*,[188] which were smuggled by devious ways into the camp. According to these, the general cry of the prisoners was heralded as: "Why should we join the Irish Brigade? We have a weekly allowance of more pay than we had as soldiers at home. We have more food than we would have as soldiers at home." This is an instance of how clever the long arm of the British secret service was in that its propaganda could reach the Irish camp in Germany. To all Irish leaders, and to the present generation, such methods are easily understood because they know of the subsequent regime of terror of the Black and Tans in Ireland. This instance illustrates the great difficulties that were in the way of Casement and Plunkett in coping with the situation in Germany during the first half of 1915.

During the first few weeks after the arrival of Joseph Plunkett, I was given to understand that my superior officer on the Irish side was Commandant Plunkett and Captain Boehm on the German side. I was personally acting in the capacity of intelligence officer and assistant to both. My principal duty was contacting recruiting agents in the camp. Plunkett decided that we would have to take steps to interview each man individually in the camp. It was arranged that this would take place outside the camp. The object of this arrangement was to ensure that afterwards no single man in the camp could say that the reasons why he had been asked to volunteer to fight for Ireland were not made quite clear to him. Leaflets had been composed and edited by our immediate O/C, Commandant Joe Plunkett. These leaflets were distributed in the usual manner through Fr Nicholson to the Irish-American papers, the *Gaelic American* and the *Irish World*.[189]

---

[188] Both papers were pro-Redmond and the Irish Parliamentary Party and in favour of Irishmen joining the British army.

[189] The *Gaelic American* was the paper of Clan na Gael and was edited by John Devoy. The *Irish World* was a New-York based pro-Irish paper owned and edited by Patrick Ford, which was generally at loggerheads with the *Gaelic American*.

One of the best examples of the work of Joseph Plunkett is contained in an appeal to the Irish prisoners of war in Limburg:

IRISHMEN

Here is a chance for you to fight for Ireland and in Ireland. You have fought for England, your country's historical enemy for 700 years. You have fought for Belgium and a scrap of paper in England's interest, though it was no more to you than the Fiji Islands. Now, are you willing to fight for your own country with a view to securing the complete independence of Ireland?

With the moral and material assistance of the German government, an Irish Brigade is being formed. The object of the Irish Brigade shall be to fight solely for the cause of Ireland, in conjunction with the Irish Volunteer army in Ireland, and under no circumstances shall it be directed to any German end. The Irish Brigade shall be formed and shall fight under the Irish flag alone. The men of the Irish Brigade shall wear a special distinctive Irish uniform and have only Irish officers. The Irish Brigade shall be clothed and fed and efficiently equipped with arms and ammunition by the German government as a free gift in the cause of Irish freedom. It will be stationed near Berlin and its members will be treated as volunteers of Ireland and as guests of the German nation.

If the war ends without the objects of the Irish Brigade having been attained, viz., landing in Ireland, the German government undertakes to send each member of the brigade, who so desires it, to the USA with the necessary means to land in that country in accordance with the immigration laws. The Irish societies in America are providing money to support the brigade as Irish soldiers of Ireland.

If you are interested, see your German soldier-interpreters in the camp who will put you in touch with the Irish Brigade recruiting agents or with the headquarters staff in Limburg town office.

Irishmen! Remember Bachelor's Walk and the murder of Irish citizens in Dublin.

GOD SAVE IRELAND!

With the arrival of Commandant Joseph Plunkett, the IRB Military Council delegate of the Irish Volunteers, the German Foreign Office adopted a more promising attitude towards the matter of Irish recruitment in Limburg camp which up to that time had been almost a complete failure. In fact, things were so bad that Casement had decided, before the arrival of Plunkett, to return to America. I was to go with him as I was an American citizen and would manage to get Rory bold safely to the USA in whatever way I could. Sergeant Dowling was to go directly to Ireland. The remaining six recruiting agents were then to be withdrawn from the camp and given suitable employment in civilian life in Germany. The chaplain, Fr Nicholson, being an American citizen, would return to his own country.

Joseph Plunkett had made his way to Germany following a very dangerous trip. From now onwards, Casement and he were given every facility and help by the German authorities. A Pullman car was placed at their disposal in order that they might visit the German Chancellor who was at the time temporarily in Charleville, France – general headquarters of the army. Casement and Plunkett came back after a week's visit to France and Flanders, and after this week they were quite convinced that the propaganda which described atrocities carried out by the Germans in the course of the war was exaggerated – and false in many instances.

They had spoken to citizens of Belgium and France and investigated for themselves. Plunkett was a great French scholar; in fact fluent in the language. He spoke German in very small quantities. I remember him saying during the course of a conversation, when he had heard the story of the British soldiers' attack on Casement and of our own uphill task regarding recruitment for the Irish Brigade, that he was more surprised that we had stuck it out; in fact, he said it was almost a miracle that we had been able to do so.

Here we had the candid opinion of Commandant Joe Plunkett, one of the greatest members of the Irish militant movement and one of the leaders in the GPO during Easter Week 1916. He also said that if we didn't get those West British Irish soldiers out of the camp, we would have to "shanghai"[190] them out of it. Our difficulty will be easily understood at that time after six months of the World War. The Germans had given us, and the 2,500 Irishmen in the Irish camp at Limburg, every facility. The recruiting campaign was obviously a failure with us until the arrival of Commandant Plunkett. This was on account of the extensive propaganda throughout the world which said that the Irish were volunteering in their tens of thousands at home to fight for the freedom of Belgium and the other small nations. To overcome this obstacle we had to devise other means, and we knew it would be a slow process.

---

[190] The word comes from the name of the major Chinese seaport and refers to the historical practice of forcing men to join a ship's crew by underhand means.

The first step was the sieving out of all elements that had frustrated our success in the camp. During the time that Casement and Plunkett were visiting the Western Front lines (they went to within 50 yards of the front French lines), Captain Boehm, Fr Nicholson and I went down to Limburg to see to and superintend the removal of all the antagonistic elements from the camp. Our headquarters was about half a mile from the camp proper. About 100 Irishmen came to us daily and each man was interviewed individually by Sergeant Dowling and myself. Plunkett didn't actually take part in the interview for obvious reasons, because of his planned return to Ireland. During the preparations for our recruitment, Captain Boehm and I found it necessary to enforce strict censorship on parcels and letters. The reason for this was that there were various means of smuggling anti-Irish papers, such as the *Cork Examiner* and the *Irish Times*[191] into the camp. During the previous months, large numbers of these had got into the camp.

Up to the class of old Landsturm[192] reserve officers, the German military authorities were very friendly to this Irish camp, but so far they had underestimated the extreme value to the German people and war machine of the Irish camp, and failed to realise that there were 20 million Irish people in America who were also proving themselves pro-German, and were against the common enemy of Germany and Ireland, even more so than the type of immigrant who left Germany for America. When we had surmounted these difficulties, we came into a better field of operations.

After the first week of the recruiting campaign under Commandant Plunkett we had quite a number of recruits for the Irish Brigade contingent. There were elements in the camp in strong opposition, especially certain West British garrison-type NCOs who did everything in their power to prevent the Irish countrymen from joining. They had even divided the German soldiers in camp into two separate opinions as regards the pro-Irish and otherwise.[193] These and various other attempts were made to prevent successful recruiting to the Irish Brigade.

---

[191] This newspaper was strongly pro-unionist at the time.

[192] This was the name given to the last reserve in the German army, which was never called out except in time of war.

[193] Commenting on the German attitude, Quinlisk wrote: "It would have been far better if some of the Germans in charge at Limburg had been shifted, because they undoubtedly hindered K[eogh] at every step, and were nearly as friendly towards the English as the West Britons themselves. We never could understand this cringing attitude displayed by most Germans towards the English." See "The German Irish

The method adopted by us to procure men for our project was simply this. Each man spent almost a full day in the special recruiting barracks outside the camp. He was then facilitated with food during that day and, after full consideration, decided to join or not to join. If he did decide to join, we had no other way of getting him safely out of the camp than to send for his kit through the German soldier interpreter, because if the Irish soldier had gone back to the camp to procure same he would be severely treated by the pro-British element.

After two weeks, we had some 50 men duly sworn in by Commandant Plunkett as volunteers for the Irish Brigade and for Irish liberty.[194] I wish to emphasise here that by arrangement with the Irish representatives and the German government, we had decided not to take as brigade volunteers any married ex-British army Irish prisoners of war. The reason for this was that we had foreseen possible future reactions against the families of these men at home in Ireland. However, we were unable to stop one man from joining the brigade volunteer contingent even though he was a married man. This man's name was Michael O'Toole. He had been a second-division civil servant in civilian life. He was a native of Dublin and a fluent Irish speaker and had

---

Brigade: Diary of Casement's Lieutenant," in *Land and Water*, 6th November 1919, p. 20.

[194] The following is a draft, written by Plunkett, of the declaration to be made by members of the brigade:

In the name of God and of Ireland, we, the members of the Irish Brigade formed in Germany of prisoners of war on … May 1915, hereby declare:

That as we entered upon this war as members of the British army in the full belief that we were fighting in the cause of liberty and justice, and thereby helping to secure and maintain the independence of our country Ireland and the rights and liberties of her people; and as we have assured ourselves and are completely certain that we were most wantonly and cruelly deceived; that the British state is now as always the implacable and deliberate enemy of our country and our people; and moreover that in this war which has been forced on the world by England, the cause of truth, liberty and justice is the cause of the Germanic nations:

Now, therefore, we have, after due deliberation and with a full sense of responsibility, taken the only honourable course open to us of severing all connection with the British army and state, of rejecting all offers of rewards and emoluments for the services we have rendered, and of volunteering for service in this brigade to fight for Irish independence. To further this end, the Imperial German Government has generously undertaken to arm and equip the brigade, and we may therefore hope with the assistance of Divine Providence to achieve our independence victoriously or to die fighting for the glory of God and the honour of Ireland. (National Library of Ireland, Ms. 10,999/1).

joined the civil service in 1902. He was an Irish-Ireland, physical-force advocate and a member of the IRB Dublin Centre.

O'Toole made himself known to me and asked if he could not speak to the Irish delegate, Commandant Joe Plunkett, as he knew him personally. I was very surprised at this but later on I found out how he had arrived as a soldier in Germany. Commandant Plunkett said he could not stop him and that it would be impossible to prevent his entrance into the Irish Brigade volunteer corps. He said he would try, when getting back to Ireland, to arrange that O'Toole's wife and child would be looked after. All this became known at the trial, on 29th June 1916, of Roger Casement, because the actual names of the men who joined the brigade in Germany were known prisoners of war. The British army allowance to the family of O'Toole in Dublin city was suppressed.

The question of the family allowance by the British was the reason why we had decided to recruit only single men in our adventure. For this and many other reasons the recruitment had progressed very slowly. The propaganda of the British secret service in London against us had had time to do its dirty work. During the progress of the now more drastic recruiting campaign, Joseph Plunkett had proposed various means of getting Irishmen from the camp, in sections, to work, and there we would have a better chance to get them to understand the purpose.

The majority of Irish prisoners of war in Limburg had thought it would be like the former Polish prisoners of war on 23rd, 24th and 25th August 1914, when at the Battle of Tannenberg a quarter of a million Russian soldiers were captured, among them many Polish-born troops. The future president of the Polish Republic, Marshal Joseph Pilsudski, had formed a Polish Brigade, made up of Polish prisoners of war, to fight with the Germans for the freedom of Poland against the Tsar's imperial Russian armies of occupation.[195] Again, there was another volunteer contingent of Czechs, which was formed by the Russians from former Austrian army prisoners of war to fight against their historical enemy, the Austrian Holy Roman German Empire. It is unnecessary to quote to any student of Irish history from 1913 onwards that the

---

[195] This is not altogether accurate. In the early stages of the war, Pilsudski raised a Polish Legion, made up not of Polish prisoners of war from the Russian army but of Polish volunteers. For the first part of the war, this legion fought on the side of Germany's ally, Austria-Hungary, against the Russians. But Pilsudski later found himself at odds with the Germans and was imprisoned by them for the latter part of the war.

Northcliffe press[196] and London government scattered British propaganda throughout the world. During this time, it stated that Irishmen were being recruited in Germany for the German army. This had to be refuted.

The German authorities had almost lost hope of any success for the Irish Brigade project because of the thousands of Irishmen whom they were aware were decoyed into the British army after the split in the Irish Volunteers in September 1914.[197] It must be understood that due to the efficiency of the German secret service, the German authorities always knew the exact facts regarding what was taking place in Ireland. Notwithstanding this knowledge, they could not understand how after all the trouble and expense involved in concentrating in one camp 2,500 men, Irish prisoners of war, there was so little success in the recruitment, with every chance to fight actually on Irish soil solely for Irish freedom.

Around 25th May, about two weeks into the small support so far for the Irish volunteer corps recruitment, Casement, Plunkett, Fr Nicholson and I decided to send immediately those 55 volunteer recruits to their new home – a German army barracks which was to be the Irish Brigade headquarters training camp and was situated at the Prussian Guards' military training grounds at Zossen. It was 30 miles south west of Berlin, in the province of Brandenburg. Arrangements were made to put the recruits into the Irish Brigade uniform.[198] Then with photos and pamphlets and other leaflet propaganda, Commandant Plunkett had decided to restart a further campaign at a subsequent suitable time.

---

[196] Alfred Harmsworth, Lord Northcliffe (1865-1922), founded the *Daily Mail* and *Daily Mirror* newspapers. His papers were jingoistically pro-British Empire. He was virulently anti-German and had been for many years before the war began in 1914.

[197] See above, Chapter 2, fn 2.

[198] Quinlisk described the appearance of the uniform and how the other prisoners at Limburg reacted on first seeing it. "The uniforms were designed by Sir Roger and were to be of a fine grey cloth, with harps on the collars to distinguish them from German uniforms ... We arrived in Limburg the following morning at nine o'clock and were received by K[eogh] and Fr Nicholson, who led us to the Alte Poste Hotel where we stopped. The next morning we donned our uniforms and went up to the prisoner-of-war camp. The prisoners were all out in the big field, playing football, cricket, and trying to while away the irksome hours as best they could. As we walked up the path in our field-grey Irish Brigade uniforms, the fellows were absolutely flabbergasted. Some smiled, others scowled, but most of them bore looks of vindictive hatred on their faces. We felt as we looked at them that we had a tough job in front of us, and that we took our lives in our hands when we went into barracks alone." See "The German Irish Brigade: Diary of Casement's Lieutenant," in *Land and Water*, 6th November 1919, p. 20.

It is most unfortunate to be forced to say here that the phlegmatic mind of the Teutonic army and prisoner-of-war camp disciplinarians failed to understand and carry out several vital requests made to them by the Irish leaders.

After a few weeks, I received a letter which had been specially sent from Zossen by Sergeant Dowling. The majority official mind of the German Foreign Office and also the more arrogant Prussian army type of mind of the General Staff refused to facilitate the men quickly at Zossen. Sergeant Dowling sent a full report to me. This I immediately gave to my O/C, Commandant Plunkett, who was then sojourning at the Order of Palatine Fathers' monastery at Limburg an der Lahn.

The real facts of the case were that contrary to our request, the 55 men had not been sent to the barracks at Zossen so as to be attached to the German 203rd Infantry Regiment there. Instead they were brought to another camp some three miles further on at Wünsdorf, which was known as the "Half Moon and Crescent" camp and was really a propaganda camp for the North African and Indian Mohammedans who were soldiers of the Allied armies. There were coloured soldiers in this propaganda camp. Some of them were already in Turkish uniform, trained by Turkish officers and NCOs, and according as a regiment had been completed, these former French and English army soldiers were sent on to Turkey and the Sultan's imperial army, which was allied with the German and Austro-Hungarian armies.[199]

As a result of this information, we had no option but to proceed to Zossen immediately and leave the Limburg recruiting campaign for a further period.

Roger Casement, Commandant Plunkett and I, together with the German General Staff officer, Captain Boehm, proceeded immediately to Berlin. There Roger and Joe Plunkett got in touch with the German signatory of the Irish-German 10-Point Agreement, State Secretary Herr von Zimmermann at the Foreign Office.[200] This approach was the correct Irish-Ireland diplomatic procedure. The result was that Casement and Plunkett, accompanied by Count von Wedel, who was Foreign Office Military Attaché, then visited the General Staff of the German army. Here the reasons were given for the appeal against the

---

[199] Quinlisk was scathing in his comments on what happened to the Irish Brigade volunteers when they left Limburg for Zossen. "The German officer Boehm had promised the men that they would be housed in a German barracks and trained and treated as German soldiers. When the men arrived at Wünsdorf, they were without much ceremony pushed into a camp tenanted by all the coloured savages of the Allied armies." See *ibid.*

[200] Zimmermann was still Under Secretary of State for Foreign Affairs at this time.

counter action of the military authorities at Zossen, and it was very definitely pointed out that it was a breach of the Irish-German Agreement of 12th November 1914.[201] The army authorities at Zossen had stated that they had no proper barracks to house the Irishmen in. Yet they were as usual adamant and maintained that they had acted in accordance with the agreement so long as Irishmen were in another camp, and away from their English associates, since it would be only a very short time when proper barracks would be suitably constructed. This was done in the course of one month.[202]

On 4th July 1915, Commandant Plunkett and Fr Nicholson, the Irish Brigade chaplain, with Chief Roger Casement, visited Zossen military training camp to say goodbye to their compatriots before leaving for America.[203] Certain decisions were arrived at during the last days of this farewell visit.

---

[201] Actually 28th December 1914; see above: Chapter 5, fn. 3.

[202] Both Roth (*The Irish Sword*, vol. 19, no. 78, p. 324) and Quinlisk (*Land and Water*, 13th November 1919, p. 16) said that the men weren't housed in barracks at Zossen until November 1915.

[203] This date is too early in view of the following letter that Casement wrote to Michael Keogh from Munich on 16 July 1915:

> Your letter reached me three days ago while I was ill – I have been ill since last Friday in bed with the doctor attending. I sent the 40 Marks as part "pay" I thought at the time; I really forget what was in my head when I sent it. I fear I cannot possibly send you money for clothes and boots; besides from a letter I got from Berlin the same day that yours arrived, I was told the men at Zossen would be "*very soon*" [Casement's emphasis] put into barracks and into their uniform. I had already asked that you and the two poor fellows who have been left stranded there for so long should be removed from Limburg.
>
> I now send you 45 Marks, which represents three weeks' pay. You must keep account of it and tell me the dates it covers from the three of you at Limburg.
>
> I want you to realise that in all things we are not our own masters and that nothing can be done for us save by the good will of the government here. To get anything done at all costs me more anxiety, pain and trouble than you can at all realise. You must not therefore think you are neglected. I can do no more for you than I have done and am trying to do.
>
> The authorities are greatly disappointed that only 55 men have been obtained and they cannot regard this as a brigade in any sense of the term, but they will keep the promise to put the men in uniform and barracks as a result of my insistence – and for that only. You must prepare for much weariness and waiting and much disappointment too – but I suppose it is light [in comparison to what] thousands and thousands are suffering in this ghastly war. You see, as a matter of fact, our effort has failed and if help does not come from America, we cannot have even the semblance of an Irish contingent formed and publicly announced.

The Irish Brigade contingent was to be composed of 20 machine-gun teams, with three men per team. This meant that the number by that time enrolled in the Irish volunteer corps almost sufficed for a composite company. Commandant Plunkett had promised us, as well as Fr Nicholson, that when they would arrive at their destination, certain overtures would be made to the Irish insurrectionary leaders in the USA and Ireland to try to send Irishmen directly from Ireland, or Irishmen of Irish descent from America, to reinforce the Irish while guests of the German fatherland as soldiers. After celebrating 4th July and the Declaration of American Independence (Fr Nicholson being an American citizen), Commandant Plunkett and Fr Nicholson left Germany and went via Holland to the USA.

During the last month of Commandant Plunkett's sojourn with us, I accompanied him to Spandau, a camp for engineering and general technical units to train them to do special work. There he underwent a short course of two weeks' training in explosives and in other matters which afterwards proved useful to him.

As already mentioned, the Irish Brigade was transferred from Limburg to a barracks in Zossen. There was a misunderstanding

---

I have left no step untaken that lies in my power, but remember I, too, am cut off and alone and unless I get help form America, I shall be in a hopeless position. My chief anxiety since I left you at Limburg has been to get the promise made to the men who volunteered (the 55 of you) carried out so far as it is possible to carry it out – and this I now learn definitely will be done "without delay". I sent copy of part of your letter to Captain Boehm. I have not heard at all from him. I am writing him today asking him to try to get you three and the two others transferred from Limburg as soon as possible. There is no object in writing you till I have something to tell you, and I have been writing daily – and nightly – to get replies to my reiterated request that the men should be put on military footing as was promised.

You must bear in mind there are difficulties for the German authorities too, and not least the fear that they will be rendered ridiculous by so poor a result. Of course the shame and failure fall on my shoulders, for the responsibility is mine. I can only beg of you to bear brave heads and face whatever comes cheerfully and loyally, feeling that all our trials are part of the trial – the exceeding hard trial – to *do* [Casement's emphasis] something for Ireland.

As soon as I get any news of certainty I shall write you again. As you will, I hope, soon be in barracks with your comrades and in uniform, you will not need clothes and you will then be in military kit.

Read this to Dowling and Quinlisk and *try* [Casement's emphasis] to be cheerful – in difficulties I know well.

Your friend,
Roger Casement

Reproduced in Doerries, *Prelude to the Easter Rising*, pp 136-7.

between the German government and Casement and Plunkett due to the fact that the German military authorities were not sufficiently informed who the "civilians" were who were arriving in Zossen. These civilians were, of course, the ex-Irish prisoners of war who had been taken out of khaki and put into civilian clothing while awaiting the uniform of the Irish Brigade.

General Schneider was the GOC of Zossen, the largest training camp in the whole of Germany in 1915, with at least 20,000 men training for the various battle-fronts in France, Russia and the Balkans. He was an old 1871 Franco-Prussian War veteran and, as can be imagined, he was a strict disciplinarian. When the ex-Irish prisoners, and now free Irishmen, were sent to the camp, they were put into the barracks with the German regiment to which they were to be attached, namely the 203rd Brandenburg Regiment. Therefore, several misunderstandings arose regarding disciplinary matters.

These were the circumstances responsible for the letter which Sergeant Dowling had sent to me. He was extremely dissatisfied with the transfer of the Irish prisoners to the Mohammedan propaganda camp at Wünsdorf. The negotiations that Casement, Plunkett and I had with Count von Wedel in Berlin brought about a change and the whole thing was settled to the entire satisfaction of the two Irish leaders. The future title of the Irish contingent was then decided upon. It was to be known in English as "the War Irish Volunteers" and in German as "*Kriegsfreiwillinger Irlander*". From this on, the German soldiers understood that these Irishmen were duly and fully recognised under the Irish-German 10-Point Agreement for the formation of the Irish volunteer armed contingent.

As stated above, the men were attached for rations, bedding etc. to the 203rd Brandenburg Infantry Regiment. New life had come into the Irishmen. They had suffered much disillusionment since they had joined the cause for Irish independence, but now these field-gray clad soldiers were full of new hope and their marching songs were what is now the national anthem, 'The Soldiers' Song', and the traditional 'Vive la the Irish Brigade', the song of the Irish Wild Geese in European history from Dunkirk to Belgrade for over 300 years.

Here I want to mention that after consultation with Commandant Plunkett, Roger Casement, Fr Nicholson and our temporary O/C, Captain Boehm, and on the recommendation of Casement and Plunkett, it was decided to try to get the world-famous Major John MacBride of the Irish Brigade that fought with the Boers, 1899-1902, to come from Ireland to Germany. He would be well known to all the Irish prisoners of war at the Limburg camp. This was decided upon because Casement's object was to launch another recruiting campaign among the 2,000 odd Irishmen still at Limburg. In this as in many other matters finance was an obstacle. It was from the Irish in America and from the Irish leaders there that Casement was subsidised. The principal person in this work was Mr Joseph McGarrity of Philadelphia. He was a well-known Fenian and Clan na Gael leader in the USA. He was a hotel owner and also involved in real estate and was of long years' intimate acquaintance with Casement.

It is a fact worth recording that the ambassador of the Irish race turned down an offer of an introduction to the crowned head of the Hohenzollerns in the spring of 1915, not long after the arrival of Joe Plunkett in the capital of Prussia. In doing so, Rory of the Gael, who foresaw the rise of the plain German people, displayed his democratic principles and instincts. His general attitude in this domain can be illustrated by a simple incident which occurred in Riederau am Ammersee, near Munich, in the summer of 1915, while he stayed in the quiet wayside inn, *Zum Schwartzen Adler*, or The Black Eagle, looking out over the peaceful waters of Lake Ammersee, with a range of the Bavarian Alps some eight miles distant, and on their summit an isolated monastery. To this abode of recluses he paid periodical visits, principally to enjoy the friendship of an old Irish monk long resident in the retreat, reputed to have been founded by the renowned Irish missionary, St Killian.

Dr Charles Curry, an Irish-American professor of Munich University, had a summer residence in Riederau, and his brother, Mr Laurence Curry, superintended the extensive farm attached to the villa. But the Irish patriot preferred the solitude of the lakeside inn to the generous hospitality of the villa, for he never allowed himself to intrude upon the private life of his well-wishers in Germany. Dr Curry had been for many years a much-honoured president of the Ammersee Yacht Club, patronised by members of the royal Bavarian household, including King Ludwig II.[204]

One particular Sunday in June 1915, a party of Munich notables and high-rankers in official war circles came to Riederau for a sail on Lake Ammersee. This meant the inclusion of the president of the yacht club and his most seaworthy racing yacht. One other condition remained: the inclusion of Casement and a five-mile cruise down the lake to the little town of Dessen, where a military band concert was being held. Dr Curry's son, a youth of

---

[204] Ludwig II (1845-1886) of Bavaria was famous for his eccentric building of fairytale castles. He drowned mysteriously in Lake Starnberg, having been pronounced insane a few days before.

some 17 summers, was to take the wheel. This afforded Roger an easy way out of uncongenial society. He laid a wager with young Curry that he would walk the intervening five miles between Riederau and Dessen, using the railway line along the shore of the lake, against the yacht, the stakes to go to whoever arrived first at the landing stage at Dessen. It was man versus yacht.

Rory fairly outstepped his opponent, the wind being somewhat in his favour. Dr Curry, in describing this adventure, said: "The occupants of the yacht were simply astounded at the prowess of this son of Hibernia."[205] Casement thus explained the incident: "I much prefer the more humane discourse gleaned from association in everyday life and companionship with the ordinary Ammersee peasant. Far less do I value the polished tongues of a pampered society."

His best friend in the long walking tours through the fastnesses adjoining the shores of Lake Ammersee was an Irish terrier owned by Dr Curry and renamed "the Rebel". He would relate with glee the various exploits of the Rebel, especially one with a wild cat. It was a fight to the finish, but full of anxiety, not only for the terrier bred in the Green Isle but for Roger himself. He could not help his canine friend, the battle ground being on the edge of a precipitous mountain crag. The Rebel got the first blow home, and retained the grip of death until the kill; but the scars of the fray were very visible at its termination.

Mr Laurence Curry, as a farmer, adhered to methods most adaptable to that part of Bavaria. It was not customary there to allow milch cows to roam over the green pastures as in Ireland. They are kept continually in stall, and rarely enjoy the aftergrass in the autumn season. Casement took particular notice of this

---

[205] Robert Monteith confirms Casement's speed as a walker. Monteith took over the training of the brigade when he arrived in Germany and he tells of Casement accompanying them on some of their long marches. "On these marches we always walked together and he always talked of his hopes and fears for Ireland. As a walker I have not met his equal. He usually joined us at a crossroads on the outskirts of Zossen and would, after acknowledging the salute 'Eyes right', step into pace alongside me. Then the trouble would start. I always had my work cut out to hold him down to military marching pace. He could easily cover five miles per hour. In Africa, he told me, he had on several occasions covered 50 miles in one day. On these beautifully kept roads he simply carried me along. Slowly, almost imperceptibly, we gained speed; forgetting all in the charm of his conversation, I would awaken to the fact that we were almost a mile ahead of the column. Then we would wait until the men caught up with us, headed by the sergeant-major [Michael Keogh], puffing and blowing, all red face, overcoat and sword. His pathetic greeting on one occasion made The Chief laugh heartily. 'Aw, Sir Roger, you're killing us!'"
See Monteith, *Casement's Last Adventure*, p. 102.

during his occasional visits to the farmyard. One day Mr Curry happened to visit the nearby town and, on his return, was astonished to find some dozen of his milch cows absent from their usual quarters. He searched the adjoining fields, and there he found Roger, with the Rebel, enjoying the pranks of those victims of prolonged captivity. Another instance of Casement's belief in natural freedom!

The sultry days of August 1915 saw the German army, under the command of Field-Marshal Mackensen,[206] sweeping the hordes of the coloured-mingled Allies right through the Serbian and Montenegrin territories to the very seashore of Salonika. Roger had come down to our camp. We walked to the little town of Zossen, about a mile and a half from the camp; and, being in a hurry to catch the Berlin train for an important engagement, his time was limited. On reaching the main roadway from the camp, we found a battalion of the 203rd Brandenburg Regiment marching ahead, to the strains of the regimental band. We were accompanied by the Irish Brigade interpreter, Corporal Zerhusen.[207]

"Come on, Zerhusen," Rory remarked, "and I will show you how I often marched for hours, as a simple exercise, when a younger man, along stretches of sandy seashore in South America." I leave it to the imagination to picture this towering Irish giant, with his powerful stride, as he endeavoured to encourage those who were taking at least two steps to his one. In serious tones, he uttered a wish not easily attained in 1915. "If only Erin's voluntary army possessed such well-disciplined and armed soldiers as those in field grey, the hope of releasing her from the seven-century bondage might easily be realised with the assistance of her quarter of a million physically fit men. The future may afford us that chance; and we must all work in that direction. I know our good friend Zerhusen would gladly join, and legitimately so, for is he not almost half an Irishman? The tutorship gained through his excellent Irish wife should have made him by this time a whole Irish Fenian."

Many minutes had not elapsed before this little band of Irish-Irelanders were on marching terms with the foremost ranks of

---

[206] Field-Marshal August von Mackensen (1849-1945) commanded the German Ninth and then Eleventh Army in eastern Europe during World War I. He finally crushed all resistance in Serbia by the autumn of 1915. He was one of only five recipients of the Iron Cross during the war.

[207] Franz Zerhusen was married to an Irish woman and had been a member of the Gaelic League in the US. He acted as an interpreter to Casement's Irish Brigade for a time. His role in that regard is much disputed. See Roth, "'The German soldier is not tactful,'" in *The Irish Sword*, vol. 19, no. 78, p. 324, fn 87.

these stern Trojans of war, numbers of whom I knew to be veterans of the battlefields of Europe and Asia. The full war-strength battalion of a thousand warriors sang in harmony with the regimental music. Patriotic airs enlivened the sultry autumn atmosphere. The soldier diplomat of Young Ireland seemed highly elated, particularly on being recognised by the commanding officer at the head of the troops. This officer called me to ask if that was not the great fighter for Irish freedom, Roger Casement. He then requested me to ask Roger if he would grant him the pleasure of a few minutes' conversation. In sending me on this errant, he added: "I can also sing 'Come Back to Erin'; my wife is an O'Neill from Ulster."

So side by side, they marched in perfect military pace, and no one was more surprised than Roger himself when the 203rd Regiment Depot Band struck up 'O'Donnell Abu!'. The bandmaster had acquired the music from one of the men of Casement's brigade. The German officer with an Irish wife of the famous Clan O'Neill had been for many years resident in India, when he held a high position in a German-Indian tea-importing company. In fact, he was only visiting the Fatherland at the outbreak of the World War and got caught in the meshes of this holocaust. What seemed to puzzle him was England's peculiar action in bringing Indians, Chinese and various other coloured races to fight her battles on the Christian battleground of Europe. Britain courted disaster, he thought, by allowing the Yellow Man to cultivate the fighting spirit and gain familiarity with modern weapons of war – a peril of no small importance which Europe will surely realise as time goes on and the Far East awakes.

The blockade of the high seas was also discussed. "I fear I can never again look straight where an Englishman may cross my path." The Irishman made small verbal contribution but, later on, his words were meant to drive home the points which were actually in the mind of this experienced German as far as trade and commercial interests were concerned. He said: "In the past, you and I have had experience in common with many friends of the Anglo-Saxon race. If we live to see the termination of this strife and turmoil, you and I will retain the honest friendship of many liberal-minded Englishmen. It is not the bulk of the English people who are our merciless antagonists. The English government has always been hostile, is today, and will continue to be, until the marauders and the empire pirates who contaminate and pollute the ranks of Anglo-Saxon aristocracy are beaten and compelled to accept less secretive ideas of diplomacy, and consent to be governed by the open administration of democracy. The end of such an event will be attained at a time not so remote, when the plain and united people of Britain will be the deciding national factors. The English Empire shall crumple to decay through the instrumentality of the people it has enslaved."

What a tragedy and a crime that his useful life should have been cut short.

CHAPTER 8: Zossen and Captain Monteith

Gradually the men settled in to their new conditions at Zossen by Berlin.[208] The new barracks was a wooden structure raised on a brick-wall foundation, constructed especially for the Irish Brigade. It had enough room for approximately 100 soldiers. It was subdivided into two large rooms with one small room at each end, one for warrant officers and one for NCOs. Each room had all the necessary equipment, wash-hand basins etc. The ordinary Irish volunteers, NCOs and soldiers had to go to the ordinary German soldiers' canteen for their rations. These were the same as the rations for the German soldier.

Captain Boehm was temporary O/C of the machine-gun teams of the Irish Brigade, as they were called from this on. As I have already mentioned, this German General Staff Officer had a fluent knowledge of the English language in the American dialect as he had spent over 20 years in Milwaukee as a brewery manager. He had full sympathy for the Irish point of view and as a German officer could always intervene very quickly on behalf of the Irish soldiers in regard to military matters.

Up to this there had been no decisions made as to who would be the future officers and NCOs. As I had been the recruiting officer and assistant adjutant to Commandant Plunkett for the three months previously, and had been associated with Casement, I was appointed Adjutant to the first 10 machine-gun teams, who were to be known as A Company, Irish Brigade. My rank was that of First Lieutenant. There were also Company Sergeant Joseph Dowling, Quartermaster Sergeant Timothy Quinlisk, Sergeant Michael O'Toole, Sergeant Seán Kavanagh and Sergeant Julian Bailey, alias Beverley. The Corporals were: John

---

[208] The evidence suggests that this process must have taken some time. On 8th August 1915, Casement wrote to von Wedel: "It is now nearly four weeks since I gathered that the small contingent of Irish soldiers at Zossen would be quartered in some barracks where they would be regarded as soldiers. I have been hoping every day to hear that this had been done; but the only letter I have received has been from one of the men telling me they were very unhappy in their present position, and begging to see me. I cannot visit the men at Zossen and I am ashamed to answer the letter, for the men must all feel, so long as they are there, that I have deceived them." In the circumstances, he told von Wedel that he could not stay in Germany any longer, "idle and useless", and asked him to arrange a passport for him so that he could leave. See Doerries, *Prelude to the Easter Rising*, p. 139.

McGranaghan, Patrick Delamore and Seán O'Mahoney. There were four Lance Corporals: Michael O'Callaghan, David Golden, Harry Burke and Willie McGrath. This constituted 12 NCOs and 44 men, or one NCO and four men to each of the 10 machine-gun teams.

Our equipment consisted of five heavy Maxim machine-guns. We also had two trench mortars for drill purposes. The men were equipped with side arms in the usual fashion. They consisted of ordinary rifle and bayonet. By the terms of the agreement with the military officers in command at Zossen and the Irish leaders, it was agreed that the Irish warrant officers[209] would carry the same side arms as the regular German army NCOs. The QMS would be equipped with a small short duty sword; the NCOs and corporals would be equipped with regular long German bayonet. At all times when walking out, the NCOs and men of the Irish contingent would always be equipped with the ordinary belt and bayonet, and as per regulations of the German army, those of NCO rank received the customary equal salute exchange similar to the salute of officers.

Much friction arose in regard to the drill propositions, and we had arranged for the transfer of one English-speaking German officer, five NCOs (one sergeant, two corporals and two lance corporals) and 20 privates of the machine-gun company of the 203 Regiment.

Further friction arose with the Germans concerning the training of the machine-gunners, as many of the men of the Irish Brigade had been trained as machine-gunners in their Irish regiments in the British army, and wished to still carry on their drill in the manner in which they had been trained. When a little oil had been poured on the troubled waters, these men finally agreed to fall in line and also learn the German method of training with machine-guns. The five teams would carry out their usual training, and while they were thus occupied, the remainder would carry on with either throwing hand-grenades or practising musketry with rifles.

It was difficult to find a system to suit two languages – German and English. This difficulty was very well faced and greatly lessened when we had the German NCOs attached because all of them spoke very good English. In this way the training was greatly expedited. The training hours were the usual ones required of German soldiers.

Reveille was as at 6.30 in summer time. Physical instruction followed. Then all went to the nearby ranges for the usual training

---

[209] This is a rank of officer in the British army, RAF or US navy below the commissioned officers and above the NCOs.

practices under actual war conditions. About a thousand yards from us on the firing range, a demolition company might be firing at a very low-flying bomber on the Royal Flying Corps.[210] On other days, when off duty, we had lectures on various military points, and also some of the German officers who were interested in athletics had arranged for practice and training in sports and games, where German and Irish might compete against each other. Included in this was boxing, football etc. Many of the Irishmen excelled in all these. Some of them became champions in the Irish army in 1922.[211]

The Irish leaders, Casement and Plunkett, had drawn up the pay allowances for the brigade members. This was not a regular-army pay and it was understood by the men that it was possible that it would vary. While under arms and training, the Irish volunteers would receive this allowance to defray their small-arms kit expenses and also for cigarette money. The rates of pay were to be as follows:

Volunteers – 3/- per week
Lance Corporal – 5/- per week
Corporals – 7/6 per week
Sergeants – 10/- per week
Warrant Officers – 15/- per week

---

[210] This was the title by which the Royal Air Force was originally known.

[211] On 28th September 1915, Casement wrote to Richard Meyer to say that he had been to Zossen the previous day and that "the men are *very* [Casement's emphasis] well cared for, very well treated – and I am sincerely grateful to you for the kindly way in which you are fulfilling your promises. On the other hand, there is no use concealing the fact that they are unhappy and feel themselves useless – also that they are without personal liberty at all." He went on: "Books they want badly – also a *couple of* [Casement's emphasis] sets of running costumes, and running shoes for two of the men who were famous athletes in Ireland – one a champion, I believe." See Doerries, *Prelude to the Easter Rising*, p. 147.

Quinlisk briefly summarised the situation in Zossen as follows: "The barracks was called the birdcage by our men; it was 50 yards long by 25, and enclosed all round by barbed wire, and guarded by five fully armed German soldiers. Life was much the same as in the ordinary prisoner-of-war camp, food being, however, much better, also sleeping accommodation. The men had exercise every day, being drilled by K[eogh] or myself." See "The German Irish Brigade," in *Land and Water*, 13th November 1919, p. 16.

Captain Robert Monteith had made his way to Germany from Dublin by the end of October. As he was of a military background, his initial impression of how the Irish Brigade men were housed at Zossen is worth giving: "They were housed in airy, well-heated rooms, similar to those in which the German troops were quartered." See Monteith, *Casement's Last Adventure*, p. 81.

As far as the NCOs were concerned, this was the equivalent to the German army NCO pay. The ordinary German soldier received only three pence per day, or 1/9 per week.

The name of Zossen by Berlin military training camp made the German soldier shudder, more especially the young and raw recruit. Why? I will reveal no war secret in explaining. Zossen camp was the last scene of mimic war that the ordinary youthful Prussian Guardsman experienced before his departure for the scene of actual hostilities. The most seasoned German soldier would prefer remaining at the first line of trenches to a term of duty at Zossen camp during the winter of 1914 and the years 1915 and 1916.

One old Prussian officer made the intolerable situation a stern reality there. This was General von Schneider, GOC the training camp. He was an old type of Franco-Prussian War officer,[212] the embodiment of iron discipline. In the early stages of the hurried mass formations on the Western Front, during the World War, von Schneider commanded a brigade of infantry comprising young volunteers, German students, professional men and other German intellectuals. The brigade was composed of a reserve battalion from the 201st, 202nd, 203rd and 204th Brandenburg Regiments. In the activities leading up to the first Battle of Ypres, von Schneider sent his willing and brave fellow countrymen to attack over a distance of about 1,000 yards, without the necessary tactical support of artillery fire – an indefensible military blunder in modern warfare.

The result was disaster, more especially as his men were assailed by enemy artillery fire. The brigade of young German soldiers was forced to retreat, demoralised and tragically depleted in numbers. Only a few hundred of a brigade originally 4,000 strong lived to tell the tale of slaughter. The general had only a few days' war service when he was recalled in disgrace to the Fatherland. Prior to the outbreak of hostilities, this stern old veteran filled the all-important role of Chief Forest Ranger of Brandenburg. Being, besides, a prominent political wire-puller, he managed to secure a good berth as GOC Zossen military training camp. The job suited him, that of "recruit smashing on home territories".

It was quite a common event on the Zossen highways and forest ranges to see wives, mothers and sisters of German soldiers expectorate in disgust on meeting the general. They thought of a father, son, husband or brother sacrificed on the battlefield of Flanders during those eventful days of October 1914. The

---

[212] The Franco-Prussian War occurred in 1870-71 and resulted in a victory for Prussia over France. This victory paved the way for the unification of Germany.

ordinary German soldiers, and almost all democratic German officers, vied with each other in their denunciations of von Schneider. The Irishmen of Casement's Brigade were even more outspoken against the "mad tailor".

He often plainly showed temper on mere mention of the word Irishman. "They will imbue my Prussian soldiers with a spirit of democracy" – a result of comradeship in sport hard to avoid. He felt the privileges of the brigade embarrassed his jurisdiction as military chief of the camp, though he could do but little as he did not hold complete control over the Irishmen of Casement's contingent. The German had to bow to superior orders as interpreted by the General Staff officer placed there by army HQ, Berlin, as liaison officer to the soldiers from the Green Isle.

I endeavoured to my utmost to meet the demands of the German military authorities half way. As Brigade Sergeant-Major, my duties involved a broad-minded vision of disciplinary measures, not only as seen by keen German eyes but also from the point of view of the Wild Geese under my command. On more than one occasion we came into direct conflict and had heated exchanges, where the ulterior desires of von Schneider and his like met with flat diplomatic negation. I recall one outstanding case where General von Schneider and I were at variance regarding the status of the Irish soldiers at Zossen camp in comparison with that of German soldiers. The GHQ staff officer had to give way but my passive resistance prevailed against the Prussian war code.

It occurred during one of the periodical "confinements to barracks" of the Irishmen. The old rule was being applied, as was always the feature of military punishment adhered to by von Schneider. As an old saying in militant German goes: *"Eins fur alle und alle fur eins"* or "one for all and all for one". This might suit Germans; the Irish temperament was against it. Withal, von Schneider ruled supreme in Zossen and it was my fate to have to render an account in person to this domineering man. The Irishmen were confined to military training camp bounds for some days at a stretch, not an unusual thing in those times, even for German soldiers who were found guilty of some breach of the rigid discipline always enforced there. Although Captain Robert Monteith, when he came, was not included in this measure, he also by times felt the lash of von Schneider, perhaps for the minor offence of visiting Berlin in civilian attire and without his military pass.

This time Bugler Pat Keogh was the offender. He had rolled home late to barracks from the neighbouring village of Zossen. The boxing bugler had been enjoying a night out with some German soldiers of the 203rd Regiment who were enthusiasts in the noble art and had a little false spirit through over-indulgence in German "mountain dew". In the morning, a drink of fresh water was all that was necessary to create a feeling of being actually under the influence of alcohol. Keogh from Tipperary had not managed to escape the guardroom.

He had not been particular about what pass he presented to get out of the camp, having apparently lost the official one, and so presented the first piece of paper in his pocket. It happened to contain the chorus of that fine marching song famous in Irish military history, 'Clare's Dragoons':

Vive la the old brigade,
Vive la the new on too,
Vive la the rose shall fade,
The shamrock bloom forever new.

Typed copies had been distributed among the Irishmen of the brigade. The stamped notepaper of the Irish Brigade was used for that purpose and, the German soldier not being conversant with the language of the typescript, Pat submitted it as legal military tender to the camp orderly room. The bugler had, as a result of his trial, to content himself with black bread and water for 10 days in a dark cell of a Prussian Guards' military prison.[213]

Since Joe Plunkett's departure in July 1915, Roger Casement was anxiously awaiting news from Ireland regarding the efforts he was to make to get, in the USA or in Ireland itself, reinforcements for the Wild Geese in Germany. Fr Nicholson and Commandant Plunkett told the Irish in America of the great efforts that were being made in the land of our "future gallant allies in Europe",[214] and on hearing of these efforts, the Irish in America put into operation the various requests made through these two men. One result was that the Irish-American, John McGoey, came to Germany. Another who came was John Kenny but he had to go back again via Ireland. He was an IRB courier. In September 1915, we had a visitor direct from Ireland in the person of Tommy O'Connor from Dublin. He came via New York and Holland and told us much news.

One mistake which was made by the Irish in America was the publication of Irish Brigade photographs far too prematurely. These photographs were of the various groups of the Irish machine-gun contingents in Germany and had been sent through the diplomatic bag of the German secret service to the Irish

---

[213] Monteith also described this amusing incident where the brigade bugler showed how resourceful he could be. See Monteith, *Casement's Last Adventure*, p. 127.

[214] The words are taken from the Proclamation of the Irish Republic which was read from the steps of the GPO in Dublin on Easter Monday 1916 by Patrick Pearse.

leaders in America. These photographs, with a declaration drawn up by Casement, were published in the Irish-American papers. The declaration was signed by the officers, NCOs and men of the Irish Brigade.

This declaration was a full statement of the reasons for the foundation of the brigade and its aims and objectives. In this there were many precedents in Irish history, such as the expedition in 1798 of Wolf Tone from France under similar circumstances when England was at war. This publication appeared in the *Gaelic American*, the *Irish World* and the *Irish Bulletin*215 in Philadelphia. This was a great mistake because it made the identity of the former members of the British army easy for the British, and it was a definite proof brought forward by the English at the subsequent trial of Casement in London in June 1916.

Fr Nicholson informed me by letter that he had got into disfavour with the American hierarchy because of his interference in Irish affairs in Germany, and he was not allowed back to his former home – Philadelphia – but was transported, as he said himself, out to the west. His letter came from Laramie in Wyoming. On his way from Germany to the USA, he was publicly insulted as an American citizen and searched physically when a British armed patrol boat in the North Sea stopped the Holland-American neutral ship on its voyage.

The leaders of the Irish in America were John Devoy and Judge Cohalan.216 The Clan na Gael met in September 1915. Certain friction arose on account of the misunderstanding of the 10-Point Agreement with the Germans, but especially regarding Article 7. These Irishmen in America, sitting at leisure and skin safe in big-chat conference, objected to the fact that Casement agreed to have the Irishmen of the brigade employed to fight with the Egyptians for this small nation and sister cause to Ireland. In case future historians would come to any false conclusion regarding this clause, it must be understood that it was a voluntary side issue only, and as an alternative if we were unable to get to Ireland.

In November 1915, I was delegated by Casement to go to Berlin to await the arrival of Captain Robert Monteith. He had a short time before arrived from Ireland via the USA and the coal bunkers of a Dutch steamer from New York to Christiania, thence overland to Berlin. Captain Bob was Director of Training of the

---

[215] The Philadelphia paper in question is most likely the *Evening Bulletin*.

[216] Judge Daniel Cohalan was a New York-based Irish-American politician and close supporter of John Devoy. Joe McGarrity in Philadelphia was also a leader of the Irish in America.

1st Battalion, Dublin Brigade of the Irish Volunteers and the first Irish Volunteer to be transported from Ireland in the summer of 1915.[217] It was decided that he, together with two other NCOs who had not been in Limburg before in the Irish Brigade uniform, would start a fresh recruiting campaign. This was done and the result after two weeks was three more volunteers. The question of further recruits in Limburg was at a standstill. I cannot give any reason for this other than that the majority were living in the hope of returning to Ireland just as ordinary prisoners of war. Some said that the Irish Brigade would be used to fight with the Germans in France. Many reasons had been given both to myself as a recruiting officer and to Captain Monteith when he assumed the role.

He was likely to be known only to the Dublin-born Irish prisoners of war. The men from the country did not know him and this was a drawback as regards recruiting. Captain Bob was first and foremost a military man and it is probably the case that a good soldier is seldom a good diplomat.

In the meantime, we had information from Ireland through the various IRB courier messengers that there would be a definite attempt to strike a blow for freedom in the course of the next year. We knew through Commandant Plunkett that Ireland had brigades of Irish Volunteers with enough men to make up an army corps to the extent of approximately 20,000 men. We believed we would get arms and equipment from the Germans. This situation had been very well debated in all its aspects before the return of Commandant Plunkett to Ireland.

When Captain Monteith arrived in Zossen, he took up quarters with me.[218] The machine-gun corps was divided into two companies – A and B. A Company was composed of three sergeants, two corporals, two lance-corporals and 40 men. This was the machine-gun company. With these were the attached

---

[217] Because of his activities with the Irish Volunteers, Monteith was sentenced to "internal exile" and had to move from Dublin to Limerick.

[218] Monteith was evidently impressed by what he found at Zossen. "I found that excellent discipline was being kept. The men fully appreciated their position as Irishmen and conducted themselves accordingly. The interpreters attached to the brigade had started classes in German, in order that all ranks might have a working knowledge of the language… They had also a singing class. Good singing is a great help on route marches."

He was also struck by Casement's devotion to the men: "Casement's love for those men was touching. He regarded every one of them as though he were his own son and was always ready to overlook their shortcomings, and spared himself nowise to add to the comfort of their life." See Monteith, *Casement's Last Adventure*, pp 81-2.

German soldiers from the 203rd Regiment. These consisted of one German officer, five sergeants and 20 soldiers. They were attached for training purposes to A Company. The remainder of the men, approximately 20 volunteers, made up B Company, which was an infantry company and carried out training in the use of hand grenades and trench mortars. Captain Monteith was now recognised as 1st Lieutenant of B Company of the Irish Brigade in accordance with the existing German army order regulations.

Roger Casement told me that the German military authorities had explained to him that since they had failed to capture the Channel ports, they considered it would be impossible to attempt a large armed or naval expedition to Ireland.

Because the expedition to Ireland could not be successfully accomplished, members of the brigade were asked if they would volunteer for war service in Egypt in accordance with Point 7 of the Irish-German Agreement. By helping the Egyptians to route the British from their country, they would be helping a sister cause to that of Ireland. To this proposal, 40 of the Irishmen of the machine-gun company agreed. This was done by means of the declaration drawn up by Roger Casement, and a copy of this declaration was sent to the Irish leaders in America, and with the photographs of the men of the Irish Brigade, was published in the Irish-American papers in New York and Philadelphia.[219]

The Clan na Gael and the IRB leaders called a full national convention of the US societies for the self-determination of Ireland in Carnegie Hall, New York. The attendance of 2,000 openly protested against Roger Casement attempting to use Irish

---

[219] Regarding this development, Doerries argues that "the German General Staff and the Foreign Office, apparently with Casement's cooperation, came up with a solution to rid themselves of the Irish Brigade" because no one believed any more that the members of the brigade would be deployed in Ireland. So it was suggested to Casement and Monteith that the time had come to consider the idea of striking a blow at England by joining the army for the invasion of Egypt "and helping to free another small nationality. On 3rd December 1915, Casement and Monteith informed the 56 members of the Irish Brigade. Not surprisingly, a mere 38 were willing to risk their lives for the liberation of Egypt by the Germans." Doerries contends that not only was this an end to the hope of landing Irish soldiers in Ireland, but it also appeared to have been the end of "any even perfunctory cooperation between Casement and the German government. Casement had lived through many an embarrassing financial tight spot and had suffered a lack of support from New York, but the refusal of his small troop of volunteers to fight for Germany in the Near East could only make him appear close to useless in the eyes of the General Staff." See Doerries, *Prelude to the Easter Rising*, pp 15-16.

volunteers to fight with the heathen Turks in Egypt.[220] Thus it proved that Roger Casement gained his home-run stroke to force more concentration on matters in Ireland. Reports of the proceedings of this conference were fully published in papers which arrived in Germany from America. We read all these. Nothing transpired for a while.

Captain Monteith was sent directly from Tom Clarke and the Military Council of the IRB for the sole purpose of coming on to Germany to represent the Military Council in Germany. Of course, the Clan na Gael in the USA had sent him to Germany as a stowaway on a cargo vessel. He had definite word for Casement that there would be an attempt, with the aid of men and arms from Germany, to effect a landing in Ireland in the spring of 1916, and that there would be an insurrection in an endeavour to gain Irish independence. This information was conveyed to the men of the Irish Brigade by Roger Casement and they were very well satisfied with the information given to them and were now prepared to continue their training with the object in view of their return to Ireland to take part in the rising there.

The reason Captain Monteith was told to bring the message directly from Ireland concerning the arrangements for the proposed Irish insurrection, to Casement personally, was to obviate any risk of Casement and the Irish Brigade going via Austria and fighting for Egyptian independence with the Turkish or Central Powers armies. This direct message from Ireland to the Irish patriot in Germany made Casement very happy. His one object was to give the Irish Brigade every assistance and to encourage the Germans to give armed assistance to the Irish Volunteers in Ireland and let them see that the Irish Volunteer Executive Council at home meant business. Casement also remarked to me that the declaration and photos of the Irish Brigade published in the US, helped and had "forced the issue".

---

[220] On the question of deploying the Irish Brigade in Egypt, Roth commented: "Casement pushed for an assignment to Egypt, part of an alternative plan made possible by article VII of the German-Irish Agreement, after it became obvious that the brigade could neither be militarily employed in Ireland, as anticipated in article VI, nor utilised for propaganda purposes due to insufficient numbers and English naval superiority. In December 1915, Sir Roger campaigned for the Egyptian project in Zossen with Monteith's support even though Clan na Gael had failed to ratify the German-Irish Agreement because of this very article VII and Devoy even went so far as to describe it in retrospect as an 'historical curiosity'." The German Foreign Office and military intelligence supported the project but the War Ministry thwarted the plan because it opposed the large expense that would be involved in transporting the brigade members to the Near East. See Roth, "'The German soldier is not tactful,'" *The Irish Sword*, vol. 19, no. 78, p. 325.

In the autumn of 1915 we learned of letters that had been written to the German Foreign Office from a "Mr Freeman" who was an employee of the *Gaelic American* newspaper. These letters were critical of Roger Casement and served to undermine him in the eyes of some, at least, of the German authorities. As if his task was not difficult enough already! It was a treacherous and underhand act.

I connected this incident with the old man, almost in his dotage – the ex-Fenian John Devoy. I had known him for eight years in America and I knew he was a disturber in many Irish affairs in the USA, and a political henchman of Tammany Hall smear politics for Irish vote-catching in New York. He was known for his record, both in the US and at home subsequent to the failure of the 1867 Fenian Rising, as the "Guilty, my Lord" compromising type of Irishman before English courts. It was also known that he purchased his freedom shortly after his trial by a "ticket of leave" with a free passage to New York. Besides, some nine months prior to this, around March 1915, one of his not too secret agents, Broder, had to be put in his place by forcible tact by Casement and myself in Berlin. He had admitted that he went behind Casement's back and negotiated secretly in the German Foreign Office as a so-called agent from Clan na Gael, and we discovered afterwards that the USA Clan na Gael or IRB knew nothing of him, but he had been sent by Devoy from the US and in a far too sly scheme; luckily, the German Foreign Office tipped us off in time.[221] That office, and especially Count von Wedel who

---

[221] Monteith wrote about the effect Irish-American interference and distrust had on Casement. He said that Casement's "strong, independent methods were evidently disapproved of by writers in the United States, and they were at no pains to disguise the fact... It gave me deep concern to think that men, obviously unaware of existing conditions in Germany, should be so critical of his actions and so slow in responding to his request for funds for the brigade... He knew that his work had been hampered by letters written to the German Foreign Office from apparently authoritative sources in the United States. Some of these letters insinuated that he was not a fitting representative of the Irish people, and these aspersions, he was well aware, had caused the Germans some misgivings, not only about him, but also about the genuineness of the entire Irish revolutionary movement."

Monteith went on to say that the Freeman letters were written on the official letterheads of the *Gaelic American* and that, whether they were official or not, "they succeeded in worrying the Foreign Office, much to Casement's detriment".

Monteith gave his not very high opinion of John Devoy at some length. He described him as "autocratic, intolerant of another man's opinion and decidedly vindictive as far as Roger Casement was concerned". He believed Devoy was "jealous to the point of insanity" of Casement because the latter accomplished in a few months what Devoy had spent a lifetime working to achieve, i.e., turning the

was a good friend to Casement, was thoroughly aware of all these intrigues.

In very late 1915, I proceeded to Limburg Irish prisoner-of-war camp to find out how the recruiting was going on and to investigate reports which had reached us of very poor results. After an examination of the position, I found the cause of the failure to be related to the transfer from Limburg of the prisoners who had Irish names or otherwise but who were not of Irish birth to the English prisoner-of-war camp. The Irish-born prisoners had counted these men as friends and British army comrades in their Irish regiments, but here they were an influence against the Irish Brigade project. Another aspect was that this camp to which they had been transferred at Giessen-Hessen-Nassau was known as a punishment camp and the so-called Irish prisoners resented being sent to it. The view was that revenge was being taken against them for not joining the Irish Brigade.

The three new men who had volunteered returned with me to Zossen to join the other brigade members.

Now the question of more intensified training for the men was decided on because of the likelihood of the brigade going to Ireland in the near future. Not only was there a question of the training in arms but there was also the question of using the two commands – the German and the English. This training continued throughout the winter of 1915-16. From the Brandenburg training camp of old Fritz the Great[222] who boasted of his bodyguard of seven-footers, Irishmen all, in the 18th century, the 20th century again saw a company of hefty Irishmen plod their early way to the adjacent rifle-ranges with machine-guns on their shoulders and no better sustenance than black war bread and milkless "coffee" derived from roasted barley. A Prussian Guard officer from Strasbourg and 10 German NCOs – mainly Rhinelanders in sympathy with Ireland – were attached to the brigade. Monteith aided with the commands in English. The rattle of machine-gun, rifle and hand-grenade was the chief distraction of these Wild Geese during January, February and March 1916.

Irish question into an international issue. See Monteith, *Casement's Last Adventure*, pp. 104-5, 116, 228-9.

Reid pointed out that the Freeman letters claimed that the Irish-American leaders had lost faith in Casement and regretted ever sending him to Germany. Reid considered Freeman "a busybody" who wrote the letters for "mysterious mischief-making purposes of his own" and was not inclined to see the hand of Devoy in the action. See Reid, *The Lives of Roger Casement*, p. 316.

[222] The reference is to Frederick II (1712-1786), King of Prussia, who became known as Frederick the Great. He was nicknamed "*der alte Fritz*" or Old Fritz.

At Christmas a football match was arranged, as part of the festivities, between the Irish Brigade and the German soldiers of the 203rd Brandenburg Regiment. The Irish team won. This was followed by a smoking concert, comprising Irish and German songs. At this concert an argument arose between some elderly German soldiers and members of the Irish Brigade. The Irishmen resented some remarks made by the Germans to the effect that the brigade consisted of only "home front" garrison soldiers who were too long at rest and who should be out fighting against their common enemy – John Bull and company.

A fight developed and in the melee there were some casualties as a result of the fisticuffs. Half a dozen Irishmen were arrested and about the same number of Germans. These had to go before the military authorities, and both sides were found guilty and received punishment. In the course of a few weeks, I read a distorted account of the incident in the London *Daily Mail* – it could be read in all Berlin hotels and had found its way in the Irish training camp. It said that the Irishmen "had knocked hell" out of the German Prussian Guards at Zossen.

The manner in which this could get into the English papers was curious. America was still a neutral country in 1915-16 and, knowing this, British agents, mostly born Canadians, had got into Germany disguised as Americans. Newspaper correspondents did this in large numbers. Casement was aware that this was happening and had given instructions to the men that they were not to disclose any information regarding their activities with the Irish Brigade to anyone they met in town and especially if they met foreigners.

Training went on monotonously for the first few months of 1916. In January we had a visit from Tommy O'Connor, an IRB courier from Dublin. As an IRB man, I knew him in the USA and in Ireland. I was present when he told Casement that in a very short time an insurrection would take place in Ireland. He asked Casement if it would be possible to send a courier to Ireland in a submarine when arrangements had been completed with the German authorities for the landing of arms and men on the Irish coast. This courier was to bring full particulars regarding the landing arrangements. Casement said that he would endeavour to do this when he knew something definite. Tommy O'Connor left Germany in late January and went to America.

St Patrick's Day 1916 brought sorrow to the brigade: Volunteer Patrick O'Holohan was carried to his grave on the shoulders of his Irish and German comrades. He had been in poor health for some time, having never recovered from the effects of the rigorous campaign of the first three months of the war. His life had been one of adventure. Serving in India, he escaped by a

German cargo boat three months before the war. The declaration of war found him in Marseilles, where he read the general amnesty order reinstating deserters from the British army. He sought to join the Foreign Legion, but made the mistake of informing the French authorities that he was a deserter, and so was packed off to the British concentration camp. Wounded in October 1914, he found his way to Limburg an der Lahn and was one of the first to volunteer his services for Ireland.

St Patrick's Eve I stood in attendance with a kindly German Jesuit who had been in Ireland and England and had done missionary work in India. He spoke English well and had come especially from the mission-house in Berlin for the Irish national festival as, indeed, he had been doing every Sunday for a year. At the request of Casement, I visited O'Holohan in the garrison hospital the night before, and he seemed to be sinking fast. The German sisters said that the German-speaking priest who visited daily had anointed him and prepared him for death, and that the doctor held out no hope for his recovery.

"Major," he whispered to me in his long-drawn sighs, "I shall never see the dear ones in old Ireland again. God bless them all. Say a prayer for me." I asked him if he had any particular message, and I can never forget his reply. "My dear and kind-hearted Irish mother is in heaven," he said, "and there I hope to join her soon. One sister is in Ireland, another married in the United States. Let them know some day, if you have the opportunity, that I died a true Irishman. Before I parted with him in sorrow, he added: "Bury me in my green uniform with harp and shamrock of Ireland in green and gold; let my cap with its cockade badge of green, white and gold rest on my coffin, wrapped up in the tricolour of Ireland."

I retired to my lonely bunk and, early next morning, hastened with the Jesuit priest to his bedside. His face brightened at sight of us, and he remained conscious until evening. Then, as the Angelus bell tolled in the village of Zossen, heralding the eve of Ireland's national festival, he peacefully closed his eyes in death. The good priest recited the prayers for the dead, the German soldier-patients and sisters solemnly joining in the last act of mercy.

Just as the sun prepared to sink somewhere west of the Green Isle on St Patrick's Day, Volunteer Paddy O'Holohan was borne to his final resting place with full military honours. The solemn strains of the band of the 203 Regiment kept the Prussian Guards in step alongside the firing party with arms reversed. Casement, accompanied by Captain Monteith and General von Schneider, marched to the graveside at the head of the combined German and Irish troops. As the last shovelful of earth was laid over the coffin, the sharp crack of the last volley rang out and the *Last Post* was sounded by buglers Keogh, McSweeney and O'Donoghue.

Then the learned German Jesuit delivered an impressive oration for the benefit of the German soldiers and civilians and the Irish comrades surrounding the last resting place of the Irish volunteer. He dwelt particularly on the intrepid fidelity to the Christian faith exhibited by the Irish race through centuries of religious oppression in their native land, and exhorted the German Catholics within his hearing to persevere in the spirit of Christianity ignited from the Rhine to the Vistula by Irish missionaries of the 8th and subsequent centuries. And in asking the good Catholics of Zossen to intercede and pray for the Irish in their midst, he urged them to bear in mind that countless Irish Catholic evangelists had voluntarily exiled themselves to sustain the earlier endeavours of Germany's Irish martyr, St Killian, first Archbishop of Würtzburg, Bavaria. He concluded with the announcement that the Irish patriot, Roger Casement, wished to say a few words on the sad occasion. Roger's soul-stirring address, which I find it difficult to recall, seemed to overawe his hearers, though understood by but a few.

"Fellow countrymen and comrades of the Irish Brigade," he said, "we have assembled today, the feast day of Ireland's patron St Patrick, on an occasion sad for all of us. We have assembled to pay a final tribute to one dear to us all, Volunteer Patrick O'Holohan, who has earned in full measure the honour bestowed on his last earthly march as a true soldier of Ireland. I feel assured that in coming here each one of us has contributed his share of the respect due to the Irish dead. The hope may be entertained that the memory of our comrade who now sleeps in eternal peace will be endeared to this race by his devotion to faith and fatherland. His name will be perpetuated in the keeping of generations to come, and a stone to mark his last resting place will serve as a beacon to attract admirers of the heroic to the spot which now enshrines his mortal remains. A suitable inscription will remind pilgrims to this cemetery of the sacrifice made by a faithful Irishman for his country's liberty.

"Standing over his early grave, it behoves each and every one of us to be in readiness so that when the time comes to contribute our share to the cause of Ireland and liberty, we shall do so nobly and boldly, as he did. Let us pray that the comrade who has been called away from us will intercede for us and guide our footsteps for the sake of Erin and the Irish people."

In a few days, Casement had erected a fine granite headstone over the grave, with an inscription sketched by Sergeant Michael O'Toole:

In memory of
Vol. Patrick O'Holohan
of the Irish Brigade.
Born at Waterford, Ireland.
Died St Patrick's Eve, 1916.
A Dhia, Saor Éire.

Casement also paid the cemetery committee to have the grave properly attended for a period of 20 years. Patrick O'Holohan's grave and memorial make a centre of pilgrimage for Irish exiles in Berlin each recurring St Patrick's Day.[223]

---

[223] Monteith also referred to this sad event in the history of the brigade. "As I marched with Sir Roger Casement at the head of the funeral party, my thoughts went back to the streets of Dublin, to the dull throbbing of the drums at the funeral of Byrne and Nolan [two workers killed in a police baton charge during the 1913 Dublin lockout] and to the wail of the pipes as we escorted the victims of the Bachelor's Walk massacre to their last rest in Glasnevin. Unconsciously, the words: 'How long, O Lord, how long?' came from my lips. Casement heard and echoed: 'How long!'"

Concerning the gravestone, Monteith wrote: "That lonely monument, standing in the heart of Germany, will tell succeeding generations that this is the last resting place of a soldier of Ireland. This man who had risked all, imprisonment and shameful death, to follow him who led the way and who was, himself, so soon to enter the kinship of heroes in the Great Beyond. Even in death this humble soldier serves Ireland. His grave, covered in trailing shamrocks, bears witness to England's enslavement of his motherland. In such ways as this is the history of Ireland written on the tombstones of her exiled dead. On every continent of the world are they to be found, the lonely graves of those who served in the ranks of the Soldiers of Destiny. May they all rest in peace." See Monteith, *Casement's Last Adventure*, pp 131-2.

CHAPTER 9: The Road to Easter Week

On the evening of 7th April 1916, Casement sent for me to show me a letter which was addressed to him and had come through German diplomatic channels from Berne, Switzerland. The letter was from Count Plunkett, the father of Joseph Plunkett. We didn't know at that time that the letter was from Count Plunkett, but it had the secret code word "Ashling" which had been arranged between Joseph Plunkett and Casement prior to Commandant Plunkett's departure for the USA and Dublin. This secret code word was written on top of the letter. From this we knew that it came from someone who at least knew Joe Plunkett, if not from himself. The gist of the letter was that an insurrection had been planned to take place in Dublin on Easter Sunday, 23rd April. This coincided with Dublin headquarters' decision eventually to change the date of the arms' landing by the Aud from Good Friday to Easter Sunday.[224]

---

[224] A number of things in the planning for the rising had happened before Casement's receipt of this letter, which he showed to Monteith on 6th April. The German ambassador in the US, Count Bernstorff, sent the following telegram to Berlin on 17th February 1916: "Irish leader John Devoy informs me that revolution shall begin Easter Sunday Ireland. Requests arms between Good Friday and Easter Sunday Limerick ... Longer waiting impossible. Request wire reply whether I may promise help from Germany."

Shortly afterwards, Devoy sent a more detailed memo to the German government. "... action in Ireland cannot be postponed beyond the date named – Easter Sunday, April 23rd ... The chance of getting arms and ammunition into Ireland now is from Germany. If a small expedition with a good supply of arms and ammunition – say from 25 to 50 thousand rifles with a proportionate number of machine-guns and field artillery and a few superior officers – could be sent by the northern route ... it would have a good chance of reaching the west coast of Ireland, especially if simultaneous with a demonstration in the Nord [*sic*] Sea ... Feeling in Ireland is now ripe" Devoy went on to say that if an expedition were sent to Ireland, they wished Casement to remain in Germany as Ireland's accredited representative "until such time as the Provisional Government may decide otherwise".

At the beginning of March, Department IIIb of the General Staff called in Monteith and informed him about Devoy's message. Discussions then took place with the German Admiralty about the transport of arms to Ireland. They agreed to send a ship, the Aud, with 20,000 guns captured from the Russians. There was no question of sending German officers or any demonstration in the North Sea. Monteith wasn't happy with the talks and decided to inform Casement and to try to

The letter specified (i) that the German aid should be landed in Tralee Bay between dawn on Good Friday and not later than dawn on Easter Sunday; (ii) that the expedition should consist of German officers, and (iii) that a German submarine would be necessary to block the entrance to Dublin harbour to stop

---

get him to come to Berlin (he was at a sanatorium in Munich because he had been ill).

Casement now worked out a plan with Monteith for his own immediate return to Ireland via a German submarine, with one or two trusted men from the brigade, to prepare for the landing of the German arms. Monteith would then follow on the Aud with a group of volunteers from the brigade and some machine-guns. But the Germans weren't interested in his plan and instead said he should go to Ireland (despite what Devoy had requested) with the entire brigade on board the arms ship. It seemed they wanted to rid themselves of him and the entire brigade in one move.

In his diary, Casement wrote: "The whole project really took my breath away. I had come to discuss the best means of landing arms in Ireland and I found myself confronted with a proposal for a 'rebellion' in Ireland I believed to be wholly futile at the best, and at worst something I dreaded to think of." He did manage to persuade the Germans to help him send a messenger to Ireland. This man was John McGoey, who had arrived from the US in December 1915. Casement originally planned to send him back to the US to warn the Clan na Gael leaders of the unreliability of the Germans but now he decided to send him to try to get the IRB leaders in Dublin to call off the rising and merely to land the arms safely and distribute them. McGoey got out of Germany all right but it is doubtful that he ever reached Dublin and it cannot be said with certainty what happened to him.

Casement felt he could not support an armed uprising in Ireland at this stage because it would be without sufficient military cover: "I had always been greatly opposed to any attempted revolt in Ireland unless backed up with strong foreign military help." Although he insisted to the Germans that the 10-Point Agreement he had concluded with them clearly referred to German troops, arms and ammunition, he got nowhere with them. In fact, they tried to blackmail him by threatening to notify Devoy that the long-awaited arms shipment would not now be sent because of Casement's refusal to take their offer and to take the brigade with him to Ireland. This meant all the blame would fall on him: "In other words, I was to be held up to my countrymen in Ireland and America as something far worse than a coward," that is, a traitor.

Under this pressure, he agreed that he himself would go on the arms ship but only if Berlin would not send the brigade on a hopeless adventure. He pleaded with Count von Wedel for help: "The *only* thing I can clearly see is that while I *may* sacrifice myself, I am not entitled to sacrifice those who trusted in my honour and good faith, even as I trusted in the honour and good faith of the German government." The General Staff even went so far as to try to bribe Monteith, with a generous financial offer, to take the men of the brigade to Ireland on his own against Casement's wishes. Monteith contemptuously rejected the offer. See Doerries, *Prelude to the Easter Rising*, pp 16-20; Monteith, *Casement's Last Adventure*, pp 133-140; Dudgeon, *Roger Casement: the Black Diaries*, pp 459-64; Ó Síocháin, *Roger Casement: Imperialist, Rebel, Revolutionary*, pp. 432-36.

reinforcements reaching Dublin. It pointed out that the time was very short and requested immediate action. Casement sent a reply saying that no German officers would be going to Ireland and that no submarine would be sent to Dublin either. He gave details of the cargo of arms that was to be sent.[225]

When this message was dispatched, Casement and I went to the German Foreign Office to see Count von Wedel to enquire what would be the future of the Irish Brigade in Germany and what exactly it was proposed to do now arising from the Irish request for arms. Count von Wedel told Casement that in view of messages which had been received from the Irish leaders in America and from Irish headquarters in Dublin, Casement should remain in Germany to carry on on behalf of the Irish republican movement as heretofore, and the Irish Brigade machine-gun company would be sent on the Aud gun-running ship. That ship had been specially constructed so as to conceal the machine-gun contingent en route to Ireland.

Von Wedel then said: "I will now transfer the whole matter to the Military Attachés at the Foreign Office who will no doubt give you full details of the military preparations for the transport of the Irish contingent on the Aud." The attachés were Captain Nadolny,[226] Captain Huelsen and Major von Haugwitz. A conference was arranged with these officers on the following day.

They, the German Foreign Office "Holy Trinity", opened the conference by saying to Casement: "You are already aware that you must remain here, and the Irish Brigade machine-gun company will accompany the Aud to Ireland." Casement very much resented the idea of being left behind in Germany and he informed the military attachés that they should take no further action regarding him until he would discuss the position with members of his brigade and find out what their feelings in the matter were.

We returned to Count von Wedel at the Foreign Office and informed him that we were proceeding immediately to Zossen military training camp to discuss with the men the new position which had arisen. Casement also told von Wedel that he resented

---

[225] This message was not forwarded to Berne by the German authorities and was given back to him shortly before his departure for Ireland. It seems that by now the Germans either knew or suspected the real reason McGoey had been sent by Casement to Dublin and they didn't want any more interference from him in the plans for a rising. See Doerries, *op. cit.*, p. 21; Monteith, *op. cit.*, p. 139.

[226] Casement's most recent biographer says that Count Rudolph von Nadolny, the head of the General Staff's political section, who played a central part in Casement's affairs while he was in Germany, "seems to have had the least sympathy for Casement personally". See Ó Síocháin, *Roger Casement: op. cit.*, p. 400.

the remarks of the attaché, Captain Nadolny, when he said that "the men of the brigade could be forced under martial law to leave Germany for Ireland without Casement, and Casement could be forcibly retained". Von Wedel pointed out that the Foreign Office was always agreeable to whatever Casement wished but he appreciated how Casement felt about these remarks made by Captain Nadolny. This ended the Foreign Office conversation and we proceeded to Zossen.

On the way we fully discussed the conference and Casement said to me in his usual confidential manner: "It is quite possible that the brigade may be got at by intrigue to get them to disobey my orders and to act directly on the orders of the German military authorities. But let them dare try it," he added in his usual fighting demeanour. I agreed to inform the brigade of the position and to ascertain their wishes. I felt I owed this to Casement.

When we put the question to the men at Zossen, they were in general agreement with whatever Casement thought best. They were willing to abide by his decision. We asked them to appoint a small committee to act on behalf of the men. Casement drew up an agreement. Two NCOs and two men signed this declaration on behalf of the brigade. On the following day, 9th April, Roger Casement said he would leave me in complete charge of the Irish Brigade machine-gun company in Zossen and would take Monteith with him to Berlin for further negotiations. I felt relieved of all further responsibility in the matter and determined to carry out Casement's instructions and see that the men were at least satisfied that everything was being done correctly.

Casement said that he would like to take an NCO with him to Berlin. After due deliberation they[227] decided to take Sergeant Bailey. Casement told me that Bailey was chosen by Monteith.[228] The choice was influenced by the fact that Bailey was an expert in Morse and signalling, although I had recommended Sergeant Joe Dowling or Sergeant Seán Kavanagh as best to go with Casement.[229] They proceeded to Berlin on 9th April.

On 11th April, Casement sent for me and in a last private conversation, he told me the following. "I have succeeded in securing that I will be sent on a submarine to Ireland and I am

---

[227] "They" were Casement and Monteith.

[228] Quinlisk remarked that Monteith's favourite at Zossen was Bailey, "who could twist him round his little finger". See "The German Irish Brigade" in *Land and Water*, 13th November 1919, p. 16.

[229] Concerning his choice of Bailey, Monteith wrote: "It was absolutely essential that I should have a man with me who was capable of handling a machine-gun in the event of our having to cover the landing of the arms, so I decided to take Sergeant Bailey." See Monteith, *Casement's Last Adventure*, p. 140.

taking Captain Monteith with me and Sergeant Bailey also on the submarine."[230] He thanked me for all I had done to help him recruit the Irish Brigade and for the help I had given him. He asked me to look after the men during the remainder of our sojourn in Germany, in the meantime, and in case they would be sent for after the successful landing of the Aud expedition and himself in Ireland.

He wrote a farewell letter to the Irishmen of the brigade and asked me to read it to them. This letter reads as follows and is dated "Berlin 11th April 1916":

Comrades of the Irish Brigade, we are going tonight on a very perilous journey and have been forced to leave you without a word of farewell or further explanation. It was not possible to tell you or to explain a few days ago or even now fully why we did not bring you.

One reason, perhaps the chief one, why you are not accompanying us today is to keep you out of the very grave danger we have to face. We are sure that all of you would have faced these dangers too, seeing that it is in the cause of Ireland's independence we go, but we have decided it was unfair to you to appeal to your courage in a matter where all the elements of danger are very apparent and those of hope entirely wanting.

You must therefore forgive us for going in silence from you and leaving you to the continued inactivities that have already been so harmful to you and contrary to your hopes when you volunteered in the service of Irish freedom. Should we live, you will know and understand all. If we do not return, or you hear no more from us, you will know we have gone to do our part in our country's cause according to what we deemed was right.

Adjutant-Lieutenant M.S. Boyle Keogh is commissioned to look after the wants of the Irishmen, volunteers of the Irish Brigade, during their stay in Germany. When the war is over,

---

[230] Why exactly the Germans changed their minds and decided to send Casement to Ireland in a submarine and allow him to leave the brigade men behind him in Germany is not clear. One person whom he had begged to intercede for him on behalf of his men was Count von Wedel. He had also approached "the well-known German-American, Jacob Noeggerath, and apparently successfully attempted to persuade him to intercede at the German Foreign Office". In his diary, Casement credited Noeggerath with convincing the Germans of the need for the submarine journey to Ireland. He was overjoyed that the brigade would be staying in Germany: "... joy that the men should not go ... My second victory – I have saved the men..." See Doerries, *Prelude to the Easter Rising*, pp 21, 192-203, 206; Ó Síocháin, *Roger Casement: Imperialist, Rebel, Revolutionary*, pp. 436-37.

your many friends at home in Ireland and in the USA will certainly have you in their care and affection; meantime, you may have hard and unhappy days to face, many trials and temptations too, and perhaps harsh things to endure.

Bear all with brave stout Irish hearts, remembering that in what you did, you sought to serve your country, and that no Irishman could give to that cause more than you gave. You gave yourselves. Having given yourselves so freely, keep yourselves bravely. Be obedient, disciplined and patient, and rest assured that whatever happens to us who are going from you today, you will find many friends in the world and your name will be honoured in Irish story.

This farewell letter was signed: "Roger Casement, Chief; Robert Monteith, Captain."[231]

He told me they were proceeding immediately to Kiel Harbour Naval Station and leaving Germany by submarine that night.[232]

---

[231] On the same day that he wrote this letter, Casement, showing his intense desire somehow to safeguard the fate of the Irish Brigade men, wrote the following letter to the German Chancellor, Bethmann Hollweg:

> ... I venture to bring to your Excellency's notice the situation of the small body of Irish soldiers who volunteered to form an Irish corps to fight for Irish freedom, with the wholehearted support and approval of the Imperial German Government. The terms on which they agreed to serve ... are embodied in the Agreement drawn up by myself on 23. [sic] December 1914 and accepted by the Under-Secretary of State on 28. [sic] December 1914 ... I cannot depart without recalling the situation of these Irish soldiers who volunteered for the cause of Ireland under the pledge of that Agreement, and begging that nothing should be allowed to interfere with its strict fulfilment. Today, through the channel of the Political Section [Nadolny] of the German General Staff I am informed ... that the Irish soldiers now at Zossen ... are "Deserters" or "Prisoners of War" and may be treated in any way that seems fitting to the military authorities. Dissenting profoundly from this point of view, I am forced to refer the treatment of these volunteers to Your Excellency as the highest representative of the Imperial German Government ... I have requested my friend Mr T. St John Gaffney, former US Consul General at Munich, to have a kindly interest in the men ... and am recommending him in this capacity to Count Georg von Wedel of the German Foreign Office...

See Doerries, *Prelude to the Easter Rising*, pp 21-2. The letter is reproduced in full in *ibid.*, pp 209-11.

[232] Also on 11th April 1916, Casement wrote to von Wedel:

> I am asking Mr T. St John Gaffney to do what he can on behalf of the Irish soldiers still at Zossen, and have written today a letter to the Imperial Chancellor on the subject.
>
> Such money as I still have left I am handing to Mr Gaffney to expend on the men in the way already established since they took up their quarters at Zossen.

The Aud was on its way since the day before. On 10th April, I had returned to Zossen and before he departed to Kiel, he wrote me a further letter which said:

A Chara,

Were I not to go – and I would be amply justified in stamping out the whole project of allowing a handful of Irishmen and machine-guns to proceed alone – and were I then to skulk here in safety in a matter where the entire hope of success was wanting, I would incur the contempt of all men and be branded a coward for all time.

If the boys at home are to be in the fighting line, then my place is with them, were I to perish in the attempt. Keep the gun practice going in case you may be sent for later on. Show a united front remembering that we who are leaving you behind do what we think right in the cause of our beloved country. If you do not hear from us again, or that we are no more, having given ourselves so freely, keep yourselves proudly and your names shall be honoured still in Irish story.

I think the best thing to do could be to put them to some useful occupation here in Germany until the war is over, and then to send them to America where Father Nicholson is already doing what is possible to provide for their future there.

As the money I leave with Mr Gaffney will not go very far, I fear, I am forced to recall your letter to me of 11th December last in which you stated that the sum I had refunded (Marks 8,000) would be held at my disposal should I require it at any time for Irish affairs.

It is always probable and indeed very likely that further remittances from my friends in America will be received here in the usual way. If so, I beg that they may be handed to Mr Gaffney who will expend them as seems best in the interest of the men.

In any case, I wish whatever sum you may hand to Mr Gaffney from the fund you and your friends so kindly raised for the Irish cause to be ultimately refunded to you by my friends in America. I am instructing Mr Gaffney in this sense.

I should like Mr Gaffney to have access to the men at Zossen, and I beg you as a last act of personal regard to do all in your power for them to mitigate the cruel disappointment they will surely labour under and to make clear ultimately to them how I left them without any explanation and apparently abandoned them.

I have acted throughout in what seemed to be their best interests, and in now leaving them behind I feel that I am still trying to do my duty to them...

I enclose a list of the remaining Irish soldiers at Zossen, a copy of which is also given to Mr Gaffney.

Reproduced in Doerries, *Prelude to the Easter Rising*, pp 211-12.

It would be well for all Irish historians to study closely the soldierly actions of Casement throughout his militant mission in Germany.

I assembled the men and read Casement's farewell letter to them on 12th April 1916. We heard no more until Tuesday of Easter Week, 25th April 1916, the second day of the actual Easter Week hostilities in Dublin, Galway and Wexford.

In the German daily press on 25th April a short account was given of the insurrection in Ireland. Also included in the news was an account of the landing of three men on the coast of Kerry from a German submarine. It said that two had been arrested and one was still at large. The men of the brigade were most anxious to know who the man was who was still at large. They were hoping it was Casement.

On the following day, the sad news came through that Casement had been arrested a day after landing from the submarine, and that the Aud had been sunk after being time-bombed by her crew near Queenstown. The report was that Roger was now a prisoner in the Tower of London and that Bailey was also captured. The Irishmen in the brigade, with the exception of a few, were of one opinion: "Bailey will turn King's evidence." Although even Joe Dowling seemed to hold against this, alas events were to prove the opinion all too true.

All through Easter Week the German papers published what information they had regarding the fighting in Dublin and the rest of the hostilities in Ireland. I was told that the Germans had dropped leaflets to the Irish regiments on the Western Front giving information as to what was taking place at home. Also there were newspaper reports of German naval attacks on the east coast of England – that the towns of Hartlepool and Scarborough were shelled by the German navy.

The news of the rising caused commotion among the men. They petitioned me to put forward their willingness to be dispatched to Ireland, win or lose, death or glory. The green, white and gold – the flag of Ireland – had flown at full mast over the Irish barracks but since the news of our Chief's arrest, it flew at half mast only. Baron von Malzahn was the military adjutant to General von Schneider, GOC Zossen. He sent for me as acting commander of the Irish Brigade and told me to use persuasive power to influence the Irishmen not to give any undue vent to their feelings or commit acts of indiscipline. He was a fluent speaker of the English language and possessed a remarkable knowledge of the Irishman's impulsive sentiments.

I had met him often in the course of routine military duty. He expressed feelings of sorrow for poor Roger as a prisoner in the hands of a most cruel enemy. "I am informed," he said, "from the

General Staff, GHQ Berlin, that Sergeant-Major Keogh of the Irish Brigade, Machine-Gun Company, is to hold the Irishmen of his contingent in immediate readiness and mobilised for any emergency or in case of sudden transportation to the latest seat of warfare in Ireland." The proper procedure in the event of a military urgency was discussed in every detail.

They had made a decision to confine to barracks all Irishmen of the machine-gun contingent. It was not a happy experience for me to impart the confinement order to the men. Was it not for freedom for all Irishmen that our compatriots were fighting to the death's agony for at that very moment in Ireland? We in Germany stood for the selfsame principle: freedom of action and freedom of speech against the common enemy. "Let no man set a boundary in the path of freedom and a united Irish nation." Words to that effect have immortalised the name of Charles Stewart Parnell in the hearts of all true Irishmen for all time. What party or political grouping in Ireland would dare attempt at any time to have the true meaning of those words obliterated from the minds of the freedom-loving Irish people?

It is not my intention to pose in the eyes of my readers, critics or otherwise. I am not a prophet, but this much is a positive factor in the cause of supreme Irish independence, north as well as south. Ireland's sons will ever find leaders in the van who will, undeterred, fight every vestige of Anglo-Saxon misrule and coercion that have fettered the path, for 700 years, of the tortured and peace-loving Irish race within the four shores of our beloved sireland.

In the succeeding 10 days from that memorable Easter Monday, our thoughts were with the boys in green at home. The splendid fight could surely not hold on for long and unassisted. The Aud and her valuable cargo now being at the bottom of the sea, secured in 20 fathoms of salt water, the end was awaited and with only one result. The surrender order was duly issued from the artillery-shelled and burnt-out headquarters of Erin's youngest stronghold, the GPO. It told the tale of yet another gallant stand in the defence of Róisín Dubh. In due course we heard of the sad fate meted out to Pearse, Connolly, Plunkett, MacDonagh and MacDermott, Clarke and Ceannt, and Major MacBride of Irish Brigade fame in South Africa. The British and West British firing squads had done their dirty work.

The 1916 Rising met with general appreciation in Germany, both from the civilian and military point of view. The Germans were filled with admiration at a small nation like Ireland rising against such a powerful enemy as Britain, and being able to carry on for a whole week of warfare, notwithstanding the fact that the German aid had not succeeded in landing. The arms and ammunition could not reach their intended recipients because of the sinking of the Aud by its own crew after waiting at Fenit Pier, Tralee Bay, for over 22 hours for the unloading assistance which never came.[233]

The men then seemed to appreciate fully Casement's decision not to have them sent to Ireland on the Aud, because they now understood that if they had gone, they would have been trapped by the British without getting a chance to fight. Roger had proven himself a worthy son of his father – the Young Irelander and rebel leader in 1847, Colonel Roger Casement, a true friend of his mentor John Mitchel and Thomas Francis Meagher during their enforced exile together in Paris.

Our noble Chief now calmly awaited a most cruel end in London, to be hanged like a common criminal, an action parallel to that of the Anglo-Saxon murderers in the streets of Dublin city during the first years of the last century when the blood-stained empire makers, at the behest of West Britonism and Dublin Castle, had brave Robert Emmet publicly hanged, drawn and quartered, and his head thrown among the jeering crowd of Castle hacks and their illiterate followers in the Irish underworld. In the case of Casement in 1916, had he been tried by a packed jury in Dublin, he would have met a much similar end, but England's power wanted to then draw the eyes of her empire's slaves on the capital landmark, London.

Outside Pentonville Prison, on the morning of 3rd August 1916, a howling mob of London's underworld foamed and swore in taunting jests as most befitting an Anglo-Saxon hireling crew. "Yet another traitor to the Royal Crown gone to his doom," they felt. In a remote corner of the outside walls of the prison on that memorable August day, a goodly cluster of peaceable people were gathered together in prayer. The stillness of that devout appeal to a just God of mercy took place because Irish exiles remember ever the sad story of bygone days in Ireland: their ancestors sent to the scaffold or the gibbet hill or the croppy's grave – a lonely heritage in all true Irish hearts.

Ellis the hangman stated in his memoirs about Roger Casement: "The impression shall ever remain on my mind in this life: the composure of his noble countenance which seemed to beam down from his giant-like stature, and the smile of contentment and happiness as he willingly assisted my assistant and self in preparations for the last short journey in this wicked world. The steady martial thread of his 6ft 4ins and a soldierly appearance added to the solemn echo of his prompt and coherent

---

[233] See Appendix 2.

answers to the Roman Catholic chaplain as he marched to his untimely doom. Roger Casement appeared to me the bravest man it fell to my unlucky lot to execute.

"I cherish most of all one remembrance given me during my life's experience of human tragedy, and that is Roger Casement's Catholic prayer book that he gave me on that eventful and sad morning at Pentonville Jail."

The sad chime of the prison bell sent forth the news that Ireland's true hero and martyr to the true faith was launched forth to meet his God. The lisp of fervent pleading was unfaltering and clear from the kindest of Erin's exiled sons and daughters. The silent tears of sorrow were brimful with grief. With no faltering step, but with unconquerable mien he had faced the cruel hangman's noose. "Into Thy hands, oh Lord, I commend my spirit," he said. An Irish hero he had lived, and an Irish hero he died. His last thoughtful exclamation for Kathleen Ni Houlihan was: "I die, but Ireland lives."

> Bold Roger Casement, the darling of Erin,
> Bold Roger Casement, he died with a smile.
> To be hanged on the scaffold was his cruel sentence,
> For a hero he lived and a hero he died.

CHAPTER 10: After the Rising

On 24th May 1916, the British War Office forwarded a very short diplomatic note to my mother, Mrs Mary Keogh, the contents of which read:

Dear Madam,

This is to inform you that your son Michael Patrick Keogh has taken up arms in the service of the common enemy, the German government, and as a follower of the arch-traitor, Roger Casement, now a prisoner in the Tower of London charged with high treason.

Henceforward your allotment allowance left to you by your son from his army pay as a prisoner of war is from this date cancelled.

In the voluminous missiles broadcasted from the British Empire's War Office it can always be surmised that a distinct and separate reason has been determined. However true, this was portrayed in a singular manner in my case as an Irish volunteer soldier and defender of Erin's just right in determining herself a small but nevertheless independent nation.

In the course of about two weeks after the 1916 Rising, the members of the Irish Brigade in Germany were deprived of their machine-guns, rifles and the rest. The Alsace-Lorraine officer, two NCOs and the 10 German soldier-instructors were taken from our midst and dispatched to their unit, the machine-gun company, Prussian Grenadier Guards at Spandau by Berlin. A most unwholesome air emanated from military officialdom. What next? The Irishmen seemed not to care. But one thing was clear: a compromising overture seemed to be the aim of the German officials. It was proposed to send us to an internment camp where remunerative work would be forthcoming. The 10 articles of the agreement between the German government and Casement were already waste paper.[234]

---

[234] Although Quinlisk said that the weapons were not taken from the men until June, he painted a bleak picture of the treatment they received after the rising. According to this account, the GOC Zossen, General von Schneider, "knowing we were leaderless, began to treat us as he liked. Passes were stopped, punishment meted out wholesale for the slightest offence. I myself was punished with three days' arrest because I could not identify a man who talked whilst being drilled. There wasn't a single day in which two or three men were not punished for trivial offences." See

In May 1916, I found myself fighting almost a lone hand, except for a little assistance from Mr St John Gaffney,[235] commissioned by Casement to look after the interests of the brigade for the remainder of their hard trial in Germany. (He visited the Casement compatriots only twice in the subsequent nearly three years of the cursed 1914-18 World War.)[236] At the beginning of June, Mr Gaffney informed me that the German government had decided to transfer the Irishmen to an internment camp in Danzig, West Prussia, to work in factories or, where the men themselves preferred, on farms. In the course of a few days, Hauptmann Nicolai, POW commandant of Danzig-Troyl, came to see, as he said himself, his future "pets".[237] Maps and pictures of the camp were produced, showing our barracks inside barbed wire and camp workshops where the Irishmen would be facilitated in finding instructive work and some pay, not stated.

I took Nicolai's number, having encountered such birds before, and afterwards he had good reason to know me in reality. The Irish contingent were to depart in a short time for Danzig on the Vistula, so I drew up a protest and, having it signed by all the Irishmen under my command, forwarded it to St John Gaffney, at

---

Quinlisk, "The German Irish Brigade" in *Land and Water*, 13th November 1919, p. 17.

Roth would not agree that the 10-Article Agreement was being ignored. Concerning the decision in early June to send the Irishmen to Danzig (for which see below), he wrote (his quotation is from official documentation): "Danzig offered 'conditions guaranteeing accommodation and treatment as laid out in the contractual agreement between the *Auswärtiges Amt* [Foreign Office] and Sir Roger Casement'. The Irishmen could be employed both inside and outside the camp as guards, as well as for camp, agricultural or industrial duties. There can be no doubt that the German-Irish Agreement was regarded as binding." See Roth, "'The German soldier is not tactful,'" in *The Irish Sword*, vol. 19, no. 78, p. 326.

[235] Thomas St John Gaffney was US Consul General in Dresden from 1906 and then in Munich from 1914. He befriended Casement during his stay in Germany. He was dismissed from his post by President Wilson for being too pro-German. See Reid, *The Lives of Roger Casement*, pp 310-12.

[236] Quinlisk wrote: "St John Gaffney, a former American Consul-General who had lost his job through giving a dinner for Sir Roger Casement, was requested by the latter to look after the Irish Brigade during his absence, but Gaffney, in company with a certain Dr Chatterton Hill, was only happy when drinking champagne and telephoning sweet nothings to the Austrian-Jewess proprietress of the famous *Continental Times*." See Quinlisk, "The German Irish Brigade," in *Land and Water*, 13th November 1919, p. 17. The *Continental Times* was a pro-German paper which appeared three times a week in English and was owned by a Mrs White. See Reid, *The Lives of Roger Casement*, p. 234.

[237] According to Quinlisk, Commandant Nicolai called the Irishmen his *kinder* or children. See Quinlisk, *op. cit.*, p. 17.

the same time sending a copy to Herr Zimmermann, Under Secretary for Foreign Affairs. I went further. I visited Berlin and interviewed Major von Boerley of the General Staff. This was contrary to the good discipline supposed to rule the Zossen military camp but I was an Irishman, not a German. By going to Berlin, I wrung another victory for Casement's followers.

Major von Boerley knew me well and had experience of many previous encounters. On one occasion, the level-minded major shut off that windjammer, Captain Nadolny, in my presence, saying: "Oh shut up, Nadolny! Sergeant-Major Keogh knows the situation far better than you would give him credit for. I have found his version always correct, and in detail his proposals always tended towards a satisfactory agreement." The outcome was that on 3rd July 1916, the Irishmen were transferred to Danzig-Troyl camp. The NCOs were to retain their side-arms and their status in common with the ordinary German soldiers. The Irishmen of the ranks were to wear belts when in uniform.

No sooner had we arrived at Danzig than Hauptmann Nicolai began hostile operations. First it was this and then it was that. Such questions were asked as "Why the side-arms?" etc. I had arranged with von Boerley to allow our interpreters, Unteroffizier Hahn and Gefreiter Zerhusen, to accompany us in an advisory capacity. Herr Nicolai had to back down at every step of this game of military chess. The first move I made was to continue the everyday drill routine and soldier duty in the daily life of the former camp – in every possible way adhering to German commands on parade. Hauptmann Nicolai, I might mention, was an exact duplicate of that other Nicolai, major of the military secret service whose headquarters was in Bamberger Street, Berlin.[238] The Danzig member of that Russo-Teutonic family, when given a free hand, was most drastic in his actions.

Only a few weeks had elapsed before propositions were brought forward to send any Irishman who wished to work out into the surrounding towns and villages – Dirschau, Stolp, Stargard – in fact anywhere within the Danzig Military General Command, which covered a radius of about 100 miles and extended over most of the provinces of West Prussia and Pomerania. In mid-July, about a dozen or so were sent to selected jobs. I then demanded for them, as civilians, the full rights and freedom accorded to German workers, in accordance with

---

[238] It is not clear who Michael Keogh means here. The main obstacle to Casement and the brigade was Captain Nadolny of Section IIIb of the War Ministry but his first name was Rudolf and not Nicolai. Perhaps what is meant is that Nadolny, like Nicolai, was of a "Russo-Teutonic" background, as mentioned in the next sentence above.

assurances given me by Major von Boerley a month before in Berlin. In a few days, in the company of Corporal Hahn, I visited the different places where those men were employed and investigated conditions: food, pay and restrictions, if any. In a few instances the employers had imposed restrictions. These were rectified.

Corporal Hahn was a sympathetic Bavarian, who knew my arrangements with von Boerley and regarded his retention as interpreter as the result of my good offices. If it had not been so, Hahn would have had to soldier and go to some battlefront. In Zerhusen's case it was similar. In June 1915, he escaped going to the Russian front by reason of Sgt Julian Bailey having arranged with a German officer for Lance-Corporal Zerhusen's transfer to the Irish Brigade as interpreter. I was then on special duty and away from Irish Brigade HQ at Zossen.

Zerhusen and Monteith were responsible for Bailey being selected to accompany Casement. This was Zerhusen's return to Bailey for services rendered. Monteith will, I am sure, explain some day how he came to bring Bailey (or Beverley as he was then known) on U-Boat 19, and why he did not personally ensure the safety of Casement when the aid from the Kerry Volunteers was not forthcoming at 9 a.m. on Good Friday morning, to unload the Aud.[239]

Towards the end of July, I took charge of some 30 Irishmen working in various places in and around Dirschau, West Prussia.[240] In the gasworks of that town I worked myself, in charge of three or four tradesmen, on the erection of a new gas tank and pipe installation. Engineering being in my line, I greatly enjoyed this activity and new life, except that the fate of Casement proved a hovering cloud. The newspapers in Dirschau kept us in touch with reports respecting him. In the last days of July the tragic news filtered through: "To be hanged in Pentonville Jail on 3rd August."

---

[239] Monteith did indeed explain all these things in his book, *Casement's Last Adventure*. Bailey used the alias "Beverley" while in Germany. When captured after landing in Kerry, he placed himself at the disposal of the British authorities and, guaranteed his own immunity, testified against Casement. Casement did not hold this against him and, indeed, showed understanding for Bailey's effort to save himself. See Reid, *The Lives of Roger Casement*, p. 370.

[240] Quinlisk wrote that he "succeeded in getting a job as clerk in the small town of Dirschau. Fifteen members of the Irish Brigade worked at different jobs in Dirschau and seemed to get on well – so well that three or four settled with girls, as if they never intended to leave the country". See Quinlisk, "The German Irish Brigade" in *Land and Water*, 13th November 1919, p. 17.

On that sorrowful morning, his few faithful comrades in Dirschau had Mass offered up for his departed soul. The good Polish priest seemed deeply affected and in the short sermon he gave for the benefit of the congregation, who were mostly Polish or of Polish descent, pointed out that Ireland and Poland held in common the true qualities of martyrdom for the Catholic faith. We, his compatriots, were reconciled in fervently offering up the prayer: May the Lord have mercy on his soul.

During the winter of 1916 and throughout 1917, the Irishmen were at work in different capacities and were treated as soldiers, like any German soldier. This was the case where they preferred to remain in the Irish Brigade uniform of grey-green, with harp and shamrock emblazoned on its facings, and green, white and gold cockade-button bedecking the green headdress. In the event of the Irish soldiers desiring to wear "civvies", they were treated as the ordinary civilian population, with whom they lived in general on the very best of terms.

There were a few exceptions where their impetuous Irish nature would not allow ignorant and self-opinionated Germans to besmirch Irish insurrectionary fame, or where the Hanover-German and Anglo-Saxon cousinship displayed itself too aggressively. In such isolated places where one Irishman appeared alone, an attack seemed certain, but two or more were assured of respectful aloofness. Generally, comradeship seemed to reign supreme. Irishmen showed their prowess on many occasions on the inter-town and city football fields. This, with their voluntary participation in various German regimental football contests, conduced to intercourse and camaraderie.

They were also popular and useful in the boxing ring. Corporal Seán McGranaghan, Corporal Patrick Delamore, Lance-Corporal Willy McGrath, Volunteers O'Donoghue, Keogh, McSweeney, O'Kennedy, O'Curry, O'Callaghan, goalkeeper Michael Dowling, with the writer thrown in, constituted an excellent combination on their own. Their exploits in assisting the visitors to victory were highly appreciated on many a hard-fought sporting field in Danzig, Dirschau, Stargard, Marienburg and other West Prussian towns in the years 1916, 1917 and 1918. "*Der Kriegsfreiwilliger Irlander in Gruner Uniform,*" or "the Irish war volunteer soldiers in green uniform," were the recipients of many congratulations and the subjects of sporting toasts in many Prussian regimental messes and private amateur football club rooms.

But not everything in the garden was rosy. There were people connected with semi-German officialdom who were out to besmirch the men of the brigade and had previously sought to hamper the Irish Volunteer delegate to the Central Powers,

Commandant Joe Plunkett. To be candid, I must add that some of the most active behind this movement were not Germans, but men with professed Irish-Ireland sympathies in Berlin, and at least one of whom could claim Ireland as the land of his birth. Despicable as they were, tact had to be used in countering them. It is not my intention to dwell at length on the intrigues kept on foot by the West End dwellers of Berlin and the society hunters of Munich.

The one person who stood loyal to Casement's followers among the so-called *"Nachfolgers Kasement"* (Casement successors) in the German-Irish Society was an American-born lady with some Irish blood enriched by rebel blood from the Bluegrass of old Kentucky. Her name was Frau Bulliet Grabisch, the wife of a German officer. She, at least, never failed to take the part of the Irish lads, now no one's children. If Mrs Grabisch at any time doubted the conduct of Casement's soldiers, it was simply because prejudicial tales had reached her. She invariably dismissed such reports with the remark: "Well, and if so, I don't blame the lads. They have been treated right along most shamefully by people who did not seem to try to understand their true situation."

This campaign of covert vilification had always another phase. Ere Roger had paid the supreme penalty of true Irish patriotism, vague, sinister rumours were set afloat. "Who was Casement?" the intriguers asked. English cousinship among the German Upper 10 was poisoning the inner political circles. Again, it was asked: "Why had Sir Roger Casement kept aloof from the scions of the Potsdam Military Academy?" He dropped the title "Sir" on arrival in October 1914. Was he really true to Germany and her ideals in the war against Anglo-Saxondom? There were people in Germany – and Ireland too – during the period between April and August 1916 who asked the question: "Was Casement an English spy?" Fools, knaves! His Irish felon's grave is the answer, and the proof of his consuming love for Dark Rosaleen and the Irish people.

And all this while, what of the Irish Brigade? Their fate was foretold in the words of the very Irishman whom Roger had commissioned to succour them.[241] "Let them rot," he is alleged to have exclaimed. At this time, these particular people were prominent in German-Irish Society circles under the leadership of

---

[241] Presumably St John Gaffney is meant here. Both Keogh and Quinlisk have little good to say of him. Monteith, also, thought little of him. See Monteith, *Casement's Last Adventure*, p. 219.

Professor George Chatterton Hill.[242] They were being used as cat's paws by certain German military officials and Foreign Office quacks to reconsign "Casement's Irishmen" to the status of prisoners of war, in direct defiance of the 10-Point Agreement between Rory of the Gael and the German Under Secretary of State, Herr von Zimmermann. In short, it then seemed clear to me that a direct breach of that agreement was contemplated. Such perfidy had happened in former times on the continent, where foreign governments were agreeable to negotiate with Irish diplomats and soldiers when opposed to England in war time. This and other important tendencies I pointed out to St John Gaffney before he went to the United States towards the autumn of 1916, lest he should think it well to report rumours derogatory to the Irish volunteer unit in Germany.

One charge which came before a court of inquiry was of 1,000 marks being due to the military authorities for certain specified missing articles. It was proved at the inquiry that over 90 per cent of these thousand marks (nominally £50), surcharged against the Irishmen of Casement's Brigade while attached to the 203 Brandenburg Regiment at the military training camp, Zossen, from May 1915 to July 1916, represented "barrack damages" purely and simply. The Irish Brigade quarters at Zossen were of wooden construction – flooring and window frames of inferior material, glass too thin to withstand a Brandenburg winter – and all hurriedly built for temporary use. The huts were on sandy soil about 100 yards from the camp "sewage farm", infested with the most vile specimens of rodents.

The brigade canine mascot, "the Rebel" as the red-haired terrier was affectionately called by the Irishmen, was a very demon of a rat destroyer. Rebel was often seen in action, much to the delight of the boys. Seán Treacy, the big six-footer from Tipperary, would sit up half the night at the sport. These encounters caused great discomfort generally, and interruptions to the slumbers of the German and Irish soldiers. Seán would vehemently encourage the Rebel to another kill, and the piercing

---

[242] Dr Chatterton Hill was interned in the civilian internment camp at Ruhleben at the outbreak of the war. Through Casement's intercession and after agreeing to work for the Germans, he was released in late March or early April 1915. See Doerries, *Prelude to the Easter Rising*, pp 95-7. It is clear from what follows that Keogh had a low opinion of him.

He was a former professor of sociology in Geneva. He wrote to Casement in mid-March 1915 that he was an Irish nationalist and anti-British but, when Casement secured his release, Chatterton Hill seems to have played somewhat of a mischievous role. See Ó Síocháin, *Roger Casement: Imperialist, Rebel, Revolutionary*, p. 412.

cries of a cornered rat made music *minus* the harmony. So, the Irish Brigade barracks was a veritable rat-burrow, the wooden supports, floors and foundation being gnawed into pulp. It did not, therefore, take much inspection to prove a true bill against "a barracks-damages account". The remaining 10 per cent was allotted to barracks' bedding deficiencies.

Mr T. St John Gaffney did not understand the military term, "barrack damages". He took the minority item, "blankets", into account first, although it appeared last on the list. He would more easily have fallen into line were it a profit-and-loss account plus double entry before the prevailing ascendancy power behind an election return, and which acclaimed the shady merits of a Tammany Hall candidate emerging from yet another victorious personation balloting process, due to the dexterous energy of the gas-house political gang in the underworld regions of Lower Manhattan, Chinatown and The Bowery in New York.

I have wondered at times and since those World War days in Germany about St John Gaffney and his sojourn in the land of the almighty dollar and Wall Street war-capital speculation – and this is what I have pondered on: Had this Irishman from the City of the Broken Treaty[243] adhered to the august principles of fair play concerning the commission placed on his shoulders by the Irish patriot martyr? It is most evident now that his confidential pow-wows were mere attempts of stupid Yankee bluff and tomfoolery. Gaffney certainly did not fail to tell Clan na Gael and the Irish Sons of Freedom[244] leaders in the autumn of 1916 that Casement's Irish volunteers in Germany were wallowing in the fat of the land and that our sublime isolation radiated material prosperity and mental serenity.

The ex-Consul General of Munich went to the US and came back but he seemed not to bother how his exiled fellow countrymen were progressing. In any event, the Irishmen did not seem to mind such undue inattentiveness. The majority of Casement's followers had long since taken Gaffney, Hill and company's number, i.e., wartime political place hunters of the darkest type. My confidential work with my late Chief had given me great scope in finding out exactly who was who in Berlin and Munich political and military circles. It paid to take one's time in

---

[243] The city is Limerick and the Treaty of Limerick 1691 ended the Williamite War in Ireland. There were really two treaties, one military, one civil. The provisions of the civil treaty were not honoured.

[244] What is probably meant is the organisation known as the Friends of Irish Freedom which was set up in the US in 1916 and was dominated by Clan na Gael. The organisation campaigned to defeat President Wilson's bid for the presidency in 1916 but failed.

sending a home-run shot at the heads of the then German-Irish Society warmongers and profiteers with luxurious flats in Prinzregentenstrasse in the West End of Munich. (A great change, no doubt, compared to the internee's verminous plank-bed bunk in Ruhleben civilian interment camp.)

Listen to Professor Chatterton Hill's answer to the question asked him early in 1915 by your humble servant in Roger's presence. "Will you join the Irish Brigade in the hope of getting the opportunity to fight for Ireland's independence?" The answer: "Owing to physical disabilities, I don't think I would be capable of becoming an efficient soldier, but if I can help in the literary defence of Irish rights to freedom, well I am prepared to go all out in my endeavours." Roger remarked some short time later when going over certain details with Joe Plunkett and myself: "There is Hill, for instance, who offers his services in certain capacities, most valuable no doubt, but to my mind the Irishman who would turn down the offer of taking a rifle in his hand for Ireland's cause is not worthy of the name of Irishman." So much for Professor Hill, the namesake of Sir George Hill, the betrayer of Wolfe Tone in 1798.[245]

Towards the end of 1916 and throughout 1917 the Irishmen of the brigade were mostly employed in Dirshcau, Stolp and surrounding coast-line towns along the Baltic Sea. Nothing of any great importance happened except an occasional set-to with Commandant Nicolai, whose camp staff and interpreters of King George's English language tried to make things hard for those "Rebel Irelanders". Nicolai ran foul of my tactics more than once, and at no time did I accept defeat except in a case where, for the time, there was no other alternative. I usually had the town military commander on my side. If not, it meant putting the live wires in operation by communicating with Major von Boerley, General Staff, Army GHQ, Berlin. A note from him squashed further contention as to the Irishmen's correct status as co-equals with the ordinary German soldiers. Nicolai would fain have the mere Irish as his slaves and on the ordinary footing of prisoners of war.

In this he was greatly helped by the all-too-docile Irish Brigade interpreters, Sergeant Hahn and Corporal Zerhusen, who dreaded this sordid specimen of a prisoner-of-war camp commandant. These unfortunate German NCOs were wont to

---

[245] The French expedition with which Wolfe Tone returned to Ireland was defeated by the English navy. For some days afterwards Tone, who was in French military uniform, was not recognised among the other French military prisoners until George Hill, who had been a student in Trinity College with him, saw him and betrayed him to the English.

carry out his bidding as far as possible without making it hard on the Irishmen in the towns where they were employed. Major von Schultz, town commander of Dirschau, on one occasion fairly put the wind up Herr Nicolai. The latter wanted to veto the permission given by the major to the Irishmen to go to Danzig, 30 miles away, "on pass" – the pass bearing the signature of the town commander. Major Schultz, an old campaigner of 1870, was forced to acquaint Berlin GHQ and ascertain the correct procedure. The facts that I had already given him confirmed the Irishmen's right to absolute freedom in the matter. Apart from all this, an occasional trip to Berlin GHQ helped me to unmask Nicolai's truculence towards my comrades-at-arms.

Major Schultz of Dirschau gave me full power to act in conjunction with his commands while in Dirschau Military Command. In my capacity as *Feldwebel* (Sergeant-Major), I should demand all the respect due to a German army sergeant-major and assist the town sergeant-major in carrying out the jurisdiction and military supervision over the Irishmen either as civilians or when in uniform. A similar provision operated in case I became connected with the duties of German soldiers; otherwise the guard-room was the place for all.

I never looked for trouble but it sometimes happened to cross my path through the conduct of German or of Irish soldiers, and I was often compelled to use strong persuasion. For instance, café brawls arising from drunken carousals ended in a dark cell, with the usual punishment for grievous breach of Prussian military discipline. It happened sometimes that German soldiers were not prepared to acknowledge my rank, as in the case of the German sergeant-major. First offenders were warned, but those who transgressed for a second time were made to click the heels with upraised hand at the double. To show fight meant to stick them up. A march to the nearest military guard-room followed and there was seldom further trouble.

In relating these episodes in the life of an Irish soldier in the midst of the greatest military camp this world has witnessed, I also recall a scene not easy for an Irish volunteer soldier to forget. It happened in February 1916 in Berlin. Captain Monteith and I were ordered to the Prussian capital for an important conference. It was noon-day and the Prussian Guards were marching down Strasse Unter den Linden, with music in full blast, en route to mount guard on the Kaiser's palace. The German officer in charge of the guards mounting company paid the usual compliment to the Irish officer in his jacket green. Said the captain to me, as the Prussian soldiers drew near: "Look out, Sergeant-Major. Watch the Prussian Guards ploughing up the ground for an Irish

Volunteer in the World War. Why England's power cannot demand such a privilege!"

CHAPTER 11: The Second "German Plot" 1918

Before the transfer of the brigade to Danzig, I had been approached and asked to nominate someone who would be a good German speaker and writer, as such a person was required in the counter-espionage section attached to the Foreign Office in Berlin. I nominated Sergeant Michael O'Toole, previously mentioned as a former civil servant in Dublin. He was a fluent Gaelic scholar, French being a second language as a second-division Irish civil servant, and he had become a German linguist by this time.

On 12th April 1918 occurred the capture of the "mysterious Irishman" by the Anglo-Irish forces at Ennistymon, Co. Clare, just as he boarded a train for the Irish capital. Immediately following this event came the report of what was known, during the Easter recess at Westminster, as "the Second German Plot". The man of mystery had landed safely from a collapsible rowing-boat launched from a German submarine.

The capture would never have been made were it not for the suspicion created by the stranger's attempt to exchange Dutch money at the village bank in Ennistymon. The exchange of money being necessary at all was due to the stupidity of German officialdom in Wilhelmstrasse, Berlin. In the bustle of their intriguing methods, they had set a veritable death-trap in the path of the already very perilous undertaking. Why was English money not part of the absolutely necessary equipment for such a journey?

The captured stranger was dispatched to the Tower of London, and it took Scotland Yard a full week to identify him, with the assistance of other Irishmen, exchanged wounded Irish soldiers from the Irish camp at Limburg an der Lahn in Germany. The mysterious Irishman turned out to be Sergeant Joe Dowling of Casement's Irish Brigade.

In December 1917, certain advances, in the way of plans, were made to the Germans from Irish quarters in the United States and from Ireland itself. Captain Nadolny, Major von Pfluke and others, with the Admiralty representative, set about the matter on hands in an earnest fashion. In due time I was apprised of the details by my old friend on the General Staff who was wont to notify me as to future events, so that we had become old hands at summarising possibilities. The idea was to procure the services of an Irishman, preferably a member of the brigade, who could speak his native Gaelic fluently. A most suitable candidate was eventually chosen (as I had recommended) – an intelligent and daring non-commissioned officer of the brigade: Sergeant Michael O'Toole, former Gaelic League organiser, familiar with the western seaboard of Ireland and who, besides, had played no small part as an IRB agent in the English army for about a year prior to the World War.

Early in January 1918, Micheál was called to Berlin, where he underwent a rigid course in instruction in the duties to be required of him on the mission for which he was intended. The Bamberger Strasse school of instruction was no easy academy from which to graduate or obtain a certificate of efficiency under the watchful eye of some of Europe's most noted secret-service experts. Neither was O'Toole an easy nut to crack or one to be gulled into pitfalls where work of strategy was concerned. The genial Irish sergeant had for a long time mapped out how to hit straight at England's power and at the same time damp the home fires of Britain. He found a medium in the word "coal". It would not be just to my former comrade-at-arms to divulge the details of his plan. But of one thing I am certain: his admiration for the German people ensured their spokesmen his full confidence and resulted in a free exchange of schemes mutually conceived, and calculated to release Ireland from the bondage of centuries.

The German scheme of 1918 was, briefly, to get into touch with the Gaelic-speaking population of the western seaboard of Ireland, win their sympathy, establish a submarine base and secure an outlet from the mouth of the lordly Shannon to the Aran Isles. The scheme, inspired by the ever-present danger of conscription for Ireland,[246] had for its main object the wholesale smuggling of war material into Ireland with a view to creating a healthy military diversion in this country, and so keeping Britain occupied while the German army, under the guidance of General Hindenburg,[247] was smashing its way to the coast of France at the height of the big offensive in the spring and early summer of 1918. It was the German hope that, provided with sufficient arms secretly landed from submarines, the Sinn Féin army would create such a situation as would divert tens of thousands of British troops from the Western Front and materially assist a victorious German offensive onwards to Calais and the Straits of

---

[246] Because of the great German spring offensive on the Western Front in 1918, the British cabinet was seriously considering extending conscription to Ireland.

[247] Field Marshal Paul von Hindenburg (1847-1934) was appointed German supreme commander (Chief of the General Staff) in 1916.

Dover where, from this base of hostilities, the "Big Bertha"[248] and 42-centimetre guns would be able to launch the final attack on the shores of England and strike with the horror of a death knell the quickened ears of London.

In March 1918, the German-Irish Society announced a St Patrick's Night festival and dinner to be held in Adlon Hotel, Unter den Linden, Berlin. Herr Baron von Stein, German War Minister, was to preside. A few of Casement's followers were to be invited. Four names were mentioned in dispatches: Sergeant-Major Keogh and Sergeants O'Toole, Kavanagh and Dowling. The last was the only one ultimately favoured as a guest of honour. The day following this ensemble, leading German newspapers were flowing over with war news of the great German-Irish festival at the Adlon Hotel. Kaiser Wilhelm II and Field Marshal von Hindenburg sent telegrams of regret for non-attendance, sincerest congratulations, bright hopes and best wishes for the success of the German-Irish Society in Ireland's interest.

There were few "good Irishmen and true" at this St Patrick's Day festival: the only one with an Irish heart was Sergeant Dowling. The others were purely and simply "political internationalists" of the "run with the hare and hunt with the hounds" type. This, of course, does not include all the ladies present: some of them were German to the core, others of the cosmopolitan variety. Looking down my diary, I find but two ladies who were staunch Irelanders: Frau Hand Zerhusen and Frau Bulliet Grabisch, the first the daughter of the Fenian poet, Peter Hand. The German husband of this Irishwoman was official interpreter of the Irish Brigade, and, with his Foreign Office relation, had done no good day's work for Ireland in double-crossing the initial plans of O'Toole. But in this, Daddy Zerhusen had done as he previously did when he furthered and promoted the selection of Bailey.

Still, the redoubtable Irishman in the submarine redeemed the good name of the Irish Brigade when he outwitted the Welsh Wizard and Galloper Smith. Joe's "not a word" policy of serene silence helped Mr Larry Ginnell to taunt the life out of the empire shifters on the lower benches at Westminster in the spring of 1918. Dowling had no documents in his possession; "they could not be produced," said the defending counsel. The communications were verbal. Lord Birkenhead would have it otherwise, until Jack Jones MP put the kibosh on the Galloper's

---

[248] From the German *Dicke Bertha* (literally "Fat Bertha"), it was a heavy mortar-like howitzer used by the Germans in the First World War. It was said to be named after the wife of its Krupps manufacturer. It was a portable, 42-centimetre weapon, which fired heavy shells and had a maximum range of nine miles.

German Plot, No. 2.[249] "No case" without production of documents.

Despite this, Dowling was sentenced to death, but the sentence was commuted to penal servitude for life. During his six years in his nine different English prison cells, let it be said that he never divulged a single secret in regard to his mission from Germany or of his adventurous trip to Ireland in a submarine. He also underwent a lengthy hunger strike at Wandsworth Prison in 1920 with the lads from home then interned there for loving Ireland better than themselves. The morning after his release, I gripped his Irish hand in freedom on the peat sod of his native territory of Laois.[250]

When I heard of the capture of the mysterious Irishman in Clare, I was attached to the Flying Corps aerodrome workshops at Stolp, the birthplace of the Prussian Field Marshal Blucher. A monument to the real victor of Waterloo, in his red hussar uniform, stands in the market square of his native town on the Baltic coastline of Pomerania, with its adjoining Polish Corridor territory.[251] On daily passing this memorial, I often wondered if this great soldier had not brought on his German guns and saved the Duke of Wellington's mixed forces from annihilation by Napoleon's "Old Guard",[252] how would it have fared with Britain and its grip on my own fair land? To my mind it mattered not if England's enemy were the Turk, if the Russian Bear or the Yellow Peril from the East proved the vanquisher of the British Empire, because they would be the friends of Ireland and of all true Irishmen, for they would bring us nearer to see, and live in, an unfettered and really united Ireland from the centre to the sea – an eventful day that I hope to live to see. Off, then, with the yoke that binds us, so that we may see the consummation of the old

---

[249] As Attorney General in 1916, F.E. "Galloper" Smith worked hard to secure the conviction of Roger Casement. He was given the title Lord Birkenhead in 1919. Jack Jones (1873-1941), originally from Nenagh, Co. Tipperary, was a Labour MP from 1918 to 1940. He was described by *Time* magazine as "the wittiest man in the House of Commons".

[250] For details about what happened to Joe Dowling following his landing on the west coast of Ireland in April 1918, see www.dowlingfamily.info/i1918su2.htm

[251] The 1919 Treaty of Versailles gave the territory which separated East Prussia from Pomerania to the newly independent Poland and it was called the "Polish Corridor". It gave Poland access to the sea but the port city of Danzig was made a "free city", under the protection of the League of Nations, rather than being put under Polish control.

[252] The Old Guard was the name given to veterans of the French army's Imperial Guard under Napoleon; they had served him since his earliest campaigns and were among the best soldiers in Europe.

Gaelic proverb: "To every cow its calf and to every land its people."[253]

In the middle of April 1918, it happened that one solitary Irishman, cast ashore in a collapsible boat, put the fear of God into England's ministers, including David Lloyd George, champion of the Boers against England's greed for Kimberley gold dust.[254] The new German offensive on the Western Front compelled proud Albion's admiralty lords to issue a last reserve and sealed orders envelope to every available sea-going tramp steamer, directing them to be prepared to proceed at once to bring home to Blighty her countless mercenary legions of Red, Yellow, White, Black and Tan races recruited from Hong Kong to Mandalay, Sandy Row to Whitechapel, and from the Morri Isles to the Congo. No Man's Land on the Western Front had become too hot for Lord Haig's[255] highly coloured and supposedly civilised warriors.

So nerve strained were the strings behind the powers reclining on the pin-cushions of Whitehall that the Sinn Féin leaders, male and female, were arrested wholesale throughout the length and breadth of Inisfáil.[256]

I at once took an open road to Danzig, furnished with a military pass from a well-wishing German officer who knew the Irish question from A to Z. He was a flying ace who braved the anti-aircraft guns of England's watchdogs more than once and had come out a victor not less than 80 times in deadly combat above the clouds with the Allies' aces. A sportsman through and through, he understood thoroughly my propositions, as laid out for his scrutiny and confirmation, before being submitted to the authorities in Berlin. It was possible, in April 1918, to connect up with Ireland by air route. German technique had thus far advanced then, and still continues to maintain its lead, despite the disarmament clauses of the Versailles Treaty.[257] The fearless

---

[253] In one of the earliest historical rulings on copyright, in the 6th century, the Irish High King, Diarmaid, ruled that "As to every cow its calf, so to every book its copy." The ruling was made against St Columcille.

[254] As a back-bench Liberal MP, Lloyd George vehemently opposed the Boer War 1899-1902.

[255] Field Marshal Douglas Haig (1861-1928) took over command of the British Expeditionary Force from Lord French in December 1915.

[256] Dowling's capture was the pretext for the British authorities proclaiming a second "German Plot" in Ireland (the first was the attempt to supply guns for the 1916 Rising) and arresting larges numbers of leading members of Sinn Féin and the Irish Volunteers.

[257] Under the Terms of the Treaty of Versailles, Germany was forbidden to have a military airforce.

flying captain gave me definite instructions and a free military pass to Berlin over the Danzig route. An eight-hour ride on a Warsaw-Lodz-Koenigsberg-Danzig-Berlin Express landed me safely back at Anhalter Banhof railway station, Berlin.

The men of the brigade and I could have continued working at civilian tasks in West Prussia until the war's end but when the opportunity arose to see military action again, some of us decided to take it. Two other men and I joined the Machine-Gun Company of the 16th Bavarian Infantry Regiment at Munich at the beginning of May 1918. I held the rank that was given to me in Casement's Irish Brigade. The other man was a corporal and the third was a private. This was a purely voluntary action on all our parts and was thoroughly understood as such by our Bavarian Regiment comrades in arms.

CHAPTER 12: The Last of the Wild Geese on the Continent in the World War

The truest words I ever heard were once uttered by Rory of the Gael early in the summer of 1915, in the presence of Commandant Joseph Plunkett, Fr Nicholson, Fr Crotty OP, Captain Boehm and myself, at an important conversation after our experience of the self-styled "Irish" soldiers then especially concentrated at Limburg an der Lahn for one ulterior purpose: to offer a fighting chance to the misguided Irishmen found within the ranks of England's mercenary forces at all times, peace or war.

"They know no better," he said, "having seen little but pure West British garrisonism at the street corners of Irish villages and towns during their youth. Those poor underfed creatures were denied the right to live clean and healthy lives. Their own fellow countrymen who hobnobbed with the squire-settlers had set them no other example. A loaf of bread and a cup of tea constituted the only substantial food they derived from their odd day's work. The lucky ones, with regular employment, were ever and sadly in the minority.

"In war time, and with the British lion threatened, the usual procedure was the lockout and 'Join up with John Bull or starve altogether'. The average Irish-Ireland employer was generally so hard pressed that help from such a quarter was out of the question. The emigrant ship often helped, but where was 'the cost' to come from now? There was but one alternative – and it surely was exploited by the agents of England – 'Take the shilling, Pat. Fight for Britain's glory, boys.' It broke many an Irish mother's heart but never can it be said that any self-respecting Irish mother willingly sent her son to don the red coat of England. In most cases, hunger and want in Ireland got the British recruiting sergeant his beer-money and proud Albion her best soldiers: 'the strapping lads from the Emerald Isle'."

It is pure narrow-mindedness to scoff at the majority of Irishmen who joined the English army in pre-World War days. False prophets and speculating politicians worked overtime in Ireland to augment the English army during the first two years of that war. Casement's great aim was to stop it; most of all did he want to prevent conscription. For the secret diplomacy of Downing Street was quite familiar to him.

In a further passage, he stated in relation to Irishmen prepared to go "all out" against their old enemy: "England's government fears not the Irishman who thunders forth empty phrases from the party platform. The one thing England's ministers tremble at is *action*. In determining their methods, all true Irishmen must bear one thing constantly in mind. If their efforts prove unsuccessful, the inevitable result in the generality of cases is the hangman's noose or an Irish felon's cell for life."

I took part in the big German offensive on the Western Front from May to August 1918 with the 16th Bavarian Infantry Regiment. In August the Prussians of the Nicolai gang ran me to earth after a four months' search. Some of that time I had spent with gallant Bavarian comrades in the front-line trenches, when modern warfare had become hell on earth, with practically 36 nations of the White, Black, Red and Yellow races taking part. I was not satisfied till the opportunity given me was fulfilled; at times, however, I had to shut off "the feed" to my machine-gun owing to the sickening horror of the process, shooting off at the rate of half a thousand a minute, and mowing down a retreating enemy like locusts before a hurricane on the African veldt.

Previously I had contracted the war flu, aggravated by trench fever, which went far towards shattering my usually robust constitution. War rations, even in times of abundance, find out all the defects in a soldier's frame. I lay in hospital at Namur, Belgium and later at Munich for a few weeks, and had overcome the critical stage. One day a Bavarian Guards officer visited me with full information from the Berlin War Office. This officer had no great love for the Prussians; few Bavarians had. The Berlin coterie and Kommandant Nicolai demanded my return to Danzig camp, a grave breach against the prevailing military discipline being entered against my name – desertion of my unit. The document read over to me did not state what "unit". We had been known in Danzig as *Der Kriegsfreiwillager Irlander*, "the War Volunteer Irishmen".

However, what really transpired during our conversation was what procedure I would take to defend the charge. My Bavarian regiment officers were prepared to keep me at Munich despite orders from Berlin or Danzig. Would I agree to such a course and fight the whole matter there in Bavaria? I took a few days to consider. Firstly, I knew the end of the war was approaching; secondly, I felt like fighting those concerned at Berlin and Danzig on their own ground. It would make the fight all the sweeter in the event of success, a point I was somewhat bent on.

In the end, after consultation with a few officer friends, one of whom came with me to Berlin, we interviewed at the War Office my old and trusted benefactor, Major von Boerley. A few days

fixed things just as I wanted them, and afforded me all the needed support in finally sending home the "grand finale" to the clique in Danzig. I cooked their Irish stew before I left Berlin, having placed all the necessary information in the hands of the then German Prime Minister, Herr Baron Brockdorff von Rantzau.[258]

Kommandant Nicolai foamed on seeing me, and further felt that the presence of the Bavarian officer, who informed him of his negotiations with me in Berlin. "But," expostulated Nicolai, "the necessary charges have already been preferred against Der Kriegsfreiwillager Irlander, Feldwebel[259] Keogh, and the case must go on as ordered by the 17th Prussian Army Corps HQ." I demanded my status as a soldier and co-equal with my rank: "a prisoner under open arrest", with the ordinary freedom enjoyed by any Feldwebel of the German army, by virtue of my then having as side-arms the sword of Kaiser Wilhelm II, similar to a commissioned officer of His Imperial Majesty's forces. Kommandant Nicolai was not the superior officer in this deal, the Bavarian staff captain, wearing the red badge of a General Staff officer, held the whip hand, and I could visit the city of Danzig in company with an equal rank of sergeant-major from the battalion of Prussian infantry to which the Irelanders of Casement were attached for soldiers' duty.

The acquaintance of an Alsace-Lorraine sergeant-major of the Infantry Reserve Schlawe Battalion 17/16, who was my escort, was of much advantage also. We spent many joyous hours together during the next few weeks: the end of August and beginning of September 1918. The fine music of a Danzig café kept our hearts buoyant but I was not quite over the war-epidemic flu. I fought it absent-mindedly and in the end it beat me, inflammation of the lungs setting in. I was carted away to the garrison hospital at Danzig, where I spend many delirious hours. The German Stabs-Artz (staff doctor) consoled me with the information that it would be better for me to see my clergy. Well, I did see the good Catholic chaplain, and he thought fit to administer the Last Sacraments. I felt resigned to it all. The head doctor at the Danzig garrison hospital was a practitioner of world-wide experience, and had lectured in Dublin hospitals and throughout England. He spoke to me in English when he knew I came from the Green Isle. The result of his examination was an

---

[258] Ulrich Graff von Brockdorff-Rantzau (1869-1928) was a German diplomat and became the first Foreign Minister of the Weimar Republic in December 1918. The German Prime Minister or Chancellor at the time Michael Keogh is referring to was Count Georg von Herling (he was Chancellor from November 1917 to September 1918).

[259] Sergeant.

assurance that "the old Irish heart was as sound as a bell". I had remained too long on my feet, a tendency peculiar to most Irishmen.

So for five days and nights, I tossed and turned in high fever of latest war type, known then in the German language as *Schutzengraben Krankheit* or trench fever. In the many lapses of its crisis, it was a case of "going over the top" again and again. After a month of excruciation torture, I was once more on all fours. When I again took to using Shanks' mare, my 10 stone and a half had reduced to well under the feather-weight scale,[260] but fresh air soon restored my strength. Moreover, my visitors were many and genial, compatriot Irishmen galore. Catholic priests were constantly visiting the hospital, and we would sit in the garden for hours going over Ireland's tale of woe. The good bishop of Danzig had reason to be proud of his Irish forefathers and the Wild Geese on the continent after the infamous Treaty of Limerick: his name – Bishop Count O'Rourke – betokened nothing less.

The first week in October 1918 saw me moving about again and still on the warpath. I had an account from Berlin, from Major von Boerley, also one from Dr O'Curry in Munich. My wishes were carried out to the letter. Interpreter Zerhusen visited me also – to say goodbye as he was leaving Danzig-Troyl for good, on transfer to some active service unit then at Spandau, Berlin. He seemed full of remorse for having to leave the "Old Brigade" service, but I comforted him by remarking if he had not played the henchman to Nicolai all would have remained better. He retorted that I had not heard the last of Nicolai. A hot time awaited me were his parting words.

In a few days, a telephone message arrived at the hospital. I was to attend at General Command, 17th Army Corps HQ. Court of Inquiry papers were served on me to appear that day before a *Kriegsgericht*, a court-martial. Nicolai had instituted charges against me for "deserting my unit" – the Irish Brigade attached to Lansturm Infantry Battalion 17/16 Danzig – and of joining without permission the Bavarian Garde Leib Regiment, Munich. He was not present, his astute personage being represented by a camp officer. Evidence having been read over, I was asked what I had to say; an official military interpreter was present for my assistance but I refused his services, being sufficiently conversant with the German language.

The court-martial officers were fully satisfied. The sham trial went on, cross-fire mingling with flank movements. It had

---

[260] In boxing, this is nine stones or under.

reached the juncture where Kommandant Nicolai was called upon to explain certain breaches against the actual orders of the General Staff, Army GHQ, Berlin. The presiding officer seemed greatly indignant at the non-attendance of Camp Commandant Nicolai. This action alone indicated a guilty conscience, and had the effect I sought, with the help of documentary evidence in my possession, some of which dated back to July 1916.

The court officers did not even retire to the private-council chamber; a few hurried notes were exchanged, the verdict "honourably exonerated" was uttered, and I was congratulated by a grip of a true soldier's hand. I requested a written and signed declaration of freedom, a credential most readily given by the president of the court and his officer associates. Yet another decision was arrived at simultaneously – the censuring of the absent commandant for daring to stop my weekly pay as a Feldwebel of the regular German army.

The end of October 1918 saw my parting with Sergeant Mick O'Toole in Berlin. The hopes we had cherished had gone with the fortunes of war. Madam Germania had become impoverished by prolonged warfare; her enemies were too numerous. What of Rory's Irish soldiers? Where were they to go? Could they expect aid from the German government to get over the herring pond?[261] This was doubtful, with a new Socialist Party getting a growing grip on the very throat of a war-weary German populace. I came to the conclusion that it was "every man for himself and God for us all". The majority of the Germans, official and semi-official, that one came into contact with seemed to be in a fog as to what was going to happen in their own political atmosphere. Some hinted very pointedly at red revolution,[262] and this was a possibility I had long visualised, from the way Russian agencies did their work throughout the Fatherland during the last six months of the World War. A few Germans still had faith in Wilson's Fourteen Points,[263] but those innocents knew very little of the methods of the European diplomats then expounding inter-Allied policy.

---

[261] That is, to the United States.

[262] Quinlisk also refers to the air being "heavily laden with rumours of ... revolution" in Germany in the autumn of 1918. See "The German Irish Brigade," in *Land and Water*, 13th November 1919.

[263] In January 1918, President Woodrow Wilson of America enunciated his "Fourteen Points" which he intended as a blueprint for a just and enduring peace in Europe after the First World War. The points were one of the reasons that persuaded the Central Powers to surrender in November 1918 as they seemed to promise them fair treatment in the postwar settlement. They were to be disappointed in this expectation.

My duty, I clearly understood, was to stick to the Irishmen of Casement's Brigade, despite the wavering of all then in Berlin, Irish or German. One Sinn Féin delegate from Ireland had arrived at the Prussian capital in the beginning of October 1918. Towards the end of the month, I accidentally found this out at the Foreign Office, Wilhelmstrasse, the German-Irish Society having withheld the information from me for over a week. I said nothing but awaited my opportunity to interview the Irishman "on the run" in Berlin, as I was told on pressing the point to an issue. It was most displeasing to be deprived of the opportunity of greeting a fellow-countryman in exile by a clique actuated by self-interest and the instinct to "play safe", and Irish neither in name nor birth with the exception of St John Gaffney.

When I did manoeuvre an enforced exchange with the "representative of Young Ireland", I just opened up, not forgetting to intervene on behalf of my recruited followers of Roger Casement and Commandant Joe Plunkett. He would see what could be done. The necessary steps would be taken with the Irish leaders at home and in the United States. The most singular feature of my interview with this Irish delegate to Germany in 1918 was his reluctance to give me his name; he was then sojourning in the suite of West-End rooms deluxe of a prominent German-Irish Society personage. I asked if that was part of the instructions imparted to him in Berlin. His answer typified the usual Irishman's caution, in one sense correct: He was shortly returning to Ireland, and I could understand the rest.

I returned post haste to Danzig and reported at hospital off recuperation furlough. It was my most earnest resolution to stick to the men who in May 1915 answered our appeal to join Casement and Plunkett. The first days of bleak November 1918 saw me once more in the midst of my countrymen at Danzig-Troyl. Most of the Irish soldiers were still in the surrounding towns of Dirschau and Stolp; about 20 were then attached to the Lansturm Infantry Battalion, Danzig 17/16, Prussian Army Corps. The rumours that filled the air of the great unknown were numerous in the few days prior to 11th November, Armistice Day in France, which eventuated in a passive revolution throughout Germany. An exception was a brush up on the Kiel Canal where sailors of the navy mutinied when asked to go and fight it out with the British navy, sink or swim. It is not my place to comment on this action on the part of German sailors, but this I will say: if it were the case of an Irish navy, manned by Irishmen, it would have risked "death or victory" sooner than face the dishonour subsequently at Scapa Flow and other ports of surrender.

On the first day of the German Proclamation for the Social Revolution, and the dethroning of the Imperial Government, the

Soldiers' Council HQ had issued edicts against the further use of the Kaiser's insignia in the army and navy. All officers and other ranks were to discard the Hohenzollern badge of office from their uniforms. A People's General Meeting was called to assemble at the great market place in Danzig city, at the mouth of the fast-flowing Vistula. Socialist and democratic speakers were to address the multitudes from many platforms, and the soldiers of the German people were to observe strict discipline and passiveness. Further, the millions of Allied prisoners were not to be allowed to break loose; in other words, it was to be business as usual.

The Irish soldiers attended the meeting: Sergeant Kavanagh, Volunteer Forde, Volunteer O'Callaghan and I being elected to act as delegates of Casement's Brigade to the German Soldiers' Council General Committee. Petty Officer Weber of the Baltic submarine flotilla acted as temporary president of this organised revolutionary committee. The Irish delegates were duly allotted their seats on the main platform in the market square in Danzig.

On being asked to address the meeting as an Irishman who had taken the side of Germany in the World War, I briefly summed up my reasons as a firm believer in the honest, hard-working and disciplined German people. The German soldiers of the nation had defended its people's integrity and their just right to live in peace and pursue commercial enterprise, despite the enormous odds they faced from the hireling and multi-coloured legions of 30 nations. Germany and its people had deserved well to elect whatever course was most desirable and compatible with rule by the majority. For its people en masse, a united stand in the future would eventually decide who won the World War. The oft-used proverb would then become a living reality: "When robbers fall out, honest folk get their own." *Deutschland Hoch in Ehre und uber alles.* (Germany high in honour and all things.) The meeting ended quietly but with enthusiasm. The people seemed joyous: if anything, the disciplinary spirit which ruled the day exhorted them to be just and fear not.

On my claiming that the military prisoners then under punishment for petty offences against militarism should be released, the presiding officer agreed. The German naval presiding officer and I placed ourselves in joint command; with the assistance of a fine military band and accompanied by comrades, Irish and German, we marched through the principal streets of Danzig to the garrison military prison. The strains of music gave a cheering set-off to our act of mercy. The populace were kept in the dark as to our actual mission; in fact, the soldiers themselves were not in the know until we had arrived there. The joy of those unfortunate war-weary soldiers knew no bounds on their release into freedom. Two Irish soldiers were among the many sufferers. The prison record book was strictly scrutinised prior to their release. In this way, no dangerous criminal was set free to endanger the public safety.

The first day of the German revolution in Danzig will ever remain a lively memory with me, one to feel proud of, and justly so. Mankind was created to enjoy freedom, not to be enslaved to petty transgressions against the militant pomp of class rule, irrespective of the distinct representative policy it may derive its authority from. The law of the masses, as administered by their elected legislators, is often more ill-considered than it is advisable in relation to the soldiers of any particular nation. The rules laid down in their name are in most part admittedly not in compliance with the people's wishes, but they are, nevertheless, the supreme commands issued by the people's self-elected rulers.

During the first few days of the revolution at Danzig, my time was mostly taken up with negotiating with the Head Council of Danzig Soldiers' Councils regarding the future of the Irish soldiers of Casement's contingent, and the arrangement arrived at was free railway warrants to any province in the interior of Germany. In a few days, Danzig was to be occupied under armistice provisions by a squadron of the British navy, so the Irish should vacate hurriedly. The task was not as easy as one might surmise but just the same it had to be done. So, a German name was given to each Irish soldier, on his Soldiers' Council passport, entitling him to go to any part of unoccupied Germany. A week's ration was handed out to every Irish soldier reporting to HQ Irish Brigade, Danzig-Troyl in addition to a suit of civvies and a free railway voucher to the furthest town in the south of Germany if he so wished.

I advised each one to proceed to Munich, Bavaria, to report at my old Bavarian Guards barracks, and await my coming there. Volunteer Jerry O'Callaghan had now become my aide-de-camp, the only person who had the secrets of my movements during the preceding six months' activity as an actual German soldier. It might not have been prudent to let others know as much and, indeed, events were to prove the wisdom of this course. We were the last Irishmen who left Danzig on the morning the English squadron came into Danzig bay on the Baltic coast. And so on to Munich and a two days' train journey, where we found our comrades in barracks with the Bavarian soldiers, excepting some who had remained in Berlin and joined the army of the new republic.

We set to work immediately at Munich. Dr O'Curry advised me to seek an interview with the new Socialist Prime Minister of Bavaria, Herr Kurt Eisner.[264] A selected delegation of four Irishmen came with me and we were accompanied by Dr Charles O'Curry, but it proved to no avail. Herr Kurt Eisner, the Jewish Socialist and extreme Internationalist Prime Minister of the Bavarian Republic turned us down. "Oh, what would the Allies say if the new German government supported Irishmen who were the dupes of the former imperialistic government of the Hohenzollerns? You ask the impossible, my dear Irelanders." I pressed the Israelite to afford my comrades time even to get into touch with the homeland or the overseas organisations. The Irish soldiers will be willing to do duty in the new army of Bavaria! "No, anything but that! Seek civil employment." Yes, but where, with the millions of German soldiers returning home to their former positions? A blank was drawn with Kurt Eisner, but it was no blank ammunition that was used not so long afterwards when Kurt met his reward.

The same delegates waited upon Mr St John Gaffney at his villa in Munich a day or so later – around 20th November 1918. In April 1916, Mr Gaffney had accepted the commission from Roger Casement to look after the soldiers of the Irish Brigade. Would he now fulfil his mission and, through good friends in Ireland and the USA, get the Irishmen to Mexico – anywhere beyond the main? "What brought you all to Munich?" he answered. "Why didn't you stay in Danzig? How can I help you?" Dr O'Curry was furious but could do nothing. St John Gaffney telephoned him the same day: "Those men will do something desperate." O'Curry answered: "But do *your* duty by them; they deserve a fair deal."

In the shades of night, in November 1918, the man entrusted with the last care of Casement's Brigade skipped to the Bavarian Alps; from there he later crossed the frontier into Switzerland. Some of the deserted Irishmen found employment with well wishers and German noblemen; others returned north to Berlin and Pomerania and distant places.

I met my old sergeant-major friend and true Bavarian soldier who had also seen service under Major MacBride in the Irish Brigade in South Africa during the Boer War. He was from Nuremberg, north Bavaria, the home town of my Bavarian wife. We decided to return to the historic walled city of Nuremberg. On

---

[264] Kurt Eisner (1867-1919) was a journalist and socialist politician who organised the overthrow of the monarchy in Bavaria at the end of the war. He was the first republican Prime Minister of Bavaria but lost the February 1919 election and was assassinated in Munich on his way to present his resignation to parliament.

25th November I was transferred to the General Command HQ, 3rd Bavarian Army Corps in Nuremberg. Jerry O'Callaghan came with me and here we were allotted duty on the army secret service staff. We were attached to the Ministry of War Department, then under the guidance of the new democratic War Minister of Bavaria – Herr Ernest Schneppenhorst – who proved a good friend.

In February 1919, Mrs Bulliet Grabisch of the German-Irish Society, Berlin, arranged with General Nolliet, Chief of the Inter-Allied Staff in Berlin, to facilitate the Casement Irishmen who desired repatriation as prisoners of war. But General Nolliet gave no guarantees as to the Irishmen's future in England. I found this out too late. Some 30 of them, who had already agreed to be returned as prisoners of war, were clapped into prison; in April 1919, the English Government decided to discharge the Irish soldiers ignominiously, "their services being no longer required". The army authorities warned them that if they were caught in Ireland under arms, they would be dealt with summarily. There is their story and it is for the salutary lesson it teaches that I give it in such detail.[265]

I remained in the German army until September 1919 when I got into to touch with my old benefactor, the unrepentant Fenian, John Devoy. The necessary documents over Holland were procured, with the assistance of a Count of the Papal Empire who knew the ropes, and with the material assistance of my veteran friend in New York, Jerry O'Callaghan and I saw Ireland once more. The Fenian spirit of John Devoy had proved constant when younger blood had abandoned us to fate.

---

[265] Quinlisk and another brigade member whom he identified simply as "B" decided in March 1919 to go to the English embassy in Berlin and give themselves up as prisoners of war. They hoped to be eventually able to make their way over the Dutch border. When they spoke to the general present in the embassy, he asked them why they had not reported earlier. They told him that they had been out working and had not heard anything about the release of all prisoners. They were given uniforms and left Berlin for Cologne. But B was arrested there after some days because a revolver and some incriminating documents were found on him. Quinlisk was picked up shortly afterwards and the two spent four weeks in jail in Cologne and Calais. Through the kindness of a "Captain L." they were released and crossed to England. "On April 9th, I left England for that land, love of which had caused me so much pain and hardship," wrote Quinlisk, and he concluded: "Perhaps a better day is dawning for Ireland. I can only say that the manner in which the German government broke its pledges to Sir Roger Casement augured ill for its designs towards the Irish people, for whom Kaiser Wilhelm in his proclamation professed such admiration." See Quinlisk, "The German Irish Brigade" in *Land and Water*, 13 November 1919, p. 17.

When I got back to Erin, I spent many months among my native hills "on my own keeping".[266] I went back to Germany again and returned home in March 1922. This last period, from Christmas 1918 to Christmas 1921, would make quite another story, which I propose telling in due course.[267]

It was Casement's Howth guns that made Easter Week 1916 an actual possibility from the purely military point of view, and in the course of time in Germany – from 1919 to 1921 – the Irish Republican Army would be affected materially if it were not for the remainder of Casement's Howth Mausers. Furthermore, the Mauser automatic "filter-bed" of gun-running was supervised in no small way at Hamburg by a sergeant of Casement's Brigade, known in 1919, '20 and '21 as "Sergeant Jack Neumann"[268] of Hamburg Docks military police (green uniform). His friends and comrades-in-arms in the interior of Germany did the forwarding, and "Neumann", assisted by Casey, Keegan and other IRA connecting links completed the shipments. Among the connecting links was Capt. *Maurichen* Meade of Limerick Brigade, IRA,[269] who made a success of his manning the deadly gun at the Lone Tree Crossroads ambush in Co. Limerick against the Black and Tans, when no prisoners were taken from the mocking-bird cages of Sir Hamar Greenwood[270] and their guinea-a-day occupants.

---

[266] A direct translation of the Irish "ar mo choimeád", the phrase meant "on the run" and refers to Michael Keogh being active during the War of Independence in Ireland.

[267] He referred briefly in some of his written output to his activities during this period but did not, to the editor's knowledge, write down the whole story of his involvement in the Irish independence struggle. For some of that involvement, see Chapter 14.

[268] The editor is not sure who this individual was. Apart from Joseph Dowling and Julian Bailey, both of whom it cannot have been, the other brigade sergeants were Michael O'Toole and John Kavanagh.

[269] Maurice Meade was also a member of the Casement Brigade.

[270] Hamar Greenwood (1870-1948) was a British Liberal MP. He served in a number of ministries and was the last Chief Secretary for Ireland from 1920 to 1922. In that capacity, he was responsible for the introduction of the Black and Tans and Auxiliaries into Ireland.

CHAPTER 13: A Chance Meeting

How I had to put Lance Corporal Adolf Hitler under
military arrest and saved his life

*(EDITOR'S NOTE: The following narrative from Michael Keogh does
not relate directly to German Irish Brigade affairs, but does relate
to the time that he served in the German army from May 1918, and
is of great historical interest.)*

Two first-aid men were carrying Adolf Hitler down the line on a
stretcher. He had been blinded temporarily by a wound on the
side of the head and was badly wounded in the groin. The date
was 28th September 1918. I was standing outside a field-dressing
post near Ligny, on the French border, and it was the first time I
took any notice of Lance Corporal Hitler. Somebody nearby said
sympathetically: "Kaput!" So it seemed for the nondescript
dispatch carrier I had come to know by sight in the front line over
the past two months. It was said afterwards that it was that
stomach wound near Ligny that kept him from marriage until the
last moments of his career. For this wound, it seemed, made it
impossible for him to become a father.

Hitler, like myself, was then serving in the Bavarian 16th
Infantry Regiment. He was in the Second Battalion. I commanded
the machine-gun company in the First – the List Battalion – with
the rank of field-lieutenant. We were part of the so-called "spring
offensive", which was to be the last great offensive on the Western
Front – the final push ordered by the Kaiser to win the war. It
almost did. We advanced 100 miles in some places and brought
Paris within range of "Big Bertha". Then, in June, the Americans
came in and the Allies launched their final smash.

It was strange that I, an Irishman and former lieutenant of
the American Fighting 69th Regiment, had come to be fighting at
the head of a machine-gun company in the beaten German army.
I had not come to Germany in 1914 to die for the Kaiser and his
jackboot regime. But it was true that I was now a Bavarian citizen
for my own soldierly protection and I had a German wife.[271] I wore
a German uniform and I spoke German like a native Bavarian.

---

[271] Her name was Anna-Marie Seuffert and she came from Wissenheidt Castle,
Unter Franken, Nuremberg, North Bavaria.

Because of the vicissitudes of Casement's Irish Brigade, I found myself where I was.

Now, in the retreat of stubborn battles as the Allied artillery chopped us to pieces and their aircraft were dropping, instead of bombs, leaflets with Wilson's Fourteen Points (guaranteeing a fair peace if the Kaiser was kicked out), I had more to feel sorry for than the Germans. Casement was hanged, his good name fouled, his character trampled upon.[272] The Irish Brigade was a failure, its handful of men scattered and demoralised. And the Irish rebellion of two years earlier appeared to have been abortive: the leaders had been shot and thousands of the Volunteers interned when I last heard of them.

The stretcher bearers disappeared into the dressing station with their burden. I thought I had seen the last of Lance Corporal Adolf Hitler.

A couple of days later, having been marooned for three nights with my machine-gunners in an outpost position and under shelling from both sides, I went down with trench fever. On the home front that winter it was the terrifying Black Flu of 1918. But to the men in the mud it was trench fever ... and it killed more than the shells and bullets did. I was put on a hospital train at Namur for Berlin, but ended up at Danzig after a week on the rails. And I finished the war in the military hospital in Danzig. When I got out of bed I weighed nine stone. I had lost three stone since Ligny.

Armistice Day in Danzig was a ferment. Everywhere the revolutionary soldiers' committees had been set up to take over command of the German army units. Officers took orders from the committees. There was a meeting of delegates from all units of the Danzig garrison in the main market place that afternoon (the 17th army corps formed the garrison). I was warned leaving the hospital not to wear my officers' epaulettes. So I cut them off with a knife.

I went onto the platform at the meeting. There was no word of Communism among these men. They were the best elements in the army – tradesmen and technicians, sick of the war and sick of Prussian generals. They spoke of peace at all costs, freedom for the German people, bread and work. And they sent greetings to the peoples of the world, asking for a fair peace for the German nation and guaranteeing to end the Hohenzollern regime themselves.

---

[272] Michael Keogh is here referring to the use British intelligence made of Casement's so-called Black Diaries which seemed to reveal evidence of promiscuous homosexual behaviour on his part.

I gathered all the Irishmen from the Irish Brigade that I could find ... about 40. And I obtained free travel for them to Munich, to Turken Strasse Kaserne barracks. They were attached to my regiment – the Bavarian Guards – for duty and rations while we awaited demobilisation and a future that was uncertain. That Christmas I went on leave to my wife's home in Nuremberg. That was how I came to miss the Communist rising in Munich.

Kurt Eisner, Bela Kun (later the Red dictator of Hungary) and the Russians Levine and Karl Radek set up their Soviet "government" in Munich in January 1919.[273] They freed 5,000 Russian prisoners of war in a camp five miles from the city, armed them and put them in control of Munich.

I was back in Munich in the late spring of 1919 when, after some days of bitter fighting, the *Freikorps*[274] and the regular army had overthrown the Reds. I had fought my way into Munich as a captain in command of the machine-gun company in the Freikorp Epp – led by General (later Field Marshal) Epp.[275]

A few weeks later I was the officer of the day in the Turken Strasse barracks when I got an urgent call about eight o'clock in the evening. A riot had broken out over two political agents in the gymnasium. These "political officers", as they were called, were allowed to visit each barracks and make speeches or approach the men for votes and support.

---

[273] Bela Kun (1886-1938?) was founder of the Hungarian Communist Party. He ruled the short-lived Hungarian Soviet Republic from March to August 1919. It was overthrown by the invading Romanians and Kun fled to the Soviet Union. He was killed in the Stalinist purges of the late 1930s.

Karl Radek (1885-1939) was a Russian Bolshevik and international Communist leader who assisted in the setting up of the Bavarian Soviet Republic in 1919. He was imprisoned during the Stalin purges in 1937 and died in prison.

Eugen Levine (1886-1919) was a Russian Bolshevik who had been educated in Germany. When Kurt Eisner, who was the first republican premier of Bavaria, was assassinated in February 1919, Levine became leader of the Bavarian Soviet Republic that was then set up on the Russian Communist model. He was executed in July 1919 following the crushing of the soviet by the German army.

[274] The *Freikorps* (Free Corps) were paramilitary organisations that sprang up in Germany after the war as soldiers returned from the front. They were formed by demobilised, unemployed and disillusioned veterans who joined them for the familiar military stability they provided. They received considerable support from the German Minister of Defence, Gustav Noske, who used them to crush Communist uprisings.

[275] Franz Ritter von Epp (1868-1947) was a regular officer who rose to the rank of general-major during World War I. He was an early member of the Nazi Party, as was his chief of staff, Ernst Roehm. He retired before World War II but was arrested after the war by the Americans and died in prison.

They came from all the new parties that had sprung up as a result of the new freedom existing in Germany. And they were very active in Munich just then because municipal elections were coming up in a few weeks. But many soldiers awaiting demobilisation, tired of war and already disillusioned with peace, had little time for politicians.

I ordered out a sergeant and six men and, with fixed bayonets, led them off at the double. There were about 200 men in the gymnasium, among them some tough Tyrolean troops. Two political agents, who had been lecturing from a table top, had been dragged to the floor and were being beaten up. Some of the mob were trying to save them. Bayonets – each man carried one at his belt – were beginning to flash. The two on the floor were in danger of being kicked to death.

I ordered the guard to fire one round over the heads of the rioters. It stopped the commotion. We hauled out the two politicians. Both were cut, bleeding and in need of a doctor. The crowd around muttered and growled, boiling for blood.

There was only one thing to do. One of the two men, a pale character with a moustache, looked the more conscious despite his beating. I told him: "I'm taking you two into custody. I'm putting you under arrest for your own safety." He nodded agreement. We carried them to the guardroom and called a doctor. While waiting for him, I questioned them.

The fellow with the moustache gave his name promptly: Adolf Hitler. It was the Lance Corporal of Ligny. I would not have recognised him. He had been five months in hospital in Passewalk, Pomerania. He was thin and emaciated from his wounds. He told me he was still on sick leave and was still getting his lance-corporal's pay and rations.

Then he began to talk about his "new party". The other with him was Zimmer, later a close friend of his. They had come to the barracks as political agents for the new National Socialist German Workers Party (NSDAP), which Hitler and six others had founded.

It was plain from the start that it was not a party which appealed to decent men like the veterans at the Turken Strasse barracks. They saw their country falling apart and their people starving, a country where housewives raided farms and dug up the potatoes with their bare hands, a country where a one-legged veteran would hack another two inches off the stump of his severed leg to win an increase in his disability pension.

It was a country of blank despair and the veterans at the Turken Strasse had no time for Hitler and the other political prophets. But Adolf Hitler that night was not cowed. He would have carried on his political arguments in the guardroom if I had bothered to listen. The man I left behind me in the guardroom that night was brimful of his own convictions. And yet, if one of those kicks had landed on his old stomach wound...

He was transferred next day to hospital in Nuremberg, after the doctor had stitched up his cuts.

The next time I saw him, he was no longer in need of a guardroom for his safety.[276]

---

[276] See Postscript.

CHAPTER 14: Plots and Homecomings

The British government unearthed yet another "German Plot" for the wholesale smuggling of arms and ammunition from Germany to Ireland in the latter half of 1921 – in other words, an attempted breach of the truce between the British and Irish Republican forces then in place.[277] Whence came the dope? Not from a pure German-Irish source but through some of the Anglophones then living in Berlin. The Oxford and Trinity chums were most active in the secret haunts of the Prussian capital during the six months of the Anglo-Irish truce prior to the Treaty of 1921.[278]

But they underestimated the skill of the grey-haired "Invincible" who had for many years made his home in Germany. Nor had the intriguing political agents of the Galloper[279] duly accounted for the vigilant young German-Irish sleuth hounds, who managed to scan the actual daily and nightly visiting-cards or otherwise tipped-off record of interlopers passing through all doors of the splendid buildings of the Unter den Linden and Wilhelmstrasse, with the British coat of arms on the mast bearing the Union Jack. The Irish people have just reason to thank a few unselfish Gaels and Germans for the oft-repeated threat of immediate and terrible war not having become a reality in October 1921.

In the summer of that year, I had occasion to partake of another pleasure trip in the bunkers of a cargo tramp, and the blind passenger route was not a new experience. I had crossed and re-crossed the Atlantic in those sea-hells, so a short passage down the Irish Sea and the Channel added little of novelty to my experience. In any event, no time could be found to coddle *mal-de-mer*, especially when one had to assist in regulating the motion of a slow-plodding merchandise steamship.

During the course of a short stay in the capital of the Gael, the Anglo-Irish truce had come into being and many days had not elapsed until it was found necessary to return to Germany. Prior to that undertaking, I had an interview with General Michael

---

[277] The truce referred to is that which brought an end to the hostilities of the Irish War of Independence in July 1921.

[278] On 6th December 1921, a Treaty was signed between delegations representing the Dáil and the British government.

[279] F.E. ("Galloper") Smith, now Lord Birkenhead, was at this time Lord Chancellor in the British government.

Collins, to whom I was already known through General Joseph Plunkett.[280] I also met Arthur Griffith[281] and Erskine Childers[282] prior to my leaving for Germany towards the end of July 1921.

In summing up the situation then, a few weeks after the cessation of active warfare, one was compelled to ask oneself: Would there be peace or renewed hostilities? The question, on the whole, appeared to me to be an acute one. The World War interpretation of the defence of small nations had, at length, found the bulldog breed not wanting in its old resolve to civilise the native of Hibernia. Sir Hamar Greenwood and his ticket-of-leave mercenaries[283] had been typical of the way England wielded its power.

Would the rulers of proud Albion rest on their laurels? As one Irishman, I found the answer in the negative. The centuries-old adage – *divide et impera* – remained the motto of Anglo-Saxon secret diplomacy. In dealing with these, Ireland's representatives would be well advised in keeping the "Green Table" game an open one – direct, to the point and without secret sessions. In the end, the Irish people must act in the capacity of judge – their decision the final one.

Once more in the Fatherland with my family, I found Germany and its people the same old self-reliant unrepentants. Well-wishers of Ireland were brimming over with joy at the

---

[280] Collins was Plunkett's aide-de-camp during the 1916 Rising. Michael Collins (1890-1922), a member of the GAA and the IRB, fought in the GPO during the rising. He afterwards took a leading role in the Irish Volunteers, especially as Director of Intelligence, which proved so vital during the War of Independence. He also played a leading role as Minister for Finance in the Dáil governments 1919-22 and as Chairman of the Provisional Government 1922. He was killed in an ambush in August 1922during the Irish Civil War.

[281] Arthur Griffith (1871-1922), journalist, editor and propagandist, founded Sinn Féin in 1905. Although he did not take part in the rising, he was imprisoned afterwards. He was President of the Dáil during de Valera's absence in the US 1919-20. He led the delegation that signed the Anglo-Irish Treaty and was President of the Dáil from January 1922 until his death in August of the same year.

[282] Erskine Childers (1870-1922), was an English-born writer and civil servant of Anglo-Irish background. He became a convert to Irish nationalism. He was Minister for Publicity in the Dáil 1919-21, opposed the Treaty and fought in the Civil War, during which he was captured and executed.

[283] During the War of Independence, the British government decided to reinforce the Royal Irish Constabulary by recruiting ex-soldiers (who became known as the Black and Tans after a famous pack of greyhounds in Ireland at the time) and ex-officers (who formed the Auxiliaries) who had fought in the Great War. They were well paid, the first group receiving 10 shillings a day and the second a guinea a day, as well as full board and lodging. They developed a reputation for brutality and were guilty of committing a number of atrocities during the conflict.

success Sinn Féin had achieved against its brutal oppressors. A short spell of inactivity followed, but this meant only that proper soundings were being taken. I was not long in finding the true bearings of the Irish ship then in Berlin.

The same old reliables were standing by, particularly my tried and trusted friend, Ferdinand Hansen, the unrepentant Hun as the Northcliffe Press and the *Times* were wont to style him. Nor had the Wilson administration forgotten his activity with Jeremiah O'Leary in New York and all over the United States prior to America's entrance into the World War.[284] In 1917, Hansen and O'Leary jumped the freight wagon, skipped over the Mexican border and thence to Germany. A stauncher friend of Ireland's cause would be hard to find.

In Hamburg, the same old routine was still in vogue. All war materials for the Green Isle could legitimately pass the barrier of the docks. A few of Casement's followers were still operating, but with a careful watch as to illegitimate travellers in the Mauser trade, supposed to be concerned with Ireland. The small quantities theretofore adhered to were still found the safest method. In the event of a further outbreak at home, new routes were arranged for in minute detail – an absolute necessity on account of certain live wires operating on behalf of unknown personages.

"Direct agents" had been changed from the Egyptian hot-bed area to the cooler German climate. Even old Boer War veterans, with World War Distinguished Service Orders (DSOs) acquired *at base*, had wormed their way into post-war Germany. A change in the actual spelling of their names did not assist some of them very much. In at least one supposed Irish-Ireland office at Berlin's West End during 1921-22, the only newspaper to be seen was the London *Times*, undoubtedly a necessary asset for the education of an aspiring lawyer. Another ambitious aspirant had a Dáil Éireann passport in his wallet but neatly tucked away in his hip-pocket was Lord Curzon's[285] ticket-of-leave. Yet others concealed their Bachelor of Law degrees, acquired at Temple Bar and King's Inns, London.

In Berlin, in 1921-22, they became aspirants to representative commercialism between Ireland and Germany. One old spark, when leaving for a trip to Paris, was heard to remark: "Oh, those wretched Irishmen again. The next thing they will attempt, I suppose, is to put a clock-bomb in my suite of rooms."

---

[284] Both Hansen and O'Leary campaigned in the US against America getting involved in the war on the side of Britain, France and Russia., which it did in 1917.
[285] George Nathaniel Lord Curzon (1859-1925) was a Conservative politician. He was Viceroy of India from 1899 to 1905 and Foreign Secretary from 1919 to 1924.

A real Irish-Irelander of worldwide fame was, on another occasion, saved from the compromising position of rehearsing his opinions to supposed friends on his way through Berlin, a secreted Dictaphone having been planted instead in his room in the Anhalter Banhof Platz. The wily foxes never enjoyed the record-plates or the confiscated Dictaphone, but they read their own well-meant phraseology in a type-written note which proved them defeated accomplices.

The tea-room gossip type of "Irish student" had now a fixed abode in Berlin on the Spree, both sexes being represented. University degrees are not easily procured in Germany. But after a few terms, students of brass could return to London or Dublin and there air the handles to their names as tokens of the latest German scholarship. The prefixed Doctor may be used in that way but at a risk, for the curious are always liable to look down the degree lists of the German universities. It is not easy to set bounds to what is possible. Even this happened in Hamburg in October 1921.

The "bogey" of another German Plot smuggled its way to the horizon of publicity. The night-life café crowd of Berlin's cosmopolitan West End were having a royal time. In the day time the typewritten code messages were dispatched by various routes, some over Milan, others via France. In the latter country, Robespierre's knife of red revolution had spared the life of many a Huguenot *provocateur*; hence it was that Bohemian pretenders ran amuck.

In Berlin during the latter half of 1921 was a certain government official, full cousin of a prominent English Jew and son of a great international banking magnate who once materially assisted a scion of English royalty. The wandering members of this lost race were firmly rooted in Berlin and had got a sound footing in the post-war financial crisis of revolutionary Germany. The Berlin cousin had reached a pedestal in this political machine. It took Irishmen to unseat him.

A question arose over the interchange of documents pertaining to German-Irish relations during the war-criminal trials at Leipzig in 1920. The documents relating to the Black-and-Tan warfare in Ireland were to be put before the English attorney sent to Leipzig to try soldiers of Germany for supposed crimes committed during the World War. The documents were to counter-stroke what Lloyd George's government were doing in Ireland. The papers were mislaid, "accidentally on purpose", and it turned out that a Jewish official knew something about them. The "graduate of Oxford University" suspected nothing until cornered like a rat in a trap, and on looking down the barrel of a

Mauser automatic, he sobbed in blundering and open confusion. Oh yes, the truth is sometimes very sour.

The vital hours were drawing near and Anglo-Irish affairs were becoming more strained. We in Germany were watching every move and effort, and little was done in London but was known in Berlin the next day. One wondered why certain negotiations were not being conducted in Dublin. Why all in London? Had not Lloyd George asked for a truce – an open admission of defeat? The Crown forces had been vanquished at their own game; besides, world opinion was on Ireland's side, not on England's. One is forced to admit that England bided her time in reversing this situation. Her offer of terms of peace did the rest. Something for nothing, and a partitioned Ireland to boot.

There were times during the Anglo-Irish truce when England's rulers gave up the ghost. The rebels were not so easy! The game of give and take was lost. England's tools and henchmen in Germany caught a tartar when they thought to camouflage "a miscellaneous cargo ship" while, cleverly decked away below the hatches were thousands of rifles, with corresponding ammunition, meant to be landed on some remote spot on the coast of Erin, tipped off as genuine to some easily beguiled Irish rebels, and duly intercepted by Crown forces of the British army then in occupation of Ireland! But the barrier at the mouth of the Elbe was not reached when a German revenue gun-boat hauled the jolly Briton into the net and searched him. The coasting tramp steamer was unloaded at Hamburg docks of her nefarious cargo of war material, reloaded with her balance of goods, admitted by customs and sent on her way to the high seas.

A stampede occurred from certain quarters of Berlin – scurrying for the nearest frontier. One culprit was caught but another quick-change artist broke through the meshes. He had bought a ticket for the German-Belgian frontier over Aix-la-Chapelle but changed trains and crossed the Dutch frontier on to Paris instead – "a fine specimen of a bird, and no doubt about it," was the reference made to him by German detectives. His wings were then somewhat clipped, but some other time his reward may be even more appropriate than tarring and feathering.

He forgot his trunks, to the number of 20, in his hotel suite of four rooms which, when searched, presented some fine foliage. The one thing remained unaccomplished, but £25,000 was saved the English taxpayer. The credit account of the Downing Street secret service yearly budget was the real gainer. The German government confiscated the guns and ammunition, which eventually proved to be tainted goods, bought and paid for. This the Irish people could read of a few days later with amazement, but Lloyd George's statement bottled up the real stuff. The main thing was: the British plot had failed.

The midnight Treaty of 5th-6th December 1921 came in due course as an alternative. So I got the Irish-German families in Germany to get ready for the home journey. This took three months to arrange. In the end, Seán Kavanagh, with his wife and child, and my wife and two children and I were to sail on 12th March 1922 on the Hudson US steamer, but our passports were refused by the American authorities at Bremen. The passports of the *Irish Provisional Government*[286] needed a visa from the *English Consul* before going on board this American ship – sailing from Bremen to Bordeaux, and thence over to Cobh, on the way to the United States. An American steamship, not even touching English waters, required Irishmen to have a British visa to Irish Provisional Government passports. No, I would see them all to Jericho rather than accept such terms of transit to the Cove of Cork.

The American official of the United States passenger steamship company at Bremen, on that Monday morning in March 1922, had, I thought, gone out of his way to hinder two Irish-German families embarking on the SS Hudson. The German priest who accompanied us to the US Lines office intervened on our behalf. "They are Irish citizens, not British subjects," he said. "Why hinder them in declaring themselves as freemen?" But to no avail.

Forthwith I wired the Irish Envoy at Berlin to the effect: "Dáil Éireann passport not recognised without English visa. US steamship agent refuses to accept Irish money." Mr O'Brien, an Irish Envoy courier from Tipperary, arrived post haste the same night, the Hudson being due to sail the next day. He tried to make ends meet but Seán Kavanagh and I refused point blank to entertain the suggestion of a British Consul visa on our guarantees of Irish nationality. We would wait a few weeks for the ship called the City of Dortmund. And so back to Hamburg, two hours' railway journey from Bremen.

We waited for the Irish cargo steamship, City of Dortmund, 1,000 tons, which sailed a few weeks later from Hamburg docks, the funnels painted green, white and yellow, and the Irish tricolour at her masthead. We sailed away on 25th March 1922, the first mate and the second mate vacating their officers' quarters for the midship bunks of AB's roost. For five days and five nights at sea our wives and children battled along until we

---

[286] The Provisional Government was set up in January 1922, under the terms of the Anglo-Irish Treaty, to take over power from the British government.

finally reached the harbour of Cobh and up the Lee without ever taking on the customs officers.

The bay bristled with gun-boats and cruisers. It was the morning after the Ballycotton affair, when the British tug Upnor was deprived of her war material by the IRA.[287] Captain Martin, his genial officers and crew will please accept this token of thanks for their many words of encouragement during the trip of the very first ship that flew the Irish tricolour on the high seas. My Bavarian wife had faced the Black and Tans in many raids during her former sojourn in Ireland, but rather than allow a British Consul visa on my passport, and accept admission as a British subject, I would sleep in the crow's nest during the whole five weary days and nights between Germany and Ireland.

It is an ill wind that does not blow an Irishman some good. My two children, Joe Plunkett Keogh and Roger Casement Keogh, three years and one year old respectively, suffered badly from the whooping-cough. When Roggi took a turn for the worse he had to enter a Hamburg hospital. The good doctors and kindly sisters spared no pains to save the little Irish-German baby. At times for over a week, it was a case of life and death, with a double rupture of the stomach added to the whooping-cough.

On St Patrick's Day, 1922, Seán Kavanagh and his wife (a Hamburg woman), with my wife and I, visited the hospital. For days my wife was distracted, owing to the hospital authorities deeming it not advisable for her to see our child. I could understand the reason: mother and child being previously inseparable, a meeting would in no way relieve a sick infant on the point of death; excitement, indeed, might only aggravate the compound malady. But St Patrick, patron saint of Ireland, assisted by Roger Casement in his martyr seat, evidently watched the sick cot of little Roger, and we all rejoiced on next seeing him apparently on the mend. The German nurses were untiring in their attentiveness to the *Kleine Irlander* when they became conversant with his name. Who is it in Germany since 1916 that did not know and understand the illustrious name, Roger Casement, the true Irishman and great friend of the German people in the World War?

In due course the time arrived to embark on the good ship City of Dortmund. The doctors and nurses begged my wife and

---

[287] On 29th March 1922, members of the Cork No. 1 Brigade of the IRA captured the British ship, Upnor, which had a cargo of military supplies it was taking back to England. The cargo was landed at Ballycotton pier in Cork. As Ireland drifted towards civil war, the incident caused a heightening of tensions between the pro- and anti-Treaty sides and between the British government and the pro-Treaty Dáil and Provisional Governments.

me to leave little Roger with them in safety and come for him later when he was completely recovered. "No doctor on board the cargo ship – why he will die if a relapse of the rupture results from the whopping-cough." What could I do, possessing little of this world's goods? I took Roger out of hospital on the eve of departure from Hamburg, but had to sign a document to the effect that such a course was against the wishes of the hospital authorities. This was necessary to their protection in case anything detrimental to the child's life might occur at sea.

The nurses in the hospital ward where Roger had lain for over two weeks were greatly affected, and again and again appealed to my wife not to risk the danger. The brave child seemed to assure them all would be well. He laughed and cooed their tears away on parting – for womankind in all lands are sympathetic and at one where nature's laws are being transgressed. How indifferent are the majority of mankind! As the father of a family, who fears but his Creator, the Father of all mankind, I hold that if the Motherhood of the entire civilised people of this world of probation were but given their well-deserved influence in matters of peace and war, future generations would be ensured against such a further human holocaust as that of the World War from 1914 to 1918.

The City of Dortmund weighed anchor at 4.30 p.m. on Lady Day. Down the majestic Elbe, the green, white and yellow standard of Irish freedom proudly fluttered from the top of the mast, proclaiming to the British and all nations' shipping that Ireland's sons were going to sea. Captain Martin seemed jubilant in his ocean-going togs. To use his own words: "I feel much more elated when I realise my guardianship of Roger Casement's friends and young Irish-Germans." The March winds blew a gale as we reached the mouth of the Elbe, the North Sea tide was full and choppy. Up to now, the City made good time, and rode the waves steadily, for she drew her full complement in tonnage displacement. Suddenly, conditions pointed towards a stormy five days' passage ere we turned Spike Island and the Cove of Cork.

As the Irish vessel entered the open sea at dusk, a most pointed World War revelation hove in sight. The monster ocean-going passenger ship, the *Vaterland*, now the Leviathan of US Lines, loomed up in our wake. What a stupendous salt-sea greyhound, as she rode the waves, a veritable floating hotel, all lighted up and winning general admiration for Teutonic workmanship. Personally I felt quite at home on the bridge with Captain Martin up to now, but ere long the SOS cry of sea-sickness had set in below: my wife and children were first attended, then Seán Kavanagh and his family were advised how best to combat the terror of a salty feeling – no joke where sick children were concerned.

The remainder of the five days and nights my hands were full. Kavanagh made a bad salt-water trooper, service with the Hamburg mounted dock-police being more in his line of rough-riding. To bed, to bed was the trumpet call and the 8ft x 6ft x 8ft cargo-ship officer's bunk offered little but the double-decker space. I slept on a couch improvised from two deck-stools but it mattered little where I snatched a few hours' repose. I had crossed the Atlantic between Cobh and New York six times, first in 1907, when I was really sea-sick. The Irish Sea was then, in 1922, no new thing either, having negotiated it another half-dozen times – so I could safely ride on the rigging on a four-master.

The second day down the Hook of Holland, and well out in the North Sea, a new phase was entered. The City of Dortmund was bound for Cork city, Dublin and Belfast; to the latter port, capital of Carsonia, this Sinn Féin ship was making her maiden call. The Irish tricolour painted on her funnels must not remain then, else she would stand danger of being shattered by the Ulster Specials[288] and the Orange forces then prowling over the territory that in former days gave birth to the United Irishmen. It was also the province that had ushered into being the spirit of the Red Hand[289] and such Irish patriots as Red Hugh O'Donnell, Henry Joy McCracken and heroine of 1798, deathless Betsy Grey.[290] On this trip, in the 20th century, the City of Dortmund – a commercial ship and trader in the interests of Irish nationality – must obliterate her national colours, much to the dislike of the Irish-Ireland skipper, passengers and crew.

---

[288] The Ulster Special Constabulary was set up by the British government in October 1920 as an auxiliary force to the Royal Irish Constabulary in Ulster. It was mainly recruited from the loyalist Ulster Volunteer Force. Most Catholics saw it as a Protestant paramilitary vigilante force and it became a sectarian police force.

[289] The Red Hand was the symbol of the ancient Gaelic Irish family, the O'Neills.

[290] Aedh Rua or Red Hugh O'Donnell (1572-1602) was the leader of the Gaelic Irish O'Donnell clan of Donegal in the late 16th century. With Hugh O'Neill of Tyrone, he led the resistance to Queen Elizabeth I known as the Nine Years War which ended in defeat at the Battle of Kinsale in 1601.

Henry Joy McCracken was a Presbyterian founding member of the United Irishmen. He led the 1798 rising in Antrim and was executed in July following its suppression.

Betsy Gray, also a Presbyterian, is said to have fought at the Battle of Ballynahinch in 1798 alongside her boyfriend and brother. All three were killed in the retreat following the defeat of the United Irish forces.

By this time I had an intuition all would not be well when we reached Irish waters. I am born of a northern Irish mother, a daughter of the old Fermanagh clan McMahon. So, with a Wexford father's blood in addition, I had every reason to remember the Irish airs from "the Red Branch Knights in Danger" down to "Who Fears to Speak of '98?"[291] Hence the past and its sad tale of disaster and woe flashed now before me as we rode the waves towards Inisfáil. What did the future hold for my native land? I often taxed my mind at sea for a correct answer. Hopes came to me of a united people, despite a partitioned island, and a gloomy prospect if Clause XII of the Anglo-Irish Treaty was not adhered to.[292] I kept subtracting two counties from the actual six paled off by the 1920 Partition Act.[293] Could the four wee counties withstand the fulfilment of Clause XII? The answer that presented itself to me was in the negative.

Saturday night, 1st April 1922, was the roughest and darkest I had yet encountered on the brine during 15 years' experience. The storm never abated from dusk to dawn, the Irish Sea raged at its deadliest, and Captain Martin, with whom I stood on the bridge, had just cause to remark: "Keogh, I hope to God my deck cargo of heavy machinery does not shift." I went down with him and saw to the lashings. The waves shot over our bows, to crash at our very feet, and at times we were in danger of being washed overboard or smashed against large cases and ironclad boxes of huge dimensions. It proved a difficult task to make the necessary inspection. All was well.

My wife and children, with the Kavanagh family, said the Rosary in the one tongue common to us all for years – German. This particular sea storm left impressions, and I feel assured those German mothers will never care to leave their adopted home again. The ocean path we traversed was all the more

---

[291] The phrase "Led the Red Branch knights to danger" occurs in Thomas Moore's 'Let Erin Remember the Days of Old'. The line "Who fears to speak of '98?" is the opening line of John Kells Ingram's 'The Memory of the Dead' (indeed, the opening line is often taken as the title of the poem), which was first published in *The Nation*, the paper of the Young Ireland movement, in April 1843.

[292] Clause XII gave Northern Ireland, set up under the Government of Ireland Act 1920 and in existence since June 1921, the option of opting out of the jurisdiction of the new Irish Free State within one month of the latter's coming into being in December 1922. If Northern Ireland did so, a Boundary Commission was to "determine in accordance with the wishes of the inhabitants, so far as may be compatible with economic and geographic conditions, the boundaries between Northern Ireland and the rest of Ireland".

[293] The two counties in question would have been Fermanagh and Tyrone, which had nationalist and Catholic majorities.

dangerous on account of being directly in the course of transatlantic liners. The fog-horn of the City of Dortmund shrieked unceasingly its sailor's warning, beware, beware, as our good ship nosed her way through an impenetrable black fog, rain and swift south-west wind. "The worst I've tasted in my 20 years' ploughing of the deep," Captain Martin assured me.

Towards daybreak on Sunday morning, 2nd April, the anger of King Neptune eased off. The danger was nigh in the leeway. At dawn we found ourselves hugging the coast line of the old Sireland whose hills are so dear to all Irish exiles:

Breathes there a man with soul so dead
Who never to himself hath said?
"This is my own, my native land."[294]

As we drew nearer, everyone seemed possessed of the one impulse – to shout: "Old Ireland, I bid you top of the morning." The skipper shook hands with me, remarking as he did so: "Were I to live to be a century, never shall I forget this eventful voyage, especially as it was with true friends and compatriots of our martyred dead of Easter Week." I do not pretend to repeat his exact words, but Captain Martin meant all he said.

About 7.30 a.m. on that Sunday morning, we were verging around the three-mile limit into the Cove of Cork. The captain pointed out the buoy beside the spot where the 1916 gun-runner, the Aud, transferred to the sea its cargo of war material that would have gone a long way in achieving Irish freedom. "Bravo, Captain Spindler, you at least stuck to your word of honour. You would not let the boys of the bulldog breed defeat you," I thought to myself. An Irish Volunteer soldier of Casement's Brigade was the first victim of the Anglo-Saxon firing squad in the 1916 Insurrection: the man from the Aud that would not speak. He met his death bravely, as an Irish soldier and a man, in a Scottish prison yard: Seán McGoey, the lad from the fair hills of Donegal. Go ndéanaí Croí Íosa trócaire ar a anam.

As we crossed the barrier into the milder waters of Cobh, a strange coincidence arose before me: the SS Celtic taking on passengers for New York – the exile ship on which I first went to America on 7th March 1907. Sixteen years of God's own time had passed away since, as a boy of sixteen summers, I started out from Cobh. On entering the harbour, I was busy with the children and with family affairs in the 10-foot square dining saloon of an Irish cargo steamer. How time changes one's path!

The skipper ran down from the bridge, saying: "Keogh and Kavanagh, the bay is bristling with gun-boats and cruisers. All

---

[294] The extract is from Sir Walter Scott's poem, 'The Lay of the Last Minstrel'.

the decks are cleared for emergency. I am running right through without waiting for customs officials. Opposite the landing jetty, under the shadow of St Colman's Cathedral, I'll slow down and take on the pilot 'on the run'. Don't appear on deck as something is radically wrong. Perhaps a new war is on."

"Right oh, we'll carry on through the porthole," I replied. I focussed my sea-going glasses. Sure enough, a warlike game was in progress. The Jack Tar[295] officers were also doing just as I was – scrutinising from stem to stern. In drawing my lens into better position, I noticed plainly each pointed motion in the City's direction. It looked like a "call to halt" any moment, but at least one thing did make me act: a gun-piece was being trained on us. What next? I hastened to the port side to ascertain our approximate position from the shore of Cobh. The captain had played a good trick on the Jolly Briton by getting inside berth between the Britishers and actual land, then but a few hundred yards off.

So, with the pilot up the sea ladder and on to the bridge, our flag the Irish tricolour was waving gleefully on the City's mast when, lo and behold, we were dipping colours to a resourceful Sinn Féin boy who waved the old flag of 1916[296] from a top window in a large hotel directly on the shore front. The British sea officers must have thought we were going to halt in the narrows for the customs officials. Not at all! We were now proceeding up the Lee, full steam ahead. The pilot knew the ropes and in two hours we hove to at Cork city docks.

Commandant Buckley and Captain Fitzgerald of Terry McSwiney's[297] own battalion, the 1st Cork Brigade, IRA, stepped aboard the City of Dortmund. We shook hands and got down to business. Disembarking was the next move. The British Tommies were over on the far quayside, loading up and skipping out, bag and baggage. We all had accepted the skipper's invitation to dinner, it then being 11.30 a.m., Sunday morning. But we were

---

[295] This was a common way of referring to seamen of the British Merchant and Royal Navy, especially during the days of the British Empire. It was not an offensive label and was used by the seamen themselves as well as members of the public. For instance, Gilbert and Sullivan's *HMS Pinafore* used "tar" regularly as a synonym for sailor, including the songs, 'The Merry Maiden and the Tar' and 'A British Tar'.

[296] Two flags flew over the GPO during the rising. One was the tricolour and the other was green with the words "Irish Republic" emblazoned in gold lettering on it.

[297] Terence McSwiney (1879-1920) was a member of the Gaelic League, Sinn Féin and the Irish Volunteers. He was elected Lord Mayor of Cork after the murder of Tomás MacCurtain in March 1920. He was arrested in August 1920 and imprisoned in Brixton, where he died after a 74-day hunger strike.

not even seated when up the Lee ran a customs and excise motor cutter and aboard the City of Dortmund rushed two or three officials, demanding from the captain an explanation of the breach of maritime customs law.

"Hello, passengers!"

"Yes. Irish families from Hamburg, Germany."

"Indeed, so. Well, well, passport please!" – and very Cockneyfied was the last order.

"Certainly, old top!" – handing him our passport, with its simple wording: "Mr Keogh and family ... being of Irish nationality, have permission from Dáil Éireann to land in Ireland."

"No, no, not good enough. Why not a British Consul visa at Hamburg before leaving? You must all remain on board ship until I bring those passports to the head offices at Cobh and see if anything can be done to let you land. But, of course, not today, it being Sunday."

I let him shoot off his mouth in the British or West British way: six of one and half-dozen of the other – a West Briton, in my estimation, being the more despicable of the two. Enough was said before I chimed in. "You, my dear sir, cannot demand my staying aboard this ship; neither are you getting my Dáil Éireann passport. So, just do as you please. We are all going ashore after we have dined with Captain Martin, but we go as Irish citizens, not as British subjects."

The juniors in the case spoke not a word but our contemptible old viper fumed: "Impossible, you can't." The skipper called him aside, brought him into his cabin and introduced him to Comdt. Buckley and Capt. Fitz. What a change resulted from this! Short and sweet came the question: "Anything to declare for duty?" He wouldn't see the dutiable stuff anyway, so my answer, "I don't think so," had to satisfy him. We stayed in Cork city that night – at the Thomond, George's Street – and up to Dublin next day.

I found dark clouds over Irish-Irelanders; while their ranks were split asunder, England's diplomacy was rampant. What did the divided leaders of a former united camp really intend to do, with the British army still in Ireland? It is either late or premature now to go into the details that presented themselves to me in the Ireland of 1922-23. I had a taste of internecine strife also in Germany in late 1918 and 1919, when it was my ill-luck to witness human beings being made to dig their own graves and be then shot into them.

I feel the one consolation that it was my luck not to be called on to stain my rifle against my fellow countrymen in 1922-23.[298] The only animate creature I did shoot during that time was a rabbit, to win a wager and a round of the house, while helping my good friend Captain C. Weston (Tom Ashe's comrade-in-arms at Ashbourne in 1916)[299] in bridge-building and road reconstruction at Ardtully and Kilgarvin, Co. Kerry, during May and June 1923. Some 100 Irish tradesmen live today to tell this tale of marksmanship – 350 yards was the sighting of the rifle used – as I had learned it with Custer's 7th USA Cavalry on the Pawnee Flats, Kansas, and for over four eventful years during the World War.

With these memories agitating my mind and other minds today, may I appeal to all Young Irelanders, and all old Irish-Irelanders, to rejoin, co-ordinate, heal the wounds of Mother Erin, and do what you owe to the dead to emancipate her. They saw that England's difficulty was Ireland's opportunity. England's difficulty is chronic. Your opportunity is constant, if only you will rise to it.

---

[298] The Irish Civil War lasted from late June 1922 until May 1923.

[299] Thomas Ashe (1885-1917) commanded the Fingal (north Dublin) Battalion of the Irish Volunteers during the Easter Rising. He won a major victory at Ashbourne, capturing a significant quantity of arms and up to 20 RIC men. He spent a year in prison after the rising. Rearrested in 1917, he died as a result of force-feeding during a hunger strike in Mountjoy Gaol in September.

POSTSCRIPT

The next time I saw Adolf Hitler, I was standing on the fringe of a vast crowd. The place was Nuremberg and the year was 1930. The month was August. Hitler was on a massive platform, furled in the Swastika flags of his National Socialist German Workers Party, much better known by its abbreviation, Nazi. One month later, his party won 107 of the seats in the Reichstag.[300] And the fate of Germany lay in his hands.[301]

I missed death by 20 minutes in Hitler's "Night of the Long Knives",[302] the bloodbath that put the one-time lance-corporal I had once arrested for his safety in control of the Third Reich. Nobody will know how many died between dusk on 30th June and dawn on 1st July, 1934. But it was nearer to 5,000 than the official figure of 500 put out by Goebbels.[303]

I had been back in Germany for six years in an engineering job. Inflation, starvation and anarchy, hand in hand with Communism, stalked the land. I rejoined the Steel Helmets, the old comrades association of the German army, which I had served in years before. I still have the Siegfried Dagger of Honour – the "Long Knife" – presented to me then by Ernest Roehm.[304] One blade is inscribed in German, with the words, "All for Germany", and the other has "Eternal Friendship from Ernest Roehm". The

---

[300] The Reichstag is the seat of the German parliament and is situated in the Platz der Republik in Berlin.

[301] It would take another three years, and many twists and turns, before this came to be the case.

[302] The Night of the Long Knives (30th June 1934) was when the Nazi regime executed hundreds (at least) of people for political reasons. The main target was the SA (*Sturmabteilung* or Storm Battalion), the Nazi paramilitary organisation led by Ernest Roehm which had helped Hitler to power. But Hitler also used the occasion to get rid of other potential opponents and to settle old scores.

[303] Paul Joseph Goebbels (1897-1945) was Minister for Propaganda and Popular Enlightenment during the Nazi regime from 1933 to 1945. Estimates of numbers killed range from 200 or 250 to as high as 1,000 or more. Hitler told the Reichstag that 74 had been executed.

[304] Ernest Roehm (1887-1934) served in a Bavarian regiment during World War I, rose to the rank of captain and was decorated for courage in combat. He joined the Nazi party in 1920 and became head of its paramilitary section, the SA, which protected party meetings and attacked political opponents. Once in power, Hitler perceived the SA as a threat to his getting the support of the army and industrialists, and so he eliminated Roehm.

same Roehm stood alongside our 500,000-strong Steel Helmets against the Communists in 1931.

Within two years, Hitler was firmly in power, and a great drive was under way to get 10,000,000 people back into employment. And a split was widening between Roehm and Hitler, one of the causes being Germany's ally, Mussolini. Bavarians like Roehm could not forget the way the Italians treated the German population of South Tyrol[305] – they were ordered to change even the inscriptions on the family graves into Italian.

I had my own reason for disliking Hitler's methods. In May 1934, I sat down and wrote an angry open letter to Goebbels after a gang of Hitler Youth thugs attacked a Catholic Boy Scouts' camp. Three boys were injured. One of them, my son Roger, a 14 year old, had his arm broken. Goebbels did nothing but a number of the Catholic newspapers published the letter over my name.

And so on the night of 30th June 1934, with a pistol and my "Long Knife" as arms, I was on street patrol in Berlin with 20 Steel Helmet men. The night was full of menace. Rumours buzzed everywhere. The Communists were planning to overthrow the government – so the rumours went. Posters went up that morning announcing "a victory march". Around midnight, it became clear that open revolution against Hitler was near to exploding. I could see it in the groups of noisy agitators we were breaking up outside cafés and bars, which in Germany stay open until 2 a.m.

Twice in half an hour we were called to rumour-tense Voss Strasse, near the office of von Papen, the Vice-Chancellor.[306] Twenty minutes after my last patrol left, a dozen men piled out of cars and forced their way in. Von Papen escaped by a back

---

[305] South Tyrol was originally part of the Austrian and then Austro-Hungarian Empire. But the Treaty of St Germain, signed at the Paris Peace Conference in 1919, gave South Tyrol to Italy even though 92% of the region was German speaking – a move that was contrary to President Wilson's principle of self-determination.

[306] Franz Joseph von Papen (1879-1969) was military attaché to the German ambassador to the US during the early part of World War I. He was expelled from the US and fought on the Western Front and in Palestine for the rest of the war. From 1921 to 1932, he was a member of parliament in Prussia. He was Chancellor of Germany from June to November 1932, having been appointed by President Hindenburg. To attract Nazi support for his government, he lifted the ban on the SA. He had to resign as Chancellor due to lack of support in the Reichstag but intrigued to have Hitler appointed to the position, with himself as Vice-Chancellor. Afterwards he criticised Hitler and only his friendship with the ailing and elderly President Hindenburg saved him on the Night of the Long Knives.

window. Two of his aides were shot dead. The SS[307] had struck, just as they were striking at different points all over Germany.

Roehm and 40 of his Storm Troopers were staying at a hotel outside Munich. They were taken from their beds at 6 a.m. by 600 SS killers and all but two of the 40 men were butchered. That was to be the fate of huge numbers of SA men all over Germany on that fateful and infamous night.

I disappeared for a week to a friend's farm. My letter to Goebbels had marked me out for suspicion. I had been warned and I had acted on the warning.

Two years later, on 8th September 1936, I left Germany for good. The Nazi regime was transforming the country. It was a case of back to Ireland for me. It was a quiet return – unlike a journey from Germany 16 years before when I reached Dublin wearing a moustache and carrying a fake American passport made out to "George King". I used this name because it was King George backwards!

At that time, I met General Michael Collins at the Spa Hotel in Lucan and laid plans for gun-running from Germany. And I went to war on a bicycle – to the battle of Mount Leinster. This was in 1920. A score of Volunteers had set up a training camp in a shooting lodge half way up the mountain on the Co. Kilkenny side. They were drilling carelessly in daylight.

Three of us were detached from the Midland Brigade to instruct them in guerrilla tactics. We set off with a guide from Gowran. But we were too late. More than 100 Auxiliaries and Black and Tans were closing in on two sides of the shooting lodge. They were climbing the mountain in skirmish line and exchanging fire with the 20 Volunteers strung out above them on the slopes.

We opened fire from a little road on the attackers' flank. The battle became a running fight as the Volunteers retreated over the mountain summit. And the four of us rode out of battle the way we had ridden in – on bicycles.

Machine guns, disguises, knives, murder – and bicycles. It's been a mixed-up life. But my last war is done. I have outlived almost all the men I fought. I have no enemies. I am at peace.

---

[307] The SS (*Schultzstaffel* or Protective Squadron) was originally Hitler's own personal bodyguard, appointed in 1925. He made Heinrich Himmler leader of the SS in 1929. Originally part of the SA, the SS became independent of it in 1930 and Himmler introduced the all-black uniform in 1932. The SS grew from 280 in 1925 to 52,000 by 1933. It organised and carried out the Night of the Long Knives and was probably responsible for some of the worst atrocities during World War II.

APPENDIX I

Interview with Fr Nicholson[308]

Fr Nicholson, whose name has been so much before readers of this narrative in connection with the activities in Germany of his friend Roger Casement, has just paid us an unexpected visit and, in the course of an interview, stated as his opinion that the Irish question is primarily a moral question, and concerns not Ireland's interests merely but a principle which involves the peace of the whole world. Explaining why he considered the Irish question primarily a moral question, he said:

If you were asked what the English have been doing in Ireland for 750 years, and you answered truthfully, you would have to admit that they have been deceiving and robbing the people most of the time, and murdering them whenever it suited their whims, their interests and their inhuman impulses. The staggering amount of the robbery fairly baffles conception. Consider the most tangible to begin with.

The finding of the Financial Relations Commission, appointed by the English government, was that Ireland was overtaxed beyond three million pounds sterling annually.[309] Presumably this condition existed since the amalgamation of the treasuries in 1817, or virtually 110 years, making the first item 330 million pounds at the minimum. The compound interest on this would finance several Shannon Schemes.[310] Observe, however, that is only the amount they admit taking publicly by taxation.

Roger Casement, once an English diplomat, who knew more than the ordinary individual of governmental deeds that are dark and ways that are devious, and incidentally refused a king's ransom to publish what he knew, maintained that the above-mentioned amount represented about one-third of

---

[308] The material in this appendix was first published in *The Catholic Bulletin*, June 1928, pp 749-753.

[309] The Financial Relations Commission, set up to assess how Ireland was taxed, published its report in 1897.

[310] The Shannon Scheme was the building of a hydroelectric station at Ardnacrusha, Co. Clare. It was begun in 1925 and completed in 1929. Its purpose was to provide an electricity supply to the new Irish Free State.

what they actually did take, making the a mount approximately 10 hundred million, that is, a billion pounds. The compound interest involved would solve the problem of emigration. But we have not got well started yet.

Let us now consider the land robberies. Confining ourselves to the reigns of Henry VIII, Elizabeth, James I and Cromwell, the amount of land plundered from the rightful Irish owners was between 10 and 15 million acres. As can only too easily be seen, the plunderers had an eye to business and grabbed the best land they could find. It could hardly be considered an exaggeration to state that it would sell today at an average of over £100 per acre, which adds about two billion pounds to the account, plus interest. This does not include the vast amounts which others had to pay in the form of forfeits, fines, bribes etc. to save their holdings from the devouring land-sharks especially nurtured by the English government.

Less tangible to estimate, but not less damaging in its results, was the destruction of Irish industry and commerce. This is not merely a matter of loss in financial returns, vast as that is, but the loss of the commercial and industrial sense of the people. It would be hopeless to try to compute the loss, not to Ireland alone but to the world, of Irish art, a condition that naturally follows loss of prosperity. This loss is all the greater, as, according to the English Ruskin,[311] the Irish are an artistic people.

The most intangible but the most stupendous loss is still to be mentioned. You will understand this if I ask you how much you would take in exchange for a broken heart. I believe it could be safely said that you would not take all the wealth of the British Empire. Well, it cannot be gainsaid by anyone familiar with the conditions that the number of Irish hearts broken by England amount to millions. The bleaching bones of the hunted exiles that strew the bed of the trackless ocean, or that were consigned to nameless and unhallowed graves in the slave plantations of the Barbados and the American colonies, or that filled the fever-pits by the banks of the lordly St Lawrence, proclaim to an astonished world that the "heart balm" which England owes to Ireland is beyond human computation.

Add to these the brutal barbarities of soldiers, savage, soulless and sin-seared, infected with the most debasing

---

[311] John Ruskin (1819-1900) was a writer, poet and artist but is now mainly remembered as an art and social commentator. His writings had a major influence on Victorian and Edwardian England.

vices that degrade human nature, repeatedly let loose on a defenceless people to terrorise, mutilate, ravage and murder them, as recently occurred with the abhorrent Black and Tans, and add again the studied, fiendish, debasing, insulting, torturing treatment of Irish political prisoners, which drove many to more welcome insanity and others to the cruel refuge of an early grave. Now try to translate all that diabolical injustice into pounds, shillings and pence: it cannot be done by any known arithmetical or geometrical formula yet discovered; but it may give a slight inkling of England's debt of retribution to Ireland.

The seemingly righteous Gladstone, in the noted Neapolitan Letters about 1855, fumed with fury because of the treatment of prisoners in the state of Naples.[312] He described it as an "outrage on religion, civilisation, humanity and decency," but, outside the case of some MPs, the same Gladstone was as silent as a clam regarding the indescribable atrocities which afflicted Irish political prisoners, compared to whose lot the conditions in Naples were a paradise. Nay more, when certain Irish leaders protested against some of the injustices suffered by their country, the philanthropic Gladstone coolly and cynically informed them that "the resources of civilisation are not exhausted". German reparations are child's play compared to the reparations due to Ireland from the sister isle.[313]

The situation would scarcely warrant the position of those who say that Irishmen have no complaint or grievance against the people of England but against the English government. Just at present the English people are proclaiming to the world that their country is a monarchy only in name, that the King is only a figurehead, and that their nation is virtually a republic. In a republic, the people are responsible for the government, but whether England is a virtual republic or not, no government could carry out its policy without the support of the majority. There were Tories

---

[312] William Gladstone (1809-1898), one of the most famous British statesmen ever, was leader of the Liberal Party and Prime Minister on four occasions between 1868 and 1894. In 1885, he declared himself in favour of Home Rule for Ireland and introduced the first Home Rule Bill into parliament in 1886. His Neapolitan Letters were published in 1851.

[313] Clause 231 of the 1919 Treaty of Versailles declared Germany was responsible for starting World War I and imposed swingeing reparations which were payable to the victorious Allies. The reparations amounted to some £23.6 billion, calculated on the value of the pound at that time. Had Germany been forced to pay the full amount, the country would have been making payments up until 1984.

at the time of the American Revolution who tried a similar cackle and, strange to say, their echo is still heard. But the Fathers of the Revolution spiked their cannon when in the immortal Declaration of Independence they expressly laid the blame for the crimes against the colonists at the door of the people of England.

You may have known of Englishmen who favoured Home Rule for Ireland, or even independence, but have you ever heard of an Englishman protesting against profiting by the robbery of Ireland or insisting that his country should return the plunder? This is where the peace of the world is involved. Whatever may be their faults or defects, men have a deep-seated resentment against injustice when directed against themselves. Most quarrels, whether between individuals or nations, are the result of one party taking something which belongs to another, or to which another has a prior claim. To put it another way: injustice is almost always, if not always, the cause of wars.

For over a quarter of a century, we have heard of peace leagues and peace movements that have made no progress. I believe that it will be found that they never insisted on justice as a condition for peace. If we could have civic peace only on the condition of burglars and bandits retaining their plunder, it would be a very unpleasant world for many. To avoid such unpleasantness, the strong must help the weak or the consequence must be chaos. Ireland is weak and is entitled to help. To be conscious of another's wrongdoing, without using reasonable means to prevent it, is to be considered an accomplice by the moral law, and even human laws consider it accessory.

If the League of Nations[314] were anything more than an expensive pink tea, it would have to give due consideration to Ireland's claim to reasonable reparation. English politicians and statesmen have shown remarkable shrewdness when dealing with world questions; they have shown remarkable stupidity when dealing with Ireland. They might as well understand sooner than later that Irish friendship is a chimera, and the Irish question but a smouldering volcano, as long as no reasonable effort is made to right the wrongs of

---

[314] The League of Nations was set up by the Paris Peace Conference of 1919 on the advice of President Wilson of the US. Its purpose was to try to prevent further wars from breaking out. One of its greatest weaknesses from the start was that the US refused to join. It was to prove a forerunner of the United Nations that was set up after World War II.

centuries, and as long as a vestige of English power remains on Irish soil.

If sceptics are inclined to smile a sickly smile at the thought of Erin's slender wand defying John Bull's once omnipotent trident, they might recall that there was once an Irish "youth to fortune and to fame unknown"[315] who attended the Christian Brothers Schools and devised a plan to paralyse the British navy. That youth was John P. Holland, and his plan resulted in the invention of the first submarine, the "Fenian Ram". It will also be remembered that an Irishman was among the first who conquered the unknown perils of the North Atlantic,[316] and it is not beyond the range of Irish genius to devise a means to make John Bull's island tremble like an aspen leaf in the autumn wind. The moral appeal should be especially forceful to Mr Bull since he poses before the world as a very moral gentleman. Does he not print bibles by the ton and scatter them among the heathens to convert them to his views of Christianity? If he could possibly be induced to look inside those bibles, he might discover one of those "physician heal thyself" arguments such as "pay what thou owest".

Asked if he considered Casement's mission a failure, Fr Nicholson said it was far from it.

While he did not accomplish all he had expected, his main purpose was advanced, namely, to realise the ideal of Thomas Davis and remove Ireland from the status of an English province in the region of international politics.[317] The same may be said of the effort to organise an Irish Brigade among the prisoners of war who called themselves Irish. It will be remembered that when the war started, the air in Ireland was black and blue with verbal and pictorial lying about German atrocities in an attempt to inveigle

---

[315] The quotation is from Thomas Gray's (1716-1771) famous poem, 'Elegy Written in a Country Churchyard'.

[316] Presumably the reference is to St Brendan the Navigator (c.484-c.577) who, according to legend or semi-legend, was the first European to reach America. Tim Severin, in his book *The Brendan Voyage* (New York, 1978), has shown that it is quite possible that Brendan reached America and has proved such a trip possible for the type of boat described in the 9th-century *Navagatio Sancti Brendani Abbatis*.

[317] Thomas Davis (1814-1845) was the main force behind the Young Ireland movement that grew out of Daniel O'Connell's Repeal Association. In 1842 he co-founded and became editor of the *Nation*, an enormously influential weekly. He wrote the poem, 'A Nation Once Again', which was the anthem of Irish nationalists for many years, and contains the lines to which Fr Nicholson was alluding here: "And Ireland long a province be/ A nation once again."

unsophisticated Irish youths to be slaughtered in the continental shambles, ostensibly to save little Belgium but in reality to save John Bull's trembling hide; while some of those who should have been their logical protectors remained shamefully silent.

The first purpose in view in forming an Irish Brigade was to stop this infamy and, when work on the brigade started, recruiting in Ireland met a sudden and unprovided death. Because I told those prisoners who said they were Irishmen that they had a country of their own and that that country was Ireland, and their first duty in an emergency was to their own country, and that England had been its inveterate and only enemy in the world, English propagandists (which means England's paid liars) termed this corrupting the men. It will be news to students of history that when any corrupting is to be done some outside assistance is needed by the nation that made an admiral of Drake the pirate (the people of Cuba, whom he repeatedly plundered, called him the dragon), made a lord of Nelson, the moral degenerate, an Irish peer of Clive, and deluged the honest but helpless Chinese with opium,[318] not to mention the varied products of royal and noble indiscretions that have been highlights in English and Anglo-Irish history and society.

When told there had been some difference of opinion as to the measure of support extended to the Irish Brigade, Fr Nicholson said that a note from Casement might throw some light on the subject. The note reads as follows:

> Hotel Vasauer Hof., Limburg a/d Lahn,
> 9.30 a.m., Monday, 3/6/15
>
> Dear Father Nicholson, – I am so sorry to miss you. I walked to Balduinstein yesterday and part of the way back, too, and was very tired when I got here at 8 p.m., or I would have called. Father Berkessel will go with you to Coblenz, to see

---

[318] Francis Drake (1540-1596) was a privateer and slave trader. He frequently raided Spanish galleons carrying bullion from the Spanish colonies in South America back to Spain. He was known to the Spanish as "El Dragón" (a pun on his family name).

Horatio Nelson (1758-1805) was a famous English admiral. Although married, he had a prolonged, well-known affair with Lady Emma Hamilton, by whom he had a daughter. It is most likely to this affair that Fr Nicholson was alluding when referring to Nelson as "the moral degenerate".

Robert Clive (1725-1774), known as Clive of India, promoted the British conquest of India by means of the East India Company.

The British fought two "Opium Wars" (1839-42 and 1856-60) with China to force that country to import British opium.

the Consul there. Consult Lieut. Boehm if you want any German pass. Tell Joe and J.D. all I said to you the other day, and impress on them the great importance of backing up the handful of men in arms. You have worked nobly and untiringly for the thing you came to do, and whatever success exists is due to you and your unselfish and untiring efforts. I leave a card you might give the Heppels. Au revoir and God speed.

Roger Casement

Asked if he thought the language question was of any importance in Ireland, Fr Nicholson replied:

People who master two languages have an intellectual advantage over those who know only one. In the Canadian province of Quebec, it is virtually impossible to fill a position of importance without knowing two languages; but it is not necessary to go as far as Canada. If you cross to little Belgium, over which tender-hearted John Bull once shed crocodile tears, you will find a large number of people speaking four languages. It could be noticed amongst the war prisoners that men who had been associated with the Gaelic League manifested a superior intelligence and more rational outlook.

Concluding, Fr Nicholson said the indications are that Ireland's political and economic future is largely before her, if guided by courageous, resourceful and prudent hands, while England's future might not unreasonably be compared to the witches' cauldron in *Macbeth*.

APPENDIX 2: What Should Have Been in 1916

An arrangement was worked out at 14 Budapester Strasse, Berlin, GHQ of the General Staff of the German army, by the genial and lion-hearted Commandant Joseph Plunkett and Roger Casement, for German military assistance to the Irish Volunteers in Ireland. This arrangement was concluded on 25th March 1915.[319] The Irish and German landing force detailed here was to coincide with naval battles and to take effect when the gun-running ship Aud had successfully armed approximately 20,000 Irish Volunteer soldiers. Owing to Dogger Bank fog in the North Sea not allowing the Battle of Jutland to take place prior to 31st May 1916, King Neptune saved England again as at Bantry Bay.[320]

The following are the details of the Irish and German landing force:

- 10 transport ships, with naval escort and Zeppelin and submarine squadron protection
- One general officer commanding (major general), three brigadier generals and six staff officers (colonels) – all English-speaking officers
- Two infantry brigades comprising 20 staff officers, 300 officers, 1,200 NCOs and 10,000 men (one-third of this infantry force with a conversational knowledge of the English language and in most part seasoned campaigners)
- Two artillery brigades with 40 field guns (light), 10 field guns (heavy) and 10 heavy guns (motor conveyance)
- This brigade to consist of 10 staff officers, 60 officers, 200 NCOs and 1,000 men – officers and NCOs to be English-speaking Germans
- One German machine-guns corps with 100 machine-guns and consisting of four staff officers, 30 officers, 100 NCOs and 500 men

---

[319] This date is too early because Plunkett did not arrive in Germany until April 1915.

[320] The Battle of Jutland was the only real naval battle of World War I. It was a technical victory for the Germans but counted for little because their High Seas Fleet did not put to sea again for the duration of the war.

In December 1796, the French sent a fleet of more than 40 ships with some 15,000 soldiers and Wolfe Tone on board to Bantry Bay in Cork but bad weather, among other factors, caused the expedition to abort.

- Irish Brigade of 10 machine-gun teams, O/C Captain Robert Monteith, with eight officers (three Irish, five German), two warrant officers (Irish), 10 NCOs, 50 men

This is exactly what was arranged with a view to a successful expedition to Ireland from Germany in April 1916.

In February 1916, the Supreme Council of the IRB in Dublin under the leadership of Mr Tom Clarke (the unrepentant Irish Fenian who had undergone 15 years' imprisonment in English prisons from 1883 to 1898) had agreed to the original plan conjointly mapped out by Commandant Joseph Plunkett and Roger Casement in Germany. This plan was intended for two separate landing forces, one in Co. Kerry and the other on the Co. Wexford coast. In this way a double action was meant for a safety-valve plan of campaign in Ireland in conjunction with the Irish Volunteer army.

It will be noticed that the geographical situation of those separate expeditions was very wisely picked out. The Co. Wexford landing was allotted to the south-east coast and was meant to serve as a feeding block to the 1798 seat of insurrection. The Co. Kerry expedition would serve as a centre of concentration for the Irish Volunteer forces from Cork, Kerry, Clare, Limerick in the south west and Galway and the extreme western seaboard of Connacht. The IRB courier, John Kenny, in conjunction with Tommy O'Connor as the dispatch carrier from Dublin, had negotiated the confirmation of this arrangement between Tom Clarke and Casement through New York and Joe McGarrity and others in the US. Any other stories are but bluff and guessing at the truth.

Apart from all this, the German Foreign Office had received other overtures from the Irish-American Revolutionary Tribunal in New York – and as events turned out, it was too late when the Military Council, planning the insurrection in Dublin, learned at the end of March 1916 that the German authorities were then decided on accepting the Irish-American proposals as final. Although the German intention was good, it was beyond all doubt a fatal decision for the Irish home forces.

Besides, one other vital point had to be taken into consideration and that due to the fact of the German secret-service eyes in Ireland knowing of the divergence of opinion then existing in Ireland between the two militant camps representing the Irish Volunteer army and the Irish Citizen Army under the leadership of Commandant James Connolly. At this time, during March 1916, the German submarines were very active around the coast of Ireland, and had at least two distinct bases from which to direct their sources of information. I remember Captain Monteith remarking of certain hints that were passed by some German officials as to the obvious division in the Irish insurrectionary camp.

Monteith was a very staunch supporter of the view that Commandant James Connolly and his Citizen Army would strike a blow for Irish freedom, even if he were to do so alone with his few hundred superb citizen-soldiers. Casement held the same view of the Irish militancy at the time. "Connolly," he said, "I admire, not only as a pioneer socialist worker whose doctrine aimed well to propagate the teachings of James Fintan Lalor,[321] but as an unwavering Irish patriot, capable of guiding the Irish peasantry and workers on the roadway to Irish independence. I have followed the writings of Connolly for years past and his book, *Labour in Irish History*,[322] has fulfilled its part in making me see eye to eye with James Connolly as far as Ireland's position can be considered – at present just as in the past."

He we witness the innate instinct in Casement which led him to be a true defender of the "bottom dog" in the make up of the modern and unequal civilisation of the 20th century in Ireland.

We need not anticipate in placing the names of Casement and Connolly on the one pedestal as Irish patriots. Each of them had recognised as the backbone of Irish nationality the peasant tiller of the soil and the equally sweated worker in the industrial and commercial life of the country. In future Irish history, the true story cannot be written of Easter Week 1916 without emphasis on the shining light radiating from the names of Casement and Connolly as uncompromising Irish exponents of equality and fraternity in a common brotherhood of man – such a history would be null and void without such an emphasis.

Sir Basil Thomson, ex-CID chief, New Scotland Yard, London,[323] in an article on the "Truth about Sir Roger Casement" in *Life* magazine in April 1925, maintains the British secret service was well instructed as to the different events surrounding Roger Casement's mission to Germany. I have no grounds to doubt this princeling of secret intrigues – the English hidden

---

[321] James Fintan Lalor (1809-49), a Young Irelander who wrote for the *Nation*, argued the case of the land of Ireland for the people of Ireland, i.e., land nationalisation, and as such had an especial appeal to the socialist Connolly.

[322] First published in Dublin by Maunsel and Co. in 1910.

[323] Sir Basil Thomson (1861-1939) was a barrister who worked in the Colonial Office. In 1913 he was appointed Deputy Commissioner of the Metropolitan Police. Five years later he was made head of the Special Branch (Scotland Yard). He was instrumental in securing the conviction and subsequent execution of Roger Casement.

diplomacy has always found leakages and, moreover, has never failed to undermine the narrowest channels of Irish insurrectionary movements. It did not even stop in manning the innermost conclaves of Irish rebel secret societies. The most dangerous candidates the Irish revolutionaries had were the Irish themselves – from Strongbow's and MacMurrough's time to the 20th-century period of Hamar Greenwood's Black and Tans.

The fact that England's spies played an important role in Germany during the World War does not by any means imply that Downing Street was apprised of the exact details in the matter of Roger Casement and his mission so far as the immediate tactics went prior to his landing off the coast of Kerry from a German submarine on the shore of Bannow Strand on that memorable Good Friday morn at daybreak, Eastertide 1916. The master spies undoubtedly knew something was being enacted but how, when or where exactly they could not possibly have unearthed until the bombshell had fallen in their midst.

Proud Albion had expended much restless energy and some hundreds of thousands sterling during the latter half of 1914, in 1915 and in early 1916. The English fleet burned so much fuel in its bunkers trying to spot the invincible gun-running ships of Rory of the Gael, from November 1914 to April 1916, that the face value in coinage representing same would more than suffice to meet the dole requirements of Britain's one and a half million unemployed in the years that succeeded the armistice of 11th November 1918. So much for the fear and dread of the British Empire's marauding government as far as Casement and his handful of faithful Irish volunteer soldiers in Germany during the early years of the World War were actually concerned.

As to what are the most marked and outstanding features attributable to the failure of the German skipper of the elusive gun-runner through the British naval blockade – the flying Deutschman the Aud – in not succeeding in unloading the much-wanted war food for the Irish Volunteer army at Tralee Bay – these features I reserve as a retainer for the astute champion of the Tralee contingent of the Irish Volunteers. A full explanation from this particular Irish Volunteer officer is long overdue. In all events, the awaited landing signal did not come because of the sad accident of a motor car turning turtle into the angry waters of the Atlantic, which sent its three Irish Volunteer soldier occupants to an untimely fate. This eventful setback may have been predestined in Irish history because that history throughout is overflowing with such ill-fated interventions.

As a rejoinder I would remark here that no small blunder was made by not ensuring a second signal party was sent on a different route and thus securing the connection with Roger

Casement and the awaiting gun-running ship – as per arrangements arrived at, by green, white and yellow lamp signals from Inistookert Island in Tralee Bay. The fault here must lie with the IRB Military Council that planned the rising, and possibly with Irish Volunteer GHQ in Dublin as well.

On Easter Saturday evening at Limerick Junction, the lion-hearted Casement was now a manacled prisoner in the hands of his own fellow Irishmen of the Royal Irish Constabulary as he was being transported to Arbour Hill Military Prison in Dublin. He was allowed the newspaper and there he read the sad news of the fate which befell Alf Monaghan and his Irish Volunteer comrades, who were dashed to pieces on the rocks in the sea while motoring hurriedly through Killorglin, Co. Kerry. He cried like a child for the brave men who sought to come to his rescue and the cause of Dark Rosaleen. A fighting chance was lost. The news of the same had already filtered through to the proper quarter in Dublin.

On Easter Sunday night, a meeting of the IRB Military Council decided to come out and fight even where the faintest hope of success was far distant. Thus was ignited the flame of Irish independence, the fires of which shall never be quenched while Irish youth inhales the memory of Pearse, Casement, Clarke, Plunkett and Connolly.

APPENDIX 3: Members of Casement's Irish Brigade

The following is a list of members of the Casement Irish Brigade in Germany 1914-1916, "A" and "B" Companies, 10 teams of Machine-Gun Corps, Irish Volunteers.

1. Sergeant-Major Michael Keogh. Assistant Organiser and Recruiting Officer of brigade. Staff Captain, Old IRA: Intelligence Officer, GHQ, 1920-21.
   Born Co. Carlow. Still alive (1960).

2. Captain Robert Monteith. Ex-Company Commander, "A" Company, 1st Battalion, Dublin Brigade, Irish Volunteers. O/C, "B" Company, Irish Brigade. Escaped to America, August 1916.
   Born Co. Wicklow. Died in USA, 1956.

3. Sergeant Timothy Quinlisk. Brigade Quartermaster Sergeant. Served in British army as a corporal in 18th Irish Regiment.
   Born Co. Waterford. Shot during Irish War of Independence, 1920.

4. Company Sergeant Joseph Dowling. Served as a lance-corporal in Connaught Rangers. Famed as Irish Volunteer soldier who on 10th April 1918 landed on Clare coast from a German submarine. Spent six years in nine different English prisons until release in 1924.
   Born Co. Laois. Died in London, 1932.

5. Sergeant Michael O'Toole. Brigade Sergeant. Member of Gaelic League and committed Irish speaker. Served in Irish Volunteers.
   Born Dublin. Died, 1936.

6. Sergeant Daniel Julian Bailey, alias Beverly. Sergeant Signaller. Served in Royal Irish Rifles. Landed in U-Boat in April 1916 with Casement and Monteith. Captured. Turned King's evidence against Casement, with latter's consent.
   Born Dublin. Died, 1929.

7. Sergeant John Francis Kavanagh. Brigade Sergeant. Served in South Irish Horse with rank of ferrier corporal.
   Born Dublin. Still alive (1960).

8. Corporal John McGranaghan. Brigade Corporal. Served in Royal Irish Fusiliers.
   Born Co. Derry. Still alive (1960).

9. Corporal Patrick Delamore. Brigade Corporal. Served in Munster Fusiliers. A trained musician and lance-corporal in band. Employed by an orchestra in Germany and remained there.
Born Co. Waterford. Still alive (1960).

10. Corporal Seán O'Mahony. Brigade Corporal. Served in Dublin Fusiliers. A native Irish speaker and musician.
Born Co. Clare. Dead (date of death unknown).

11. Corporal Michael O'Callaghan. Brigade Lance-Corporal. Served in Munster Fusiliers.
Born Co. Cork. Still alive (1960).

12. Corporal David Golden. Brigade Lance-Corporal. Served in Munster Fusiliers.
Born Co. Kerry. Dead (date of death unknown).

13. Corporal William McGrath. Brigade Lance-Corporal. Served in 18th Royal Irish Regiment. Active in Old IRA, 1920-21.
Born Co. Kildare. Died, 1949.

14. Private Harry Burke. Brigade tailor. Served in Dublin Fusiliers. Active in Old IRA intelligence service, 1920-21.
Born Dublin. Still alive (1960).

15. Private Maurice Meade. Brigade M.G. Stores. Active in East Limerick Brigade Old IRA 1920-21 and veteran of Ballylanders, Kilmallock and Lone Tree Crossroads ambushes.
Born Co. Limerick. Died, 1960.

16. Private Jeremiah O'Callaghan. Brother of Michael. Served in 18th Royal Irish Regiment. Active in Old IRA during War of Independence and killed at Mallow, Co. Cork, in 1921.
Born Co. Cork. Killed in 1921.

17. Private Patrick O'Holohan. Served in 18th Royal Irish Regiment.
Born Co. Waterford. Died and buried at Zossen, 1916.

18. Private James Kennedy. Served in 18th Royal Irish Regiment. Active in Old IRA, 1920-21.
Born Co. Waterford. Still alive (1960).

19. Private Patrick Murphy. Oldest soldier in brigade. Served in Royal Irish Regiment. Died in St James's Street Workhouse, Dublin and buried in a pauper's grave.[324]
Born Belfast. Died, 1927.

20. Private Michael Dowling. Irish Brigade piper. Served in Irish army after independence.

---

[324] It seems that Irish Brigade members received no Irish military pension similar to those received by former IRA members from the War of Independence. See Roth, "'The German soldier is not tactful'," in *The Irish Sword*, vol. 19, no. 78, p. 329.

Born Co. Kilkenny. Died, 1954.

21. Private Patrick Sweeney. A native Irish speaker. Killed during quashing of Munich Soviet after war.
Born Co. Galway. Killed in Munich, 1919.

22. Private John McSweeney. Bugler and war piper. Active in Old IRA, 1920-21.
Born Co. Tipperary. Still alive (1960).

23. Private Patrick Keogh. Irish Brigade bugler. Active in Third Tipperary Battalion Old IRA, 1920-21. First light-welterweight boxing champion in Irish defence forces, 1923-24.
Born Co. Tipperary. Died, 1940.

24. Private John O'Donoghue. Served in British army, regiment not known. Welterweight champion boxer.
Born Manchester. Dead (date of death unknown).

25. Private James McCabe. Served in British army, regiment unknown. Emigrated to USA.
Born Lancashire. Died, 1939.

26. Private Michael Collins. Served in Dublin Fusiliers.
Born Dublin. Dead (date of death unknown).

27. Private John O'Neill. Served in Dublin Fusiliers.
Born Dublin. Dead (date of death unknown).

28. Private John O'Curry. Served in Dublin Fusiliers. Active in Old IRA, 1920-21.
Born Dublin. Still alive (1960).

29. Private Joseph Stacey. Served in Dublin Fusiliers.
Born Dublin. Died, 1960.

30. Private John Barnacle. Served in Dublin Fusiliers.
Born Dublin. Dead (date of death unknown).

31. Private Thomas Wilson. Served in Dublin Fusiliers. Sergeant in Irish defence forces.
Born Dublin. Still alive (1960).

32. Private Patrick Carr. Served in Dublin Fusiliers. Died at Sennelager Military Hospital, Westphalia, Germany in 1918 and buried at Sennelager.
Born Dublin. Died, 1918.

33. Private John Greer. Served in Royal Irish Fusiliers. Active in Old IRA, 1920-21.
Born Co. Wicklow. Died, 1958.

34. Private Peadar Forde. Served in British army, regiment unknown. Active in Old IRA, 1920-21.
Born Co. Kildare. Still alive (1960).

35. Private John Davis. Served in British army, regiment unknown.
Born Co. Kildare. Dead (date of death unknown).

36. Private John Murphy. Served in 18th Royal Irish Regiment.

Born Co. Wexford. Dead (date of death unknown).

37. Private Patrick Waters. Served in 18th Royal Irish Regiment.
Born Co. Wexford. Dead (date of death unknown).

38. Private James Carroll. Served in Royal Irish Regiment. Nicknamed "Kruger"[325] because served in Major John MacBride's Irish Brigade in Boer War.
Born Co. Waterford. Dead (date of death unknown).

39. Private Thomas McGrath. Served in Royal Irish Regiment.
Born Co. Waterford. Dead (date of death unknown).

40. Private John Fulford. Served in Royal Irish Regiment.
Born Co. Waterford. Dead (date of death unknown).

41. Private James McCarthy. Served with Munster Fusiliers. Believed killed in British ambush while active in Old IRA, 1920-21.
Born Co. Cork. Died, 1920-21.

42. Private Cornelius O'Rahilly. Served in 18th Royal Irish Regiment. Active in Old IRA, 1920-21.
Born Co. Cork. Still alive (1960).

43. Private Frank Sewell. Served in Munster Fusiliers.
Born Co. Kerry. Dead (date of death unknown).

44. Private Michael Ryan. Served in Leinster Regiment.
Born Co. Limerick. Dead (date of death unknown).

45. Private Patrick McGrath. Served in 18th Royal Irish Regiment. Active in 3rd Tipperary Brigade Old IRA, 1920-21.
Born Co. Tipperary. Still alive (1960).

46. Private Thomas Tracey. Served in 18th Irish Regiment.
Born Co. Tipperary. Dead (date of death unknown).

47. Private Thomas Harte. Served in Leinster Regiment.
Born Co. Tipperary. Dead (date of death unknown).

48. Private Patrick McMahon. Served in British army, regiment unknown.
Born Co. Tipperary. Died, 1952.

49. Private Patrick McDonagh. Served in Leinster Regiment.
Born Co. Galway. Still alive (1960).

50. Private John Lynch. Served in Leinster Regiment.
Born Co. Offaly. Dead (date of death unknown).

51. Private John Daly. Served in Connaught Rangers.
Born Co. Mayo. Dead (date of death unknown).

52. Private John Long. Served in Connaught Rangers.

---

[325] Paul Kruger (1825-1904) was a Boer farmer who became a leader of the resistance to British encroachment into southern Africa in the later 19th century. He was President of the Transvaal Republic from 1882 to 1900. He went into exile during the Second Boer War and died in Switzerland in 1904.

Born Co. Roscommon. Dead (date of death unknown).

53. Private James Brandon. Served in Inniskilling Fusiliers.
Born Co. Derry. Still alive (1960).

54. Private John Mallon. Served in Inniskilling Fusiliers.
Born Co. Derry. Dead (date of death unknown).

55. Private James Carr. Served in Royal Irish Rifles.
Born Belfast. Dead (date of death unknown).

56. Volunteer John McGoey. Volunteer from New York.
Courier between Clan na Gael in US and Germany. Taken
off Swedish ship by British at Kirkwall and shot on Holy
Thursday 1916 at Peterhead Prison, Scotland.
Born Co. Donegal. Executed 1916.

BIBLIOGRAPHY

Books

Borgonovo, John, *Spies, Informers and the "Anti-Sinn Féin Society": the Intelligence War in Cork City 1920-21* (Dublin, 2007)
Daly, Mary (ed.), *Roger Casement in Irish and World History* (Dublin, 2005)
Doerries, Reinhard, *Prelude to the Easter Rising: Sir Roger Casement in Imperial Germany* (London, 2000)
Dudgeon, Jeffrey, *Roger Casement: The Black Diaries, with a study of his background, sexuality and Irish political life* (Belfast, 2002)
Inglis, Brian, *Roger Casement* (London, 1974)
Monteith, Robert, *Casement's Last Adventure* (2nd edition, Dublin 1953)
Ó Síocháin, Séamas, *Roger Casement: Imperialist, Rebel, Revolutionary* (Dublin, 2008)
Reid, B.L., *The Lives of Roger Casement* (New Haven, 1976)
Splinder, Karl, *The Mystery of the Casement Ship* (Tralee, 1965)

Articles

Casement in Germany: A Guide to the Roger Casement Papers in Clare County Archives
Keogh (McKeogh) Michael, "Roger Casement, Germany and the World War", *Catholic Bulletin* 17 (1927), pp. 1,267-80; 18 (1928), pp. 63-76, 165-77, 282-87, 396-402, 505-15, 613-22, 727-39, 749-53, 833-45, 942-53, 1,042-46, 1,155-64, 1,281-92
Quinlisk, Anthony, "The German Irish Brigade: Diary of Casement's Lieutenant", *Land and Water*, 6th November 1919, pp 18-20; 13th November 1919, pp 16-17
Roth, Andreas, "'The German soldier is not tactful'", *The Irish Sword*, vol. 19, no. 78, pp. 313-33
Irish Times, 17th October 1983; 19th November 2007

Papers

Casement-Boehm Papers, University College Dublin Archives [P127]
Michael Keogh (McKeogh) Papers, University College Dublin Archives [P128]

Miscellaneous Michael Keogh Papers in the possession of his son, Kevin Keogh, Dublin

Joseph Mary Plunkett Papers, National Library of Ireland, Ms 10999

Interview

Kevin and Mary Keogh, Dublin, 31st January 2008

Above: *Roger Casement*

Right: *Roger Casement Birth Place, Sandycove, Dún Laoghaire - seen here with Michael Keogh laying a wreath*

Below: *Michael Keogh War Medals*

Memorial Mass in Dublin Castle with Jim Larkin

Memorial Mass with Sean Lemass

Wedding Photo of Michael Keogh with wife Annamarie

The Wedding Party of Michael and Annamarie Keogh

Michael Keogh in the Irish Free State Army

Michael Keogh standing by a photo of his wedding